ONE SIGNAL
PUBLISHERS

ATRIA

DIRTY KITCHEN

A MEMOIR OF FOOD AND FAMILY

JILL DAMATAC

ONE SIGNAL
PUBLISHERS

ATRIA

NEW YORK   AMSTERDAM/ANTWERP   LONDON
TORONTO   SYDNEY/MELBOURNE   NEW DELHI

ONE SIGNAL
PUBLISHERS

ATRIA

An Imprint of Simon & Schuster, LLC
1230 Avenue of the Americas
New York, NY 10020

For more than 100 years, Simon & Schuster has championed authors
and the stories they create. By respecting the copyright of an author's intellectual
property, you enable Simon & Schuster and the author to continue publishing exceptional
books for years to come. We thank you for supporting the author's copyright by
purchasing an authorized edition of this book.

First One Signal Publishers/Atria Books hardcover edition May 2025

ONE SIGNAL PUBLISHERS / ATRIA BOOKS and colophon are trademarks of
Simon & Schuster, LLC

Simon & Schuster strongly believes in freedom of expression and stands against
censorship in all its forms. For more information, visit BooksBelong.com.

For information about special discounts for bulk purchases, please contact
Simon & Schuster Special Sales at 1-866-506-1949 or business@simonandschuster.com.

The Simon & Schuster Speakers Bureau can bring authors to your live event. For more
information or to book an event, contact the Simon & Schuster Speakers Bureau at
1-866-248-3049 or visit our website at www.simonspeakers.com.

Interior design by Kyoko Watanabe
Cover design by Laywan Kwan

Manufactured in the United States of America

1 3 5 7 9 10 8 6 4 2

Library of Congress Control Number: 2025931936

ISBN 978-1-6680-8463-2
ISBN 978-1-6680-8465-6 (ebook)

Contents

Author's Note

For twenty-two years, America held me close. Not in its arms, safe from harm, or in its palm, cradled and free, but in its grasp: one hand vise-tight around my neck, the other clamped over my mouth. In exchange for my release, my captor required a ransom: the sacrifice of life as I knew it. A ten-year ban, as if the previous two decades of entrapment—for that is what the American dream is for many immigrants—hadn't been punishment enough. Freedom isn't free.

They called us many things in the land of the free and the home of the brave. Illegal. Undocumented. Alien. My fellow Filipinos called us "TNT," brief in their derision. Playful, almost. "Tago ng tago," always hiding. It implies shame, performs shaming. As if we are somehow to blame. As if hiding, and continuing to hide, is a choice freely made. As if leaving one country and being rejected by the other were somehow the consequences of our personal failures and not that of the governments tasked with caring for the people within its borders. What talking heads on television never seem to mention is that the longer a person stays undocumented, the harder it becomes to loosen the shackles of America. That it is unimaginable, impossible, to emerge from the shadows to reveal the self. The self may never be found at all.

I wrote this book as an air-bridge, astride two lands, a way of crossing the cold vacuum between longing and belonging. These words may reach my family, isolated, unyielding, and afraid, the wretched refuse of a teeming shore. These words may reach American citizens in those hidden, soft places within their state-hardened bodies. These words may resonate with noncitizens in the exposed, vulnerable places of their fear-knotted bodies. My experiences might ring true to the complicated humanity that is often silenced by today's shouting, ratings-driven, social media–amplified news cycles of fear, blame, and paranoia.

I also wrote this book so that I could document, for myself, a migration taken by my body and spirit from secrecy to revelation. An inner journey from fear to hope that has, in every stage, been accompanied by the tastes, smells, and textures of the Philippines, where I was born and from which I have been separated for most of my life. To paraphrase Proust: when everything is gone—or hidden away, like my family and I had to be—food is always there to help us remember, allowing us to taste joy, wonder, sorrow, rage. To savor yesterday and take another bite towards tomorrow. In learning how to cook the Filipino dishes in this memoir, I have also unearthed the Filipino version of me, the one left behind in Manila, wondering where I went. My sister and I, small children upon arrival in America, learned to cosplay, to assimilate and survive. In the process of writing and cooking for this book, I came back to life amid tiny details and noisy diasporic gatherings: the finger dipped into water to barely touch the top of the uncooked rice; the tooth-squeaking, gum-fizzing, tongue-stinging tang that tells you the sinigang is finally sour enough (no measurement or recipe gets this right); the way a salo-salo dinner, which the Americans call a potluck, becomes an act of communal care. Salo, to catch. "Salo-salo, catch-catch, I got you, kapatid." *Kapatid*, sibling. Root word *patid*, to trip. Together we fall, together we eat, together we rise. Small realizations that have brought me back to life as every kapatid removed their shoes at my front door, a cacophony of homemade dishes, laughter, karaoke. These simple joys, ignored or avoided in my family's unhappy, isolated, secretive decades of being undocumented, were reacquainted to me, chapter after written chapter. Like generations of immigrants before me, cuisine has been a vessel for and a reminder of the fruits of our ancestral lands. A terroir that is flavored by soil and memory, by grief and joy. Each of the recipes in this book are as they were taught and fed to me by my family, dishes shaped by our personal and shared preferences and, often, by what was available to us. As Filipinos all over the world know, there is no one right or pure way to make or serve our cuisine. Food historian Doreen Fernandez has written about how our cuisine is not so much about its origins, but its destination: dishes and ingredients are indigenized into Filipinoness while simultaneously evolving through time and place. No matter where we are, we make our dishes with what we have, based on flavors and textures we know, on memories and longings we carry. Always, the beauty of our food is in its ability to absorb influences while undeniably remaining itself.

I also wrote this book to document myself into existence. According to the American government, I did not exist. In defiance of this, I want to understand how the caprices of powers and nations have shaped my family, my body, and the ways we have been deprived and nourished—by each other, by cultures, by countries. Which country? I now have three: a country of birth, a country of death, and a country of rebirth.

As conflicted as I was initially about including my life stories of violence and abuse, of hunger and pain—often derided as trauma porn, in order to silence those who dare speak, to justify the world's indifference—I include these stories here, flinching, afraid. These struggles are an integral part of my life, struggles made more difficult by the heartlessness of American immigration policy, or lack thereof. This is what happens to real people, to real families, like ours. There was no safety net, no running to the hospital, or to child services, and definitely not to the police. We were vulnerable, exposed, wounded, and exploited, without the aid, sympathy, or protection of a government that promotes itself globally as the exceptional leader of the free world. And my family was one of the luckier ones. No handcuffs, holding cells, or hieleras for us.

Filipino food—a blend of regions, countries, and occupations—serves as the antidote that helps counteract the poisons of family and history. This is not a story of finding life, liberty, and the pursuit of happiness in the United States. It is a story of discovering life, liberty, and the pursuit of happiness *despite* the United States.

This is more than a memoir, a cookbook, or a history book. It is a way of rejoining a world from which I have hidden for most of my life. It is an appraisal of a life of historical colonial and immigrant trauma that has manifested in my family as violence, abuse, and mental illness. It is a hand waved in the air, seeking relief from the Sisyphean punishment we have been forced to bear. With this book, I join the growing circle of undocumented writers who have sublimated their individual and unique experiences—for we are not a monolith—into a call for change and an end to inhumanity. Through the writing of this book, I am coming to terms with the thought that perhaps the decades of pain, fear, loss, rage, loneliness, depression, and grief can be of some use, after all. That it has not been for nothing. That in having the privilege of escaping and surviving, in allowing myself to finally be seen, the rest of us still in hiding may one day be closer to being seen too. To being acknowledged, welcomed, understood, and, most importantly, legalized.

For those of us who are survivors: this book was incredibly hard to write, and you may find it equally difficult to read. In unearthing my own trauma, I have been painfully aware that doing so might trigger yours. And so, go gently, particularly in Chapters 5 and 6. If you find that you need to skip ahead or step away from the book for a bit, please do. Chapter 7, on Adobo, is a good place to return to, and subsequent chapters get better from there (sorry for the spoiler!). Please know that I am grateful to be here, to have this book. I am even more grateful to have you as a reader and hope that some of my journey may resonate with yours. I also hope that, in sharing the story of my family's personal misfortunes and accumulated violences, we all might, over time, work together to reorient our systems, institutions, and personal interactions to focus on empathy, material change, and care.

Resources for fellow survivors:
Sexual violence: https://rainn.org
Domestic violence: https://www.thehotline.org
Undocumented immigrants: https://www.informedimmigrant.com

To be an undocumented immigrant is to be made invisible and silent. This book is my proof of existence. One that needs no country's permission. One that can never be revoked.

Jill Damatac
Cambridge, England

dirty kitchen /'dərdē 'kiCH(ə)n/ *noun*

A partly or fully outdoor extension and multipurpose space commonly found in Filipino houses. Used for big-batch cooking. Also for butchering whole animals, open fire roasting, the cutting of children's hair, the hand-washing and hang-drying of clothes, and the storage of provisions. There might be sacks of rice, cans of American Spam, tins of Alaska brand powdered milk. Corned beef, plastic vats of honey from Baguio, and bags of coffee from Kalinga. A maid or my yaya, taking a hot midday nap in a dark corner. Separate from the indoor, Western-style kitchen used for light cooking, plating, serving, snacking, and impressing visitors with the brand-new microwave, refrigerator, and coffee machine paid for by the eldest child, a former doctor now working as a nurse in America.

Itak at Sangkalan
(Cleaver and Chopping Block)

August 1992

T he first time I cleaved from the earth and saw oceans, I was nine. We left the Philippines six years after the end of the His and Hers Dictatorship of Ferdinand and Imelda Marcos. Hidden by night, Mama, my three-year-old sister, and I traveled by airplane. We arrived at our final destination after three airplanes and thirty hours in the sky. We went back in time by one mortal day, August 13, 1992. The longest day of my life, in both time and space.

Lay the sangkalan, ideally made of strong sampalok wood, on a flat surface.

On that journey, I saw the dawn gate in the east, the one between sky and sea, where all life begins. Where gods and spirits are born. As each day begins, they stride across the heavens on wind-light feet, cloud to cloud. They walk westward, towards death, the dark gate at dusk that leads to the underworld. They reemerge, immortal, the next morning, in the east. Start the journey anew.

By some trick of Mak-no-ngan, who my I-pugao ancestors say created our earth, we began our new life by flying eastward, against the direction of the gods. We flew from Manila, by the dawn's early light, and reemerged in Newark, New Jersey, at the twilight's last gleaming. We remained for two decades in the underworld known as the West. Worry sat in my belly during our flight, hurtling beneath the Sky World's garden of stars. Were we headed for a new life, or merely a different death?

Miles below the belly of our plane, currents of deep, heavy water pulled down on my soft, growing bones. I strained forward in my window seat. I hoped to see the glint of water, or the stars, or the unknown land that lay ahead. I saw nothing. There was only my reflection, cut in two by the double-glass window.

I was reluctant to leave Manila, forced to travel in the middle of August in my hand-me-down hot wool dress, a relic from the 1970s. The white ruffled bodice, long sleeves, and high neck itched at my summer-sweaty skin. The shame of being all wrong, a feeling that would become my only lifelong friend in America, reddened my face. My American cousins' donations were twenty years old, smelling of the mothballs packed in the balikbayan box. The dress was made for winter, an alien concept for my tropical blood.

Prepare a half cup of lemon juice or white vinegar.

"And what will you be doing once you're in the United States?" said the solemn white man with mud-brown eyes, dirty-blond hair, and a mustache to match. The US Embassy building in Ermita, Manila, was once the residence of the United States High Commissioner to the Philippines, the headquarters of American colonial control. It was built by the US Treasury Department, for our islands were a stream of revenue for America. Next door is where the Spanish had executed José Rizal the century before. He was accused of inciting colonial rebellion through his books, pamphlets, essays, plays, and poetry. Shot to death by firing squad. His dying wish was to face east, towards dawn. The commemorative statue that now stands where he stood faces west, towards the sun, as it sets each day over Manila Bay. Sentenced to gaze upon death forever.

"I wanna go to Disneyland!" I said, my smile blackened by a missing front tooth. Mama had instructed that I was to be agreeable, for once. This was my earliest lesson in how to please the Americans: do not be yourself, do not be contrary, do not be a challenge. We were to present ourselves as good immigrants. The kind that would never overstay a tourist visa, then mouth off about it in a book three decades later.

With a rag dipped into the lemon or vinegar, wipe the sangkalan clean.

Saying goodbye to family at Ninoy Aquino International Airport—another monument for another man shot to death for inciting rebellion—I hid my tears in my Lolo Pedring's arms. His warm belly muffled my sobs. He promised to visit often. I miss my grandfather's bedtime stories to this day. I hope that he reads this and sees himself in the way I let a tale unroll itself. The elders do say that we are always accompanied by our most kindred ancestors. Perhaps Lolo is mine.

"OK, time to go," Mama had said, gently pulling me away, straightening my collar, not-so-gently pounding my upper back. "Stop slouching." Good posture, cleanliness, and beauty were very important to Mama.

Her excitement at seeing Papa again gleamed from her heavy-lidded brown eyes. He had been away from us for more than two years. My last memory of him was blurred by tears: before walking into the departures door, the same one we were about to enter, Papa had turned around one more time, left hand hoisting his bag over his shoulder, his right hand waving goodbye, his eyes red, brimming with tears. The echo of my voice, lost in the crowd, shouting stay, stay, stay. The gods' itak slashing down mercilessly, taking away the Papa I knew and loved forever.

Rinse the sangkalan with clean water. Wipe dry with a soft cloth.

Before his soul was cut in two, Papa was a trained architect and virtuoso musician. Like many, he was forced by Marcos's law to become what Filipinos call an OFW: an Overseas Foreign Worker, required by law to send half of his earnings home, propping up the government's malfeasance with his own body. He traveled by sea to places with names that meant nothing to me: Philadelphia, Curaçao, Aruba, the Bahamas, Manhattan. He sang and played the piano and guitar with his band. He entertained the ship's white British and American officers just enough to escape their cruelty, which they reserved for what they deemed to be lesser crew. Papa mistook this for friendship. He would later tell me that those years were some of the best of his life.

"We were in a new place every few days, and we could disembark and go to so many different beaches, visit the towns, see New York City. And the Caribbean! The sand was pink, or white . . ." He would trail off, disappearing into a different self I would never meet. A self that forgot his wife and two small daughters far away, missing him. A different self, photographed—we would discover decades later—with many women, fingers intertwined, arms around waists, foreheads touching, legs draped over laps on the same beach lounger, or sitting together, T-shirts only, hair rumpled, in a shared bed. A smile that we would rarely see in America.

For Papa, it was better to go to white and pink sand beaches in the Caribbean, strawberry-blond girlfriend in tow, than to our humble, brown-sanded one, the kind that Western tourists never deigned to visit. Better to sing at lunch and supper in cruise ship dining rooms full of pale, wrinkled tourists and adoring female crew members, I suppose, than to lie in bed with his tired, hardworking wife, than to sing to his small daughter, his number-one fan, every night. The Beatles' "I Will" at bedtime for six years in a row can get a little old, after all.

Take a whetstone, one made of strong mineral from our home soil, and wet it with cool water.

In the years Papa was away, I sleepwalked at night. I went down the stairs in the house on Madasalin Street, where Mama's family lived. I sleepwalked past the dining room, into the sala. Lolo Baldo, my mother's father, once found me on one of the sofas, sitting upright, my eyes open and blank. He followed me as I stood up, walked to a window, arms hanging by my sides. Outside, there was nothing and no one that he could see. Lolo Baldo did not wake me. To do so might upset whichever benign engkanto had visited my body, taken me for a walk around the house. My grandfather sat, tired from a full day's work, and waited. He told me that each time he found me this way—sometimes in the sala, sometimes in the kitchen—I would eventually shuffle upstairs, back to the bedroom I shared with Mama and my sister. He made sure that I lay back down onto my banig, the floor mat I slept on. I unrolled this woven palm leaf mat each night on the floor next to the raised twin bed, which Mama and my sister shared. We had left our own house, the big marble house, months before, after Papa had boarded the ship in early 1990. After strange men began to watch our windows, circling like stray dogs. After Mama became too afraid to live alone with her two small daughters.

At night, my spirit led flesh through space, searching for a time that would never return. In search of our own kitchen, with its breakfast nook and the stools I sat on every morning. In search of our own dining table with its lazy Susan, all of us within arm's reach of each other, Papa slicing open the mangoes from our tree as dessert. We would each have a whole mango, Papa crisscrossing each half in the special diagonal way that he knew I loved. In search of our own sala, cavernous and cool on the hottest Manila days, warm and dry during typhoons, long before such storms began to regularly flood the marble house. In search of the tall double doors that opened to our cool back garden, where chickens roamed, clucking among the banana and avocado trees. In search of Mama, content and sitting, legs tucked into a rattan armchair, flipping through her favorite magazines. In search of Papa playing his piano, or restringing his guitar, telling me to stand far back, just in case one of the strings lashed out. In search of my baby sister, having just learned to walk, toddling on fat legs from one piece of furniture to the next, giggles and drool, wearing only white cotton diapers. My helpful engkanto friend and I must have sleepwalked in search of them, the family that I had lost and would never have again. A future together lost in pursuit of an alternate American reality.

Choose an itak with a sharp edge and a firm grip. Wipe the itak clean.
Run its blade through water.

Waiting to board one more flight, I scratched again at my wool dress, which made me stand out from the American children at San Francisco International Airport. They stared at my wilted collar, patent leather black Mary Janes, and bowl-cut hair, recently trimmed by my yaya in the dirty kitchen. I marveled at their translucent skin, flaxen hair, tie-dyed T-shirts, light-up sneakers, and constitutional confidence. It wasn't just the TV: white people really did look like that. How did they get to be so pale? Does living on this land do that to you? These children ignored their parents, ate Dunkin' Donuts and Burger King, played Game Boy while we waited. I nibbled at a pack of Sky Flakes from Mama's handbag, read a komik book of myths Lolo Pedring had given to me a few nights before our flight to America.

"The Greek myths I read to you? They are very good, but look at these," Lolo had said.

He had feigned nonchalance, handing me three thin books. The books were stapled at the spine and, unlike the colorful Marvel and Archie Digest comic books Papa sent me, these komiks were in black and white ink on pulpy newsprint, which smeared ink on my fingers. The cover bore intricate drawings of gods, aswang, engkanto, dwende, and sirena, beautiful against the backdrop of a giant balete tree.

"You should know these stories too. If you like them, I can send more."

Lolo Pedring had watched while I riffled through the pages, sat down to read the first one. A small, satisfied smile had creased the corner of his mouth. I remembered him as I sat there, unaware of San Francisco, just outside. I looked up at the airport gate that led further into the West, further into the underworld. Would Lolo be asleep by now? I had wondered. Would he, too, be wishing he could tell me a story from memory, as he often did?

In the myth of the divided child, the goddess Bugan descends from the highest realm of Sky World to join her beloved, a mortal man. At a hut near his village, they begin a family of their own. She bears him a son, and for a time, they are happy. But not long after, Bugan is made to feel unwelcome by the villagers. They fear her power, envy her beauty. They poison her garden so that she cannot eat. Their sharp words are knives at her back. Sad and lonely, Bugan decides to take her mortal husband and half-godly children back to Sky World. But her husband is afraid and refuses to go. Bugan makes a fateful choice: she tears their son in two, keeping the boy's lower half for herself, the upper half for her husband.

"This half, with the heart, will be easier to raise on this earth," Bugan tells him. She ascends home with her half.

Weeks later, a stench reaches the highest level of Sky World, where Bugan and her son live. Terrified, she rushes down to earth.

"What have you done?" she asks her mortal husband. Unaccustomed to caring for a child, he had neglected their son. The boy died not long after Bugan's departure.

In rage, Bugan tears the dead body into pieces with her bare hands, needing neither itak nor sangkalan to do so. Her grief brings her to the edge of the forest, where she throws the pieces away. An ear lands on soil, turns into the first mushroom. An arm transforms into the first snake. The boy's skin, I-pugao dark and brown, becomes a winged creature, that which we now call the kukuk bird. In fury and despair, we conjure great and startling things.

With even, long strokes, run the itak's blade, wet with water, across the stone. Repeat along the length of the blade until sharp, catching on the skin-edge of a finger.

On that flight to America, I listened to one song, louder than my little sister's cries for more milk. I had discovered it on the flight from San Francisco to Newark, blaring through the airplane's free headphones. I did not know what the piece was called, but I knew how to find it through my seat's menu buttons. I had a favorite section. Two-thirds of the way through, a piano in adagio gave way to a blossoming string orchestra. It ushered in a feeling of optimistic wonder, a brief comfort on a journey I didn't want to take. The floating strings were legato and unhurried, dropping down to create space. I snuggled into the window and watched the clouds pass beneath me—at dusk, over the Pacific as we flew over Taipei, then again at dawn, as we approached California. The rhapsody peaked to a dreamlike crescendo. I imagined that I was a goddess from Sky World, discovering new lands. How lucky the United States was to be heralding my arrival. Bugan, disguised in a hot, itchy-as-hell wool dress smelling of mothballs. But unlike Bugan, my family would be back together again.

That dreamy, violin-ribboned, trombone-draped passage—Gershwin's *Rhapsody in Blue*, I would discover years later—was brief. It lasted for less than three minutes. Played on repeat, it felt like the forever I had wanted for my sister, my parents, and me. When we touched down in America, the song ended, cut off halfway by the pilot's announcement. The flight attendant collected our blankets. With a gentle hand, she took back my free headphones while I jabbed at the control panel. Please, just one more play of the song.

The itak is now ready for use. Rinse once more, under running water, to remove any small, sharp metal shavings.

Clutching the thin book of komiks from my grandfather, I stepped off the airplane at Newark, my spirit cut into two, forever.

1

Pinikpikan
(Beaten Chicken in Broth)

Papa's 1960s–1990s

SERVES 6

Made ceremonially, with an elder or a mumbaki

> 1 chicken, alive, feathers intact
> 2 quarts fresh water
> 2-inch piece ginger, peeled and sliced into matchsticks
> 1 head garlic, minced
> 1 onion, chopped finely
> 3 sayote or 2 papaya, chopped into cubes
> 2 bunches pechay or malunggay
> 1 cup bayah wine
> 8 ounces etag
> A fire at roasting temperature

Grip knife. Dig. Push in. Pull out. The crunch of cartilage. The tearing from bone. Skin and flesh slipping from my grip. Yellow globules of fat beading under my fingernails. I twist the bones apart. Sinew and skin fling off the tip of my steel knife, wet pink landing on the granite's cold white. It quivers next to the open kitchen window.

When a house is afflicted with illness, the sacred ritual of ketema must be performed.

I am not making my ancestors' Cordilleran pinikpikan today. I am making tinola, its more acceptable relative. Tinola is taken for granted, made at home for pesos. Pinikpikan is taken as a curiosity, performed by the noble savage for YouTube. There isn't much to these dishes, these ulam, the part of a meal that is served with rice. They do not capture social media attention through their looks, which are pale, indistinct, and watery, or their scent, which is gingery slow-simmered chicken, or their flavor, which does not bloom, soft and gentle on the tongue, until the second mouthful. These are not dishes that are served to white tourists. These are not dishes Filipinos would order on a night out. Shame, disguised as pride.

Cordilleran pinikpikan disobeys the Philippines Animal Welfare Act, a 1998 law reinforcing the bars of empire's dogmatic cage. Do not eat dirty chicken soup made in your dirty kitchen. Instead, eat Spam, made of In God We Trust, fried in clean American-style kitchens. Buy a GE, a Frigidaire, a Westinghouse. The act codifies the prohibition of an Indigenous tradition older than the Philippines. As if the theft of our land wasn't enough. Pinik-pikan. Root word: *pik-pik*. To beat repeatedly.

In 1887, José Rizal wrote his most famous novel, an act of anticolonial defiance titled *Noli Me Tángere*. Rizal's protagonist, Crisóstomo Ibarra, just returned to our islands after a trip around the world, requested tinola as his first meal. Of all the dishes he could have had, it was this plain, clear-brothed, ginger-laced embrace that Ibarra craved. During this welcome home meal, a haughty Spanish fraile was given the worst parts of the chicken: the neck and a wing. When asked about his travels, Ibarra said, "Even if my country does seem to have forgotten me, I have always thought about it."

I lay the chicken into a steel pot. Its mirror-like gleam has made the task of forgetting easier. I think of how far removed this tinola is from its origins. Once defiant, now acquiescent. My try-hard attempt at identity as a costume. I mistake flesh for body, salt for land, food for tongue, swallowing for experience. In places, this small galley kitchen is chillier than the other rooms. A quirk of older housing, maybe. Or a spirit, lingering reluctantly at the threshold of some other spirit plane. Every home hosts a spirit or two. Some dead, some living.

The mumbaki must come. They will bring betel nuts, betel leaves, rice cakes, and other offerings in a winnowing basket. Members of the household will join.

Pinikpikan, unlike tinola, is not primarily cooked for pleasure. It is eaten as the final part of a holy ceremony, which must appease the gods and offer compensation to a displeased universe, until the ancient cycles that govern our earthly Pugao plane have been restored. This is our pamana, an inheritance of timeless tradition that cannot be governed by any law. Pinikpikan can be made to augur one's fate before journeys. The mumbaki comes to the family house just ahead of dusk, betel leaves in a sack, jar of bayah in hand. In a circle, all share a drink, passing around this holy wine of celebration, mourning, and sacrifice. They spit the juice of chewed leaves into a bowl. They stay huddled close, keeping the energetic door to the spirit world unbroken. They ask for the gods' protection, for omens to be kind, for the road before their traveler to be smooth. If the chicken's entrails, still warm with life, do not portend a safe passage, then the traveler must wait to leave another day. Perform the ceremony again and again, until the gods give their assent. The traveler may never leave at all.

All must be seated in a circle. The shared energy will open the door to the spirit plane.

I wonder if my family's misfortunes are a punishment for leaving without making pinikpikan first, without asking the gods for permission. We should have made some effort with them, even in the American suburbs. In our tradition, illness in one's mind, in one's soul can be attributed to abandonment. Abandonment by one's family, by one's lover; abandonment of our mountains, our people, our culture. Abandonment was the ultimate insult to the gods and the gifts they had bestowed.

Pinikpikan—and the act of cooking it—is a manifestation of how our mumbaki understand that our bodies are not separate from the planes of existence. For thousands of years, elders have passed down our practices of healing and divination. They have always known that soul injuries like my father's are rooted in a desecration of the sacred order. In the tearing of a harmonious social fabric. By leaving us behind, Papa may have brought the gods' retribution upon himself. But the elders have also always maintained that no one is ever alone in their guilt. That as a family that shares blood, lineage, and soul ancestry, we are all guilty of abandonment. America was our punishment.

The women will drink bayah. They will sing in trembling voices, eyes closed. Their bodies will shake.

Pinikpikan can also be cooked and eaten to help correct a disturbance in the natural order, disturbances like Papa's. When a house is inflicted by illness, madness, or misfortune, the sacred killing of a divine animal aids in the divination of uncertain fate. The priestess examines the animal's heart: Is it tilting towards life, or away from it, towards death? The gallbladder predicts healing and good fortune, or more punishment and sorrow. And to heal the disturbed, a greater animal sacrifice might be made: more chickens, if the illness is small. A goat or a pig, for deadlier conditions.

All must wait as the spirit chooses a body to possess. The chosen woman will lead the singing and the chanting, and all must follow. Memories and grievances may arise.

There is a memory, an ember from an old fire, flickering across three planes of decades. Lolo Pedring's house, a back door open. Beyond it, a cooling Manila late afternoon. The panicked flap of a chicken's wing, brown-bronze plumage drifting in humid air. My uncle, the second youngest of Papa's five brothers, shirtless in the heat. Cigarette in the corner of his mouth, hair in a thick, wavy mullet. Wooden stick in his hand—or was it some other uncle's hand?—slicing through the air. *Pikpikpikpikpik.* Death by a thousand beats. It is the only time I have ever seen violence course through my uncle's gentle artists' hands. The bird finally still. Neck broken, head swinging loose. An eye on me. Afterward, the weak spurt of blood into a bowl, spattering concrete. Red smeared later on by black, charcoal from a wood fire on the ground, brown-bronze feathers devoured by flames into ash.

I stood there, lingering reluctantly at the threshold of the dirty kitchen, one hand on the painted doorframe. My baby sister's cries echoed from somewhere inside the house. Just outside, this rooster lay dead in front of me. At six, I learned of death as a necessary counterweight to life. My Lola Rosing, my father's mother, gently tugged me away, an arthritic hand over my eyes. But I had already seen all I needed to know.

She and I went back inside, sat at the dining table to prepare the family meal. Those pots of chicken in gingered broth that I helped Lola Rosing to make: Were they tinola, or pinikpikan? I cannot remember. She kept a malunggay tree in her front yard, bushy and narrow, fed by the tropical morning sun. Whenever she made this dish, she had me pick fresh leaves from the tree, reminding me to choose only the sweet young branches. Malunggay takes effort to harvest. Its fronds are individual galaxies of small, dark leaves shooting out, in fractal order, from the parent branch and into eternity. At the table, Lola and I plucked leaves until she was satisfied with the size of the fluttering green pile. With a wordless smile she would nod, giving me permission to play outside.

We will know when the spirit has chosen once the wine has joined our blood, reached our heads. The spirit will speak through its chosen body. The circle will stay unbroken.

The mountain way of life was taught to my father's people by the gods in Sky World. They came down from their heights to shape our earth. Some playfully sculpted our green peaks, taller than the Appalachians. Others ran their fingers through these mountains, creating the rushing brown Chico River, which feeds our rice terraces. Through our holy women and men, the gods taught us how to step into the stream of cyclic life, respecting its ways so that we may live. My father's grandmothers used plants like malunggay as medicine, easing discomfort in the belly, expanding the intake of breath, thickening the flow of blood.

Our ancestors would be dismayed to find that these gifts are now exploited by elected leaders against our Indigenous people's will. So that they may strip our proud mountains of their belts of gold, copper, and minerals, families are forced from ancestral villages and lands. The very currents of the Chico River, and the roots of every tree, sold to the highest multinational bidder. Our malunggay trees, sustenance for generations, are now profitable exports, following the path of corn, tomatoes, chilies, coffee, and quinoa from our Indigenous siblings in other lands. Malunggay fronds and leaves, once grown with love in each home, are now grown for shareholders. Pulverized, sold as powders, marketed by #wellness influencers, blended into smoothies, swallowed as capsules.

The spirit is held in place by the circle. We will ask questions: Who are you? What do you want? Is there a sacrifice to be made so that you might be appeased?

In 1990s suburban America, malunggay was impossible to find. We substituted any way we could to make our tinola, using spinach or bok choy, depending on what was cheapest at the supermarket that week. When there were pepper leaves in the local Asian store, it was my responsibility to defrost the rock-hard frozen pack while I did my homework. Sauté the garlic, read chapters on plant structure for AP Biology. Sear the chicken thighs skin side down, draft an essay about Columbus. Toss in a bouillon cube to make the broth taste like time, forget about the land of my birth.

Sometimes, we used Florida green papaya in place of sayote. Sayote was a rarity for us in those early years, a cross between an apple and a squash. We missed its presence in our cobbled-together pots of American tinola, smacking our lips between hot mouthfuls. We chewed on the American papaya (the kind grown by underpaid undocumented immigrants under duress) instead of Benguet sayote (the kind grown by landless Indigenous people in debt). Sayote was a gift from our Nahuatl-speaking siblings, brought over by Spanish Manila galleons during our shared colonization. It is a rarity here, north of the Nahuatl's ancestral territories, in the place now known as the United States. Sayote's translucent flesh gives tinola a slight bite, a moment of verdant sweetness against the gentle salt of the broth. In tinola, the broth is often seasoned with patis, a fermented fish sauce common to our part of the world. In pinikpikan, slices of etag, salted pork aged and preserved in jars underground, are used.

The body through which the spirit speaks will answer, trembling. The spirit may say which animals are needed as an offering.

Our suburban, house-bound life in America was nothing like Papa's transient 1960s and 1970s boyhood. He and his brothers followed Lola Rosing and Lolo Pedring around the Cordilleras. Forced to move almost every year to follow their father's job, they had to constantly adjust to a new region, a new town, a new school. Tadian. Banaue. Kiangan. Bontoc. Baguio. Six boys, feet dusted by the soil of our ancestors, uprooted with the turn of each season, forced to sprout wherever they must. They grew to be tough, yet tender, like the gagattang that grows everywhere in our mountains, delicate thistle blooms nodding atop hard, rough stalks.

The spirit's message is complete when it has left the body, which will sigh loudly, stopping the shivering and trembling.

Papa was born between two brothers who did not live past birth. Bookended by death, my father understood isolation and separation better than his brothers, feared it more than his brothers. He often wondered what his survival was supposed to mean. I wonder now if those two lost sons were the beginning. The opening rounds of the gods' ongoing intergenerational punishment for our lineage of Damatacs.

He discovered music when he was three. Along with loneliness, music remains my father's closest sibling. It is his substitute for home soil, a talisman of safety no matter where he may be in the world. Papa feels present and safe only through music. His first instrument was the accordion, a heavy block of wood, leather, and linen almost half his size. He strained to carry it, its thick leather strap digging into his tiny shoulder blades, its breadth, fully expanded, too wide for his small arms to reach. He learned to play it on instinct, by ear. His toddler fingers strained and pressed, hoping, note by note, to earn his father's love.

The mumbaki chooses a chicken, healthy and young, as sacrifice. The bird is held upside down by its feet.

Music allowed Papa to be seen by his father, to be proudly proclaimed as Federico's son. In every town they briefly lived in, Papa would play the accordion. His father brought guests home for dinner, gathered in whichever official government house the Damatac family had been given. After the meal, Lolo Pedring would place his young son, barefoot, on top of a coffee table. The expectant weight of the accordion shrugged onto his hopeful little shoulders. And then Papa would play, my grandfather's friends singing kundiman songs, maybe something from Perry Como or Nat King Cole. In those moments, embraced by his father, Papa felt claimed, rooted. He began to see music as love, as a way of being loved. He began to see love as earned, as a conditional object to be rescinded at any time.

"Your Lolo was so dedicated to his work. He was the head superintendent, you know, of schools in the Cordilleras," Papa once told me. "He was in charge of a lot. The government wanted the American curriculum everywhere. I guess he forgot about us."

With a stick of moderate weight and size, the mumbaki begins to beat the chicken, starting with the head, so that it does not suffer.

There are pictures of Papa and his brothers, sepia-toned, from the 1960s: scowls unfaded, photographed in strong mountain sun. High and tight haircuts, American military-style. My grandparents are young, stern, formal, surrounded by their brood. Each son just physically distant enough to indicate greater distances felt within. In one photo, Papa and three of his brothers stand, awkward and stiff, with Lolo Pedring, in front of the Philippine Military Academy in Baguio. Established in 1936 by a fledgling, US-colonial-era Philippine Commonwealth government, it was built in the image of the US Military Academy at West Point, under the oversight of General Douglas MacArthur. This building was made to enable our islands to defend itself. I peer closely into Papa's face in this photo. His expression is almost inscrutable, almost like discontent.

Continuing to beat the chicken's body, all the way to the tips of its
wings, the mumbaki will ask that a fire be prepared on the ground.

In adolescence, my father and his brothers were pulled apart. The two eldest were sent down from the mountains, to Manila, to the house of Lola Luisa, their mother's mother. My grandfather wanted them to attend high school in the capital. Another understandable strategic move in a lifetime of strategic moves, my grandfather aligning with power, swallowing his personal dissent, in the hopes of a chance at survival. Eventually, my father followed, leaving behind his three youngest brothers, unable to reach his two oldest brothers, even though they lived under the same extended family roof. My grandmother stayed behind with the youngest boys. My grandfather continued to roam the northern mountains, hard at work, sowing the American curriculum, school by school, teacher by teacher, rice terrace by rice terrace, into our tribal lands.

"My brothers and me, we never really got to be friends," Papa once said. "By the time I got to Manila, my older brothers already each had their own barkada, their own crews. And then your other Titos followed, and they found their own friends."

With the chicken now beaten dead, the mumbaki will pull off all its
feathers. These are gathered and placed at the base of the fire. The
flames will consume the feathers into ash.

Manila in the 1970s was a planggana of discontent. My father had just turned fifteen. Separated from his brothers and his parents, with no friends, he must have felt alone and afraid, without control over his own life or his destiny. He began to live a solitary life, going in and out of his grandmother's house on his own time, passing his brothers' shadows at dawn, at dusk. Ate his meals of cold leftovers alone.

At that house, Papa discovered an old piano that no one played. In addition to his guitar, he played for hours at the piano, listening to radio shows for new songs. Playing them by ear. The Beatles, Stevie Wonder, Frank Sinatra, The Beach Boys, Connie Francis, Antônio Carlos Jobim, Herbie Hancock.

Eventually, Lola Luisa's house—accustomed to the din of many voices, relatives from the provinces arriving and leaving—became filled with music. Cousins would sing along. Brothers, uncles, aunties stood next to that old piano or by Papa's guitar, asking him to play one more song to sing along to before someone else's turn.

To fit in, to no longer be excluded or bullied by the lowlander urbanites, Papa the mountain boy had to change. He learned to speak Tagalog with an unassailable Manileño accent. He changed his military-cut hair, growing it long and wavy, like the musicians he loved. Bell-bottoms replaced his straight trousers. Tailored polyester shirts, all high-1970s dagger collars and long cuffs, replaced his plain, sober cotton button-downs. He claimed to be a city boy from Baguio. And he changed his name: from Ferdinand to Fernando. Maybe the name change had to do with Ferdinand Marcos, who became president when Papa was ten and remained dictator until he was thirty-one.

"I hated it in Manila, at first," Papa said to me one summer. "Hated being called Igorot by my classmates, being made fun of for speaking Ilokano. They said we were dirty, that we all ate dog and cut off each others' heads and carried spears around. Those Manileños, acting superior while trying too hard to be American. Pretending to be Spanish with their made-up census names."

I am proud of our Indigenous surname. Damatac, a name that is native to our islands, is a name of resistance. I think of our people's immense mountain rice terraces, carved upward as they retreated from the Spanish a few centuries ago. Rather than comply with the conquistadores' swords and the frailes' bibles, our ancestors chose self-sufficiency and survival, climbing higher and higher, towards the gods. The mountains and the rivers became their fortress. There, they remained mostly undisturbed, defended by both men and women warriors and the powers of our mumbaki, until the arrival of the Americans and the Japanese in the early twentieth century.

Using a sharp, long bolo, slice the chicken open from throat to belly. Let any unclotted blood run into a bowl.

One day, near the end of his final year of high school, one of Papa's older brothers took him to the Conservatory of Music at the University of Santo Tomas, the oldest university in Asia.

"That's where your dad should have gone," my uncle would tell me years later. "I tried to encourage him. But our father, your Lolo, wouldn't allow it."

Papa wanted his father's love more than any music or instrument in the world. He ignored the musical imprint left in his soul by his ancestors, for it is they who help shape our needs, our desires. Instead, Papa obeyed his father's wishes. Architecture major, with a minor in business.

"What will you do with music, anyway?" Lolo Pedring had asked him. "You can make more money as an architect. The government is commissioning lots of buildings these days, you know."

Edifice Complex. This is what scholars now call the dictator's building sprees, facades to hide corruption and death, funds received from the IMF and World Bank. Propaganda set in concrete and steel, propped up by the Americans, who saw the dictator as an essential regional ally during the Cold War, a useful extension of imperial power. And while my father may have acquiesced to his father's wishes, our ancestors' spirit of defiance still coursed through my Papa's young veins. Instead of studying, he joined university students protesting Marcos's 1972 declaration of martial law. Papa marched as the Marcos economy failed, as Marcos stole billions from the government, as Marcos signed the Labor Act into law, forcing Filipinos overseas, sacrificial bodies to atone for his theft.

"We made signs, you know ... Marcos Hitler, Diktador Tuta." He laughed. Dictator Puppy. Hippies side by side with priests and nuns, daring Marcos's police to beat them with sticks, to imprison them with no charges. To disappear them by the thousands.

The mumbaki will examine the bile-sac, so that we may know if this sacrifice is sufficient for the gods. So that we may know if our loved one can be saved from death.

Because of his role in those student rebellions, Papa lost a year or so of his university education. Marcos's pulis, long black sticks hitched on one hip, revolver holstered on the other, knocked on Lola Luisa's door, looking for him. They visited the house of his girlfriend, the daughter of a local pulis sergeant, who turned them away, denying they'd ever heard my father's name. Papa lay low for one year under Lolo Pedring's advice. There is a chance that my father was spared because of Lolo Pedring's position of power in the mountains. Perhaps my Lolo, ever shrewd, did what was needed to smooth the dictator's ruffled feathers.

It did not take long for Papa's defiant spirit to be beaten out of him. After his period of hiding, he returned as a more compliant version of himself, easy tinola replacing bloody pinikpikan. He stopped attending secret meetings, no longer joined marches. He obeyed Lolo Pedring and continued his university studies, transformed into an upper-middleish-class college kid. A happy-go-lucky guy, pockets full of spending money from his sizable allowance, nights spent drinking, hotel rooms booked for girlfriends after days of shopping. He played his music at bars and venues, opening acts and late night jams, covers of Crosby, Stills & Nash; Cat Stevens; Led Zeppelin. He furtively read the newspaper for friends' names. Once, he told me that he felt guilty. That, unlike some of his friends and his friends' friends, he was not much of a revolutionary. He sounded wistful as he said it.

Papa's efforts at transformation were futile. He failed to find a foothold in architecture, an industry whose greatest patron happened to be the His and Hers Dictatorship. He switched, near the end of his degree, to an elementary education major. He just wanted to be done. He only wanted to play music. Like many of Papa's friends, the courage and defiance in his blood were replaced by fear and acceptance. By the need to survive, even if in silence.

Sear the chicken's body over the fire, so that its skin chars dark brown-black all over. Cut the body into pieces.

During those dictator years, Papa's heart pounded not in fear, but in rhythm with music. He was kept alive by his dreams of playing music, of composing songs, tiny accordion fingers all grown up into a man's hands on frets and keys. He directed two church choirs, creating harmonies too difficult for his singers to grasp, sometimes so difficult that he would, in classic hot-tempered Papa fashion, walk out in frustration at their inability to follow. The choir, devoted and knowing Papa better than he realized, would wait until he walked back in, less angry, ready to try again.

On one of those choir practice afternoons, he met a girl. Like him, she was also a university student. As she came in for her audition, he asked her what song she would like to sing. He was softened at the sight of her, with her slim shoulders, graceful hands, and shock of long, curly, gloss-black hair. Her big brown eyes shy and heavy-lidded, her face unadorned, clean.

"'Annie's Song,' by John Denver," she said. Without music, she began to sing. And my father, hearing her steady, clear voice, followed with his guitar, the beginning of a beginning. The start of having someone to accompany, and to keep company, until the end.

Her name was Ana May. She was three years younger than him, quiet and sweet, but with a steeliness to her glance, to her posture. She was punctual and disciplined, cool yet friendly. Ana May did not chase my father, the matinee idol of the group, the ex-boyfriend of quite a few of the ladies. She did not chase anyone. She had better things to do, obligations to fulfill, engkantos of her own to leave behind. This distance she kept bewitched my Papa, and many of the other boys too.

Their first date, a year or so later, was over an ice cream.

"The bet was, if my university won the TV challenge against hers, I'd take her out for ice cream, and vice versa. I couldn't lose," he said to me.

I was there at their wedding in 1982, four years after their first date. Afloat in Mama's belly, still safe, if just for a few more months, from the final few years of Marcos. I heard their vows to each other, the songs that played at their wedding banquet. Heard him say how much na mahal kita, heard her whisper it back. Heard the ruffle of turtledoves' wings released overhead at the wedding reception, hope for the future just before they cut the cake. Felt the renewed purpose Papa was so sure he had finally found.

Their hopefulness did not last. There were so few jobs to be had in 1982, and fewer still by 1983. So that he could provide for his young family, Papa found an office job, doing something corporate at a desk for Nestlé. He also found freelance work, small jobs drafting up buildings commissioned by the government whose autocracy he once protested, modernist and brutalist facades to cover up the blood of citizens, spilled and burned into the ground. And still, no matter how much he changed himself, transformed to survive in Manila, to survive Marcos, Papa continued to face the prejudice of others.

"Your mother's brothers did not approve of me," he said.

In a prepared pot of clean water, boil the chicken along with the ginger,
garlic, and onion. Simmer over a low fire until soft.

Later on, perhaps at the wedding, Mama's brothers discovered who my
father's family was—educated and wealthier than they realized, colonial in
that American way that Filipinos love to mimic, worship, and resent all at
once. Almost every member of Papa's family was university educated, paid
in full by my grandfather, who was in possession of tracts of land, multiple properties, and secret wealth whose origins, possibly shameful, remain
unknown. They saw the fruits of my Lolo Pedring's survival instincts, and
nodded in approval.

My mother's family, scarred by Marcos's economy, began to show Papa
grudging respect, even as he struggled to find work. Still, my mother's
mother, envious and grasping, spread lies about my father. That he never
finished university, that he was an uneducated country bumpkin. When con-
fronted with her lies, with my father's diploma, his graduation photos, she
changed her story. That my mother, quite implausibly, paid for his tuition,
even though she was years behind him at university. Even though my mother
gave all of her salary to her parents.

Through his in-laws' decades of exclusion and lies, out of love for my
mother, out of pride for himself, my father never said anything in his own
defense. Perhaps he understood that life in a regime dictates that when one is
left with nothing but vanity and envy, others, like my mother's mother, may
wish to drag others down, insinuation by insinuation, lie by lie. One beat of
a stick at a time, pik-pik, pik-pik.

Those who lived through the regime know: debt ballooned under the
dictator's twenty-year reign, the cronyism and the pocketing of IMF and
World Bank funds. The Edifice Complex was just that: a brutalist edifice for
a failed state. The Philippines went from owing $600 million in 1965, at the
start of Marcos's regime, to $26 billion by 1986, at its end. "The Golden Age of
Infrastructure," Marcos's supporters call it. Architecture, roads, and bridges
as a facade for murder and theft. I suppose, for such supporters, it was not
a lie, thanks to the kickbacks they received, the way their regions benefited
while others starved.

When my sister was born in 1988, Marcos had been gone for a little over two years, flown out of Malacañang Palace via a US military helicopter. Papa seemed to come alive again with her arrival, seemed to commit to being a father and a husband. My spirit's memory associates her birth and our move into the big marble house as the real start of our family. Unlike my sister, who was created with love and intention, I had been a mistake.

My grandfather asked Papa, his architect son, to help draw up plans for the big marble house. For free, for love, Papa sketched his ideas, dreams in elevation and floor plan form: a soaring common room space with double-height ceilings, a marble breakfast bar for the kitchen, a carved wooden staircase, and, rather than an upstairs hallway leading to each bedroom, a family room surrounded, in a semicircle, by doors to each of the three bedrooms and bathroom. The lead architect embraced my father's ideas, built them into steel, cement, sand, tile, stone, marble, and wood. Between his shifts at work and on weekends, Papa worked alongside the builders on our house-to-be. He mixed and laid cement with the workers, cut timber for the stairs, fit the cast-iron grates—his own design—over the windows. His own sweat is there, forever mixed in with the mortar in the house's foundation, its walls.

The big marble house took longer than planned to be built. While we waited, as Mama's belly grew with my sister inside it, we stayed at my mother's parents' house. An unbearable indignity for my father. Some nights, he did not come home.

As it finishes, add the sayote and leaves of your choice. Add a cup of bayah and slices of etag to salt the broth. Allow to simmer for 10 minutes.

In the big marble house, we were happy, even if for only a short time. Lolo Pedring bought a puppy for me, a bulldog that Papa named Bruno. Every afternoon, I did my homework at the big dining table while Bruno snored under my feet, which did not quite touch the floor. My yaya, Alona, took care of me and my baby sister. Papa worked at his office building or at his drafting table. Mama worked at the Philippine National Bank in Makati. Friends and family, cousins and neighbors visited, played with me in the lush gardens tended to by Lolo Pedring. We snacked on the mangoes and avocados that fell from the trees, on Baguio strawberries that hung, fat and red, for children's fingers to pluck. I was the first to witness my baby sister's first steps, fat legs jiggling with each step she took on the cool marble floor, the two of us collapsing into a pile of giggles when she made it across the room to me.

For our last Christmas together, the only real one we had before everything changed, my father made a tree with his own hands.

"Why don't the trees have snow on them?" I had asked Papa weeks before, my hand in his. The shopping mall's selection of artificial pine trees didn't have snow, not like the ones in the American Christmas movies that played on our screens. And so, Papa built a tree, using a tall length of PVC pipe and branches from the trees around the house, cut so that they formed the shape of a perfect, conical pine tree. Painted white, the glow of that long-ago Christmas tree still lights my memories of that big marble house.

The engkantos, peering into our windows from the mango tree, found us boring, then. The mountain gods bided their time. Papa went to work every day. In the mornings, while he nursed a cup of coffee, I played airplane-spoon with my baby sister, feeding her mashed apricots, which mostly dribbled down her giggling, fat-wobbly chin. Kisses on all our foreheads from Mama, rushing out the door in heels and a suit. Papa dropped me off at school some days, picked me up by the tall iron gates in the afternoon. On other days, he washed my baby sister, helped me with my multiplication tables, played songs for Mama after dinner. He was a changed man, a far cry from the boy in the mountains who could not call any house a home, who missed his brothers, his mother, his father. He and Mama threw parties at the big marble house: housewarmings, birthday celebrations, christening parties. I had a regular bedtime, and I slept through each night, my spirit and breath safe in the cradle of our new home.

But perhaps Papa was not so changed, after all. The engkantos and the mountain gods must have seen that he was alien to such domestic ease, unable to embrace the relative comforts of his life. He was uneasy with the gentle rhythms of a real family, the kind he had dreamed of when he was fourteen, new to Manila, alone and motherless in a strange house. He could not accept the unconditional love of two children and a wife who never asked him to change. Became uncomfortable with the reliability of waking up each morning with all of us still there, always there. In the evening walks he took around Provident Village, on streets named Geneva and Amsterdam, did he see, flashing on the banks of the Marikina River, the telltale tempting glow of the mythical fanfanilag—which the lowlanders call santelmo—floating just above the water's surface, beckoning for him to leave by sea?

Before long, the big marble house began to fill with musical instruments and band rehearsals: covers of George Benson, Chic; Bobby Caldwell; Lionel Richie; Marvin Gaye; Stevie Wonder; Donny Hathaway; Earth, Wind & Fire; decades of Motown; '70s and '80s yacht rock. A joyful thing, for most homes. An impending sign of doom, for ours.

After my sister's first birthday, Papa did what was most familiar to his rootless feet and unanchored soul: he packed up his things, his guitars and his keyboard, and left. "I won't be gone long," he said, while I sobbed into his chest the night before his flight. He couldn't be sure. He was to play music with his band on a big Norwegian cruise ship. I can send you pictures, he said. Don't worry, anak, the money is good, and we need the money so we can have our own wealth. We won't have to owe anyone anything. Did you know, you can make telephone calls at sea these days, hush now, that's enough crying, that's my girl, you must be a good big sister.

Weeks before he left, I begged him to stay, handing him a piece of paper.

"What's this?"

"A list."

"Of?"

"Reader's Digest says that it is important to make a list of pros and cons when making a big decision. So here is the list."

Pros: the ocean, money. Cons: missing my seventh birthday, our "snowy" Christmas tree. The cons ran long, reasons to stay penciled neatly onto the back of the piece of notebook paper.

"Don't tear paper from your notebook again," Papa scolded. "It's expensive."

Later, I hid his brand-new shoes—the white leather ones he would later wear onstage—under my bed, hoping he would be forced to stay. But he was determined to be Filipino Odysseus, ready to cross oceans for twice the annual salary and for his own fulfillment. He must have found it all to be more exciting and romantic than he wanted to admit. He was setting off to sea to fight battles inside himself, a soldier in an economic war waged by Marcos against his own citizens. Against families like ours.

When the pinikpikan is done, the food is covered, held in a basket. The
mumbaki will stand over it before it is time to eat.

I am certain now that had we consulted with a mumbaki—gently beat a
chicken to death as offering, sifted our fingers through its warm organs—that
the gods would have never allowed Papa to leave. The heart and gallbladder
would have indicated sorrow and suffering. Perhaps an unfavorable death.
But I am also certain that even if our holy women made him stay at home
until the animals' omens gave way to good fortune, Papa would have broken
that circle. He would have forced his way out and found his way to the edge
of the sea. Called to the water, my father followed the fanfanilags' call and
cast himself adrift. A willful choice. The gods know that fate is just a word
we assign to the consequences of our freely made decisions. For months, I
refused to write Papa any letters. I came to the phone only to say hello, kumusta po. He folded letters into my birthday cards, explained why he needed
to be away. I did not read them.

Papa's six months became a year, almost renewed by contract into two.
Papa's odyssey of music, ports of call, and exotic white women was inter-
rupted only by the discovery that he was not earning as much as he thought.

"That Tony," he said to me, years later. "He couldn't play the guitar worth
a damn. But he was good at stealing money."

And that is how we came to be in America: through Filipinos who saw
their fellow Filipinos as a source of stolen income, a repetition of how we
steal from each other. Papa failed to see the long arm of the gods, refused
to consider that perhaps, after a year of wandering the oceans, it was time
to go back home. Instead, Papa disembarked off the gangplank at New York
Harbor and, with barely a glance at the Statue of Liberty, decided to stay in
America.

"It was your mother's fault, you know," he said to me when I was sixteen.
"She said that you weren't doing well in school. That you wouldn't eat. That
you were sleepwalking, fighting your yaya. All I wanted was to make money
for six more months, maybe a year in New York, then go back home. But she
said it would be better here, that my aunties said she could easily find a job."

I did not believe that Papa had no say in the matter. You were the one
who left the cruise ship for New York instead of going home, I wanted to say.

You were the one who left in the first place. You were the one with the colonial mentality, the one who believed the lies Filipinos have been taught by Americans to believe: that the United States is the best place on earth, that the Philippines is a toilet by comparison. That a life of debt, sadness, anger, near-poverty, and loneliness in America is better than a life of middle-class contentment in a Philippines finally free of the dictatorship you once protested on the streets.

> *"Spirits of our ancestors," the mumbaki will say. "We place this offering in the basket and we honor you. We ask that you keep away the evil spirits of the East and West, the curses of our enemies, the sicknesses that bring death. We ask that you spare our children."*

I have yet to find the courage to say these things to my father, to confront him with the mistake he made and doubled down upon for thirty years. A fatal error of thumbing his nose at the gods. These days, as I have grown older, older than even he was when he first walked off that ship and into New York City, I am learning to see his reasons, though understanding them still escapes me. At times, I think I can even forgive his wanderings. I think of the loneliness of the great ocean, the merciless stars at night, how they must have made him feel so small and alone, like childhood. I think of calling him, of making him listen to me, for once—the child whose future he threw into undocumented turmoil. I think of shouting into the telephone, like a spirit, angry at being conjured, speaking through the belly of a bonfire, grievances screaming through blood and smoke. But because I have been raised by my father to be afraid, I do not.

I call the New Jersey house when I can, when I have recovered enough from the inevitable wounds of our previous conversation. Sometimes it takes me one week, sometimes one year. Sometimes, five, straddling decades. My father cannot always converse. Often, he does not make it to the phone. He struggles to find his way, trapped there in that house by his engkantos, his stacks of boxes, his fears and paranoia.

He may have the same name, and flesh, and voice now as he did then, but I lost my real father in 1990, at the departures gate at Ninoy Aquino International. The Papa that exists now, the dark shadow self I call Dad, no longer plays the piano, which now sits, covered in dust, behind towers of hoarded boxes in the living room. He now lives only to convince himself that he did the right thing in bringing us to America. That, despite thirty-three years of evidence to the contrary, the United States might still give us amnesty, a path to citizenship. That, even if such a blessing from the gods never happens, a half-life of secrets and hiding in America is still better than a full life of belonging and selfhood in the Philippines. That destroying his relationship with his children, his family, his country is worth it, all so that America may someday embrace him. My father has yet to learn that in constantly rejecting himself—the mountain boy, the city musician, the Filipino immigrant—he allows the world to reject him too.

The mumbaki must eat first, and then we follow. Afterward, we must disperse from this site, so that the spirits know to pass healing or judgment upon us.

It has been a year since our last phone call, when he told me to stop describing ourselves as immigrants, a word which brought him shame. I pick up my phone, tap "Home" in my contacts. I hear the connection ring. I lose my nerve and end the call. I lift the lid on the tinola, check the firmness of the sayote, the greenness of the bok choy leaves. Season the broth with a spoonful of patis, a twist of black pepper, stir it in. I'm not ready to talk yet.

And then: my phone vibrates. The screen glows. "Home" is calling back. I stare at the screen, let the phone shudder on the granite counter. My finger hovers over the screen to accept. Almost touching the bright green dot, saying hello a little too eagerly. Instead, I snatch my hand back, turn my body away from it. I cannot decide. I dip the ladle into the pot, filling it with gingery broth. The phone continues to buzz. I lift the ladle to my wordless lips, sip in a curled tongueful of hot soup. I slurp in air to fan the roof of my mouth. I close my eyes. Imagine myself accepting the call. The phone stops buzzing. The screen drops to blank black. I swallow the tear-salted lump in my throat and lick the ladle clean.

2

Sisig na Baboy
(Pork Cooked Three Ways)

Mama's 1960s–1990s

SERVES 4

4 ounces pig's ears

4 ounces pig's cheeks

2 1/4 pounds pork belly

Sea salt

1 tablespoon black peppercorns

5 fresh or dried bay leaves

1 or 2 heads garlic

1 red onion

6 bird's eye chilies

4 ounces chicken or pig liver, diced

10 garlic cloves, minced

1/4 cup sugarcane vinegar

1/4 cup calamansi juice

4 eggs

At the table:

Sinangag rice

3-4 calamansi, sliced in half

Maggi seasoning, to taste

The kitchen is cloudy with smoke. The blare of the alarm pierces the Sunday quiet. I cough into a sleeve, run into the haze. Somehow, in the smoke, I find the oven door. It creaks in complaint as I yank it open. I check the trays. The pig's ears have just begun to char.

Boil the pig ears, cheeks, and belly in a potful of water, with salt, pep-percorns, and bay leaves, for 2 hours, until tender.

Sisig is a dish of making do. Of eating what must be eaten in order to survive. It is a reminder of what has been taken from our islands, of the un-wanted we have been forced to swallow. Of what remains, and how we have adapted. It reminds you, as it sizzles in its cast-iron pan, of transformation brought only by hunger, fire, and acid. It reminds you, as your teeth gnash on the crispy, chewy, and tender pig flesh, of all that it is made of. It reminds you, as its citrus-sour, chilied heat endures on your tongue, of how to swallow undesirable truths. Of how to take the unwanted, the discarded, and turn it into something desirable.

"When you're drunk, this is exactly what you want," Anthony Bourdain said of sisig during one of his show's episodes in Manila. In truth, sisig is what is wanted when one's country is leveled by centuries of occupation. When the land of one's birth is a case study of US military–occupied necro-economy. When its natural riches are pillaged by empires and multinationals. When one's family is dispersed around the world for remittance purposes, sisig is a source of comfort, fatty and crisp. Sisig is what Filipinos eat when all the best parts are taken by occupying American forces.

And besides, sisig is excellent for brunch, which is what I am making today.

Green mango, garlic, salt, chilies, vinegar: sisig in its original form did not contain meat. It was fresh, vegetal, and raw. It was a side dish, its acid bal-ancing the main ulam's salt and fat. It comes from my mother's people, the Kapampangan. Descended from Indonesian tribes, they settled in our central lowlands alongside our true aborigines, the umber-skinned Aeta. Born on lava-fertile soil, in the unpredictable volcanic shadows of Arayat, Pinatubo, and Negron, the Kapampangans understand the inevitability of fiery, life-giving destruction, whether it be from the gods or from bible-bearing missionaries. Unlike other, less wise people, my mother's people knew that the world came to be by accident. They understood our place in the universe, that we were never its center or its intent. And that like all living beings on this earth, we come from survival, not creation.

Light the grill or preheat the oven to 400°F.

Mama's childhood was not like Papa's. While Papa was raised in upper-middle-class comfort—a material security against which he rebelled—Mama was raised in poverty. Unlike my father's parents, who were educated to graduate level, my mother's parents did not finish high school. Their education was one that was earned not through books, exams, essays, and theory, but through daily tests of hunger, weekly pop quizzes of need, and the reality of transient landlessness. They did not need to read or write about a Philippines under Marcos and the shadow of postcolonial American occupation. They lived it.

"We survived, you know," she once told me. "Your Lolo Baldo and Lola Lina had to do what was needed just to have enough for the week, for the month."

Mama's parents had eloped in 1952. Alfonso Gonzales was twenty-five; Catalina Mendoza, seventeen. Did she love him? Did she think she could grow to love him? Perhaps she thought she could love him enough, this mustachioed man with a camera, a jeepney, and a dreamer's talk of far-off places like Manila and Baguio. In 1952, the Philippines was young also, and thought it had found a savior in the United States. The Americans, having relinquished its colonial grip on our islands six years before, in 1946, were an immovable stain on our soil. They were comfortable on their 147,000 acres of military-reserved land, which they took from the Kapampangans. On that land, the cooks at Clark Air Base fed the American soldiers only the best cuts of pig. They had bacon and sausages for breakfast, ham and cheese sandwiches for lunch, and pork chops with imported applesauce and mashed potatoes for dinner, all the better to flex their military-industrial might on our soil. Kapampangans, hungry outside the reservation's walls, watched the unwanted pig parts as they were thrown away. Trotters and heads piled high, rotting in the Filipino sun, year after starving year.

Town to rootless town, house to rented house, job to aimless job, Alfonso and Catalina made do with the little they had. They had one son, then two. Mama, who arrived in 1958, was their third child. Their first daughter.

Allow the boiled pork ears, cheeks, and belly to cool and dry on a rack.

In Quezon City, Lola Lina worked at what would now be called a sweatshop. She sewed women's brassieres by the dozens each day. The work was slow and finicky. She came home with stabbing pain in her eyes, her neck, her hands. She was paid by the piece. Each bra my Lola Lina sewed was piled into boxes, stacked onto trucks, and sold in stores across our islands. Before Marcos drove the nation into indentured debt servitude, our economy was focused on domestic production. On self-sufficiency, not export to pay down international debts.

Lolo Baldo found work also. He was a deliveryman for Kraft Foods, the American company. Soon, he and his brothers began a small real estate business together. Five young men with young families to feed. They worked seven days a week, from dawn to almost midnight, each roaming Manila and the areas just beyond in search of houses and land, sellers and buyers. Each brother hoped to someday own something too, a piece of land to regain what was lost.

As soon as their firstborn, Raynold, was old enough, Lola Lina gave him the task of cleaning their rented house on Molave Street. My uncle Raynold was only six, but he knew how to sweep the floors, an expert in the walis tingting, the walis tambo. Small bare feet alternating on a bunot to polish the wooden floors, Tito Raynold danced across the floorboards, the coconut husk under his right foot. He swept, scrubbed, cleaned, and polished the house his parents worked hard to afford to rent. And then he walked himself to school, ever the good son.

During those years, Lolo Baldo sold enough houses and land so that Lola Lina could stop working at the bra factory. Lola Lina gave birth to their fourth child, a second daughter. It was the 1960s, and there, living in that rented house on Madasalin Street—the street of the prayerful—it seemed like their dreams of owning their own land and house were possible. This hope suffused our islands, too, even as our economy burned, fed by longing, delusion, housing, land, greed, lies, banks, and debt. Our people chewed on mouthfuls of rice, sometimes with nothing else but hope.

On the grill, or in the oven, roast the pork ears, cheeks, and belly until golden brown and slightly burnt at the edges.

The Kapampangans understand that it is possible to create life from nothing. Before everything, they say that there was only the vast space of the cosmos. In this space was the temple of the gods, who often met at the behest of Mangechay, the deity who oversaw them and the cosmic world. During one such meeting, the gods saw that Mangechay's daughter had grown to become beautiful. Their desire for her overshadowed the purpose of their gathering.

"Allow me to marry her, O Supreme Mangechay," said one god.

"Choose me, O Highest One," said a goddess.

"I have yet to take a wife, Beloved God," said another, whose words were soon drowned out by others, all of whom wanted not only to marry the beautiful goddess but also to secure a familial alliance with their leader.

In Mangechay's judiciousness and wisdom—they had not become ruler of the gods for nothing—they decided that their daughter's hand in marriage should be won through battle. And so, the most powerful beings in the universe fought for Mangechay's daughter's hand. These gods battled for millennia, a phenomenon labeled by Westerners as the Big Bang: beams of light flung against dark masses, asteroids exploded by shards of ice, balls of superheated gas swallowing rocks hurled from other planes, which we now call multiverses. But there was no winner in this battle, for the gods and goddesses were of equal power to one another. Still, they raged on, each hoping to gain an edge, a foothold, any smallest hint of dominion over the others. Some died trying.

Then, one day, Mangechay cried out amid the boom, flash, and bang of battle:

"Stop!"

There, where the gods' temple once floated, was the body of Mangechay's daughter, life flowing out of her hands, heart, and head. Was she struck dead by flame, or a rock, or a star? No one could say. The warring gods, in their fight for supremacy, had forgotten all about her. As they circled, the gods noticed something else, just beyond her body: a rough-hewn sphere, a hunk of rock spewing steam and smoke, sputtering lava, floating in space. It must have been formed by their weapons of ice and fire. Of light, gas, and stars.

Did no one think to ask the young goddess who she might want to marry, or if she wanted to marry at all? In Mangechay's daughter's memory, and as apology, the gods ended the battle and vowed to stop fighting forever. They gave this sphere of rock, still spewing magma and steam, some water, seeds, soil, and salt. They blew air and wind into its atmosphere, laid clouds upon its lowest layer, forming a protective veil so that the sun, its closest star, could not scorch the life blooming underneath.

This is how our world came to be: at the careless hands of deities, trying to make up for the mess they had made. These gods would return to this spherical rock often, bringing gifts of flora or sea creatures. Trees and forests. Ribboned tiers of light that dance in its northern skies. And when humans came to be, the gods nurtured them, too, teaching them how to survive, how to not destroy this gift of a new world. From their seat on great Mount Arayat, the gods gave us vegetable sisig as medicine, said by priestesses to be a cure for acute imbalances: a hangover, a bad stomach, a headache. A shipful of uninvited conquistadores.

As the Spaniards descended upon our land, my mother's ancestors, feet planted on unpredictable volcanic soil, understood the fickleness of life and the futile, deadly cost of war. They did not fight and retreat into unconquerable mountains, as my father's Cordilleran ancestors did. No, the Kapampangans chose to stay and survive. Their survival among the Spanish lasted centuries, became instinct. This instinct has carried my mother's family, my mother, and our family through generations. Through empires, dictators, migrations, and other ruptures.

Kapampangan survival was not without cost or pain. As the collective stomachache of colonization took hold, sisig underwent its own holy transfiguration, going from occasional animist remedy to a daily part of the Jesus-blessed family meal. With scooped fingers and a thumb, elbow resting on a raised knee, Kapampangans would gather a pat of rice, some ulam, and a green hunk of sisig on the side. The chili-hot, acidic corrosion hardened their stomachs, balancing the bitterness blooming, silent and unspoken, in their blood. Mama's favorite snack descends from that native cure: green mangoes dashed with puckery vinegar and salty patis.

Remove the golden-crispy pork ears, cheeks, and belly from the grill or oven. Let cool on a rack.

No one was ready for the currency crisis of 1969, except perhaps for Marcos and his cronies. Their pockets were lined, garages full, houses secured, offshore accounts stuffed with money meant to build the country's industries. In an effort to become the first Philippine president to be reelected, Marcos spent money the country did not have, a continuation of his first four years in office. He propagandized IMF and World Bank debt as progress, borrowed against the unrealized gross national production of a country whose rotted industries were failing. Debt secured upon the backs of Filipinos who could barely afford to feed their children, could not afford to own a home. The administration built roads and bridges to constituencies bought with corruption, theaters and cultural centers to tell its lies, energy infrastructures to control natural resources and power alliances.

Payback time happened sooner than anyone, perhaps even Marcos, expected. Unable to pay even the interest on its loans, by 1969 the Philippines was handcuffed by its debtors into indentured servitude. As part of the IMF's debt restructuring plan, the country was forced to halt domestic production. From then on, and still today, our islands are a site of extraction, our industries oriented towards exporting everything to pay off debt. Minerals. Plants. People. In the shock of the balance of payments crisis, the Philippine peso and its fledgling, postcolonial economy crumbled.

As the peso and the economy fell, so did the Manila real estate market. Lolo Baldo's income, reliant on people buying houses and land, was reduced to ashes.

"I can't remember if your Lolo and Lola lost their down payment for the house first, or the house they were renting. But it all happened around the same time," Mama said with a sigh.

In weeks, Mama and her family were homeless. Landless. With no place to live, and with their savings sunk into the lost house and lot, my grandparents were left with no choice. They moved to the home of Tiong Dom, one of Lolo

Baldo's younger brothers. Tiong Dom was more prosperous than Lolo Baldo. All of the brothers were. Each owned a house and land, servants to sleep in servants' quarters.

"Tiong Dom didn't have servants yet," Mom continued. "So we stayed at the quarters, underneath the house. Us girls and your Lola in one room, the boys and your Lolo in the other."

My mother was eleven, her baby sister only three. The two eldest, my Tito Raynold and Tito Nathaniel, were sixteen and thirteen. My mother's family story—along with the burning will to make do and survive, which now lives on in me and my cousins—was born inside those servants' quarters underneath Tiong Dom's house. I am proud of this lineage of hardship. An inheritance not of gold, or houses, or tracts of land, or contacts and nepotism, but of iron and fire, of determination in our blood.

As the roasted pork ears, cheeks, and belly cool, set the table, so that all are ready to eat while the pan of sisig is still hot. Once cooled enough to touch, finely dice the pork into ½-inch cubes. Set aside.

Mama's family spent two years underneath Tiong Dom's house. They owned nothing besides clothes, maybe a radio. Sometimes, Mama and her brothers would sneak over to a window, the one that looked into Tiong Dom's sala, where the television sat. Three sets of sleepy brown eyes, trying to catch a glimpse of that day's news on *Pangunahing Balita*, or maybe a game show: *Pamilya Kwarta o Kahon*. As they stood outside, peering in through the window, a cousin, comfortable on the couch inside, would pull the curtain across to keep Mama and her brothers out.

"Tiong Dom's kids—my cousins, your Titas—they were my playmates, you know," she told me. "But sometimes, I guess they didn't want to share."

Take a large skillet, maybe one in heavy cast iron, forged in a fire. Preheat the skillet so that water droplets sizzle on its surface.

In Pampanga, the Gonzales family's homeland in the center of the Philippines, the addition of pork to vegetable sisig was just beginning, though we do not know exactly when. Perhaps it began in 1969, as the nation descended into the debt crisis. Perhaps it began in 1972, with the declaration of martial law, ginned up by Marcos as an anticommunism strategy, while people starved and rioted in the streets. During those years, the Kapampangans bargained with the Clark Air Base commissaries. They offered to buy, on the cheap, the discarded cuts of slaughtered pigs. All the bits the Americans refused to eat. They took these pig parts home—snouts, cheeks, feet, ears, livers, hearts, intestines—and cleaned them. Boiled them so that the embedded dirt would rise, like scum, to the water's surface, skimmed off with a bamboo spoon. Roasted them over open flame or seething charcoal, so that the pig skin went golden brown, like ours. And then, the Kapampangans took these boiled, roasted pig parts and chopped them finely, into bits small enough to stir in with their green mango sisig. Slowly, the discarded offcuts of meat took over the dish.

When it all became too much to bear and the gods' simple cure of spicy-soured raw vegetable was no longer enough, did the stirred-in pig parts help the medicine go down? Did our people think—while they chewed on the burnt, resistant, cartilaginous pig scraps—that by eating from the same animal as the Americans, we might finally be seen as part of the empire? That by ingesting the Americans' discarded remnants, we would no longer be their dirty secret?

In 1974, Marcos and his cronies found a way to make do and survive in power just a little longer. With a crashed economy and no real industries to produce gross national anything, the administration signed the Labor Code into law. This document, on the surface, appeared to be a humane rewriting of how the Filipino worker should be treated. In effect, Marcos's Labor Code consolidated workers' labor and earnings into the chokehold of state control. By 1974, our people had been working overseas for decades, almost a century, migrating to the American mainland as cheap labor, part of the commonwealth. The Labor Code turned these scraps of American exploitation into a profit machine oiled and run by the Philippine government. It was through one of these government agencies—the National Seamen Board—that Mama's two oldest brothers finally found work.

"That system, hay nako." Mama sighed. "The government took, like, half of your Titos' pay before they ever saw a single centavo. And that was before taxes."

Tito Raynold went overseas first, as the lowest-ranked worker on a cargo ship. Spat on and abused by British, American, and German officers, he worked his way up, beginning with scrubbing the ship's deck. He learned each part of her engine, her crew, how to navigate by instruments, by the stars. He saw the world, its possibilities. Learned how to dream. My uncle may have despised the island regime, the American empire, and all that they took from his family, but he found a way to make do with the scrap he was given. By the time Tito Raynold disembarked from the ship one last time, years later, he had been promoted to the rank of second engineer, all without a formal degree.

As the skillet heats, mince the garlic. Dice the red onion and chilies.

Sisig also transformed itself in 1974. That year, a woman named Lucia Cunanan began to sell her version of sisig at her food stand in Angeles City, just outside Clark Air Base. Aling Lucing, as she was called, did modest business before she created pork sisig as we know it. Made only of salvaged pork cheek and ear, her thrice-cooked sisig, seasoned with chilies and garlic and finished with Maggi seasoning, became an instant hit. Tatays, Titos, and Lolos came to Aling Lucing's. They sat in groups, drank San Miguel beer, sang Frank Sinatra and Elvis Presley to someone's guitar, ate pork sisig as pulutan into the night, until curfew, when Marcos's patrols made them go home. In those martial law years, joy was hard to find. Aling Lucing's pork sisig made each day somewhat bearable. Made it possible to get up the next day to make do and survive.

Tito Nathaniel, Mama's second-oldest brother, followed Tito Raynold overseas. He had an associate's degree in ship engineering, funded by Tito Raynold's earnings. Though Marcos's government took the better parts of their salaries from them, my uncles still managed to earn enough to send back home to Lolo Baldo and Lola Lina. Mama's family began to lift itself from poverty.

"Your Titos really saved us," Mama said, her voice quavering on the telephone. "Your Tito Raynold didn't have a degree, but he worked his way up from the very bottom. Your Tito Nathaniel became chief engineer, even though all the others were usually white men back then. And Tito Raynold paid for my university tuition."

By 1976, four years into martial law and eleven years under the regime,

Mama began her studies at the University of Santo Tomas. With his hard-earned money, Tito Raynold built a house on Madasalin Street, one side for himself, one for his mother and father. This duplex house, and the land it was built upon, still belongs to our family today. My Titos furnished their parents' house, so that finally, they could sit down in their own sala, watch teleseryas on a television of their own, and eat on a real dining table, waited on by a maid. Tito Raynold married Rea, the Bacolod-born woman of his seabound dreams, who kept all of his letters and waited for his return.

Toss all of the garlic and two-thirds of the red onion and chilies into the heated skillet. Sauté until the onion is translucent, the garlic brown, the sting of the chilies softened.

Young Ana May Gonzales went to university with goals in mind: to graduate with a bachelor's degree in business, find work in banking or in finance, and help her family continue to thrive. She was studious, detail-oriented, a hard worker not easily distracted from the path she had chosen.

I understand why Mama attracted the rich girls of UST. Daughters of senators and congressmen, Marcos cronies, beneficiaries of the regime. There are photos of Mama from these years, when she was eighteen, nineteen. Wide, doe eyes with sleepy lids, a finely shaped nose. Full lips, a square jaw. Broad shoulders, a slim frame. Long, curly hair. Shyness that belied the iron will underneath. Beautiful. The kind of beauty no amount of money could buy, even with money like the rich girls had, dictator money slipped into their fathers' pockets.

Maybe these rich girls wanted to have Ana May around to bask in her glow. To feel just as beautiful, sharp, and humorous as her, while still feeling superior to her, knowing how poor her family was. They brought her into their exclusive group, asked her to sit with them at lunchtime. Took her with them when their fathers' drivers came to pick them up after classes.

"We went shopping, sometimes a movie before or after," my mother recalled. "We'd go out to eat. When it was hot, we would go swimming in their pools. They had so many servants bringing us drinks, snacks, towels."

Over time, she pulled away from those rich girls, found friends whose families and backgrounds were more like her own. The kinds of people who did their best despite the regime. After an afternoon of leisure poolside at a senator's mansion with senators' daughters, Mama would have come home to her family's cramped apartment, the one they rented next door to the half-built house on the lot bought by her brothers. She would not have seen her brothers for a year, maybe two, depending on the length of their overseas contracts. They were paying for her university tuition, for her jeepney fares to get to campus, an hour or so from home. Eventually, her new friends—the ones who rode jeepneys like she did, who brought lunch from home like she did—convinced her to join the local church choir. There, she met the choir director, a handsome, intense young man named Andy.

"Your Dad and I were friends for a year, year and a half," she told me. "It didn't really become anything for a long time."

There is a photograph of young Ana May and young Andy, maybe their first one together, long before they became my Mama and Papa. She was in her second year of university; he was in his final year, having fallen behind one year after protesting Marcos on the streets of Manila. It was her eighteenth birthday—her debut, as it is called on our islands. In the picture, Andy is seated in a chair, next to another male friend of theirs, someone from the choir. Ana May stands between these two men, shy and smiling. She is dressed in a floor-length gown of butter yellow, her curly hair long, just past her shoulders.

"Can you see my arms?" She laughed at me, over the phone. "I didn't know where to put my hands! It would have been inappropriate to put my hands on their chairs."

T.-rex arms, bent at the elbow, hands hanging limply in front of her chest. Awkward, polite. A proper young woman, ever dutiful, always doing the right thing. By then, Ana May had grown up to become one of the most beautiful young women in town. She may not have had the figure of some of the others, but no one had her face or her brains. Sons from other families began to show interest, each positioning themselves as marriage material, just as the gods once did for Mangechay's daughter's hand.

"Marry this one," said my Tito Raynold, arranging for Ana May to meet a nice young man from a prosperous family. "His parents are dentists, and he will be a dentist. He can take care of you."

"How about this one?" said Tito Raynold some other time, after Ana May had rejected Dentist Boy. "His family does imports and exports. He's going to inherit the business someday!"

But Ana May could only shrug. She visited their houses, met their mothers and siblings, sure. But she was only being polite. Did no one think to ask young Ana May who she might want to marry, or if she wanted to marry at all?

"I wasn't really all that interested in having a nobio," she told me. "I just wanted to graduate, get a good job, help my parents and my brothers pay the bills. Maybe help send your Tita to college, like your Titos sent me to college."

Besides, she didn't want to marry someone just because he was from a nice family, or rich, or from a nice family and rich. She wanted to marry, someday, for love. She was already an obedient and dutiful daughter. She did all the right things, made no mistakes, was the family's pride and joy. She planned on giving her earnings to her family, on supporting her brothers and her sister. She didn't want to give her heart's future to them too. Love was the one thing she could keep for herself.

Stir the diced liver into the garlic, onion, and chilies. Mash with a spoon until creamy and cooked through.

No one supported Ana May when she decided to marry Andy. She planned the wedding only with Tita Rea, without help from her mother or sister. She and Papa paid for most of it, with some help from his father. Mama's family's lack of support was not because she was pregnant out of wedlock. The family disapproved of Andy, an artsy kid with a nice allowance who didn't seem to have any plans. They were disappointed in Ana May, their eldest daughter, usually so obedient. Suddenly, she was pregnant, getting married semi-shotgun, going against their will. Perhaps they hadn't realized, until then, that she had a will of her own to begin with.

"I know your Titos just wanted me to marry someone who could take care of me, someone with a stable job," Mama said. "They had the best intentions. But they weren't very good to your Dad."

In February 1983, six months after their wedding vows, I became Ana May and Andy's firstborn. That year, the Marcos regime became even bolder in its violence. Ninoy Aquino, Marcos's most prominent dissident, was shot dead on an airplane tarmac on national television. He had just defiantly returned from exile in America. I was born into those three final years of turbulence. Masses of bodies crowded in protest on EDSA in 1986, a road named after Epifanio de los Santos, a Filipino nationalist during Spanish colonization.

"People power! People power! People power!" I remember shouting at the television. As a three-year-old who had just learned how to read and write, I found words exciting, and these two words, chanted as they were by my family, felt like an incantation. My T-shirt was yellow, the color of hope, the color of the revolution in 1986. The color of the presidential campaign of Corazon Aquino, the American-educated, Kapampangan-speaking law student turned political wife of the murdered dissident. Like many of our women, she has been reduced by history—written by American men, Filipino men, and the women who serve them—to an inexperienced housewife. To me, she was more than just the first woman to be our president. She was my first real president.

Just before Papa left us for the sea, Mama had moved up in her career. She worked at the Philippine National Bank, her iron will and stellar university degree propelling her up the ranks. I remember take-your-daughter-to-work days, the thrill of riding up the elevator. I remember craning my neck at the impressive bank building in Makati, the fanciest part of Manila, where all the white people were, and still are.

"Where are all the customers, Mama?" I had asked once, my little voice echoing throughout the shiny lobby.

"No customers here," she had whispered back, taking my hand. "We do the paperwork here."

But what my mother didn't tell me then was that her bank branch had once served one very important customer: Marcos.

"Oh, the stealing of the money happened pretty regularly," she said to me, recently. "I was new to the bank, and he was still in power. I worked on the lower floors, where the public treasury vaults were. Every few weeks, you'd just see men loading stacks of cash into big bags. They'd load those bags into big shiny cars, not armored trucks or anything. Those cars were going straight to the palace. He treated the bank like it was a personal ATM."

After Marcos fled the country, airlifted out of Malacañang Palace by Ronald Reagan's helicopters, our islands continued to suffer. My Tito Raynold, who had returned to Manila, started many businesses at once, seeking to create a stability for his children that he never had. At the house he helped build on Madasalin Street, he opened a sari-sari store, selling everything from bottles of Coca-Cola to bars of American candy.

Tito Raynold went on to open many businesses: motor-tricycle rentals, gasoline tank rentals, more sari-sari stores. He built Raynold's, a small eatery in Quezon City, customers eating elbow to elbow. He made his favorite dish in the style of Aling Lucing's, pork sisig in all of its crispy, spicy-sour, fatty Kapampangan splendor, the charred smell of grilled pork and the ghosts of Angeles City hazing the air.

The diced pork ears, cheeks, and belly next go into the pan. Stirring continuously, pour in the vinegar and calamansi juice. Allow the pork to cook to a darker brown, some parts crispier than others.

"You want to know why my sisig is special?" Tito Raynold asked me recently over a sizzling plate. We were sharing a meal next to the volcano, Taal. I had just returned to the islands after twenty-two years of exile.

"Because I make it with pork belly. Usually it's made with the cheap parts of the pig, ha. Why should we eat only cheap parts? And love. You must always cook with love. Cooking is love."

And love is in giving, even if it meant giving away his own university dreams to my mother, his beloved sister. In 2019, decades after he had sent himself away to toil at sea for the sake of the Gonzales family's survival, my dear Tito Raynold finally graduated from university.

"You cannot eat too much sisig, ha," Tito Reynold said at that same meal. "You eat too much sisig, you die."

Remove the pan from the heat.

In 1990, Papa left us to work overseas, as so many other fathers and mothers have done before and since. For our own safety, Mama, my sister, and I had no choice but to live in the Gonzales family compound on Madasalin Street. Tito Raynold's sisig restaurant had closed, choked by the cost of doing business in a struggling economy, in a corrupt city.

The gods' fury and impatience, seething for so long beneath our feet, eventually spewed forth. They rumbled the earth for months, seeking justice against all of us who had set them aside. From Zambales, the fiery, volcanic rage of our forgotten gods exploded, bursting out of Mount Pinatubo on June 7, 1991, and again and again in the days after. As if to underscore the gods' message, the mountain blew its top to pieces in sacrifice, leaving only a caldera in its place, breaking the land, burning the air. The skies were plumed with ash, the land rushed upon with searing flows of superheated gas and lava. Towns and villages buried. Families crushed to death under walls and rooftops. Thousands homeless.

In Manila, at the house my uncles built, my cousins and I stepped outside one morning, in awe of the sky and the coated ground, all in the same shade of ash-white. Flakes of ash swirling, covering the ground, the houses, the cars. Years later, in America, I would be zipped into a hand-me-down coat, seeing my first snowfall, and I would think of Pinatubo's ash, drifting down onto my sandaled feet. Of far-flung aunties and cousins from Pampanga, houses wrecked by flows of lava-mud lahar. They arrived on a bus, on jeepneys, slept temporarily in Lola Lina's sala. They ate with us at the table, insistent on using their hands to eat. With scooped fingers and a thumb, elbow resting on a raised knee. The way of our elders, our ancestors.

Pinatubo's eruption equaled Krakatoa's in 1883. This was only part of the gods' plan. A few days later, they conjured a tropical cyclone from the east: Typhoon Yunya, birthed by the Philippine Sea, the skies above, and their ruling gods. Stormy winds and heavy rains flung northwest, across the ash-grayed skies and charred land, spanning hundreds of miles around Mount Pinatubo. Looking back, it is easy to see why they chose Pinatubo and southern Luzon as their site of destruction. The US military's Clark Air Base to the nearby east, in Pampanga, and Subic Bay Naval Base close by in the southwest, suffered heavy damage from the gods' punishment of explosive fire and whiplash rain. Their buildings, barracks, and hangars collapsed from the weight of lahar—hot, cement-like flows of ash, lava, soil, and water. In an evacuation lasting from June to November 1991, Americans airlifted themselves, more than 15,000 of them, to safety back to their mainland, an evacuation they called Operation Fiery Vigil.

President Aquino was busy in those months. She had her hands full, fighting off coups from power-starved men, rewriting the Constitution to create a presidential one-term limit, reducing her office's powers, reestablishing the bicameral Congress dissolved by Marcos, salvaging our dying economy. She and her government observed the Americans' evacuations immediately after Pinatubo and Yunya. They saw an opportunity to rid our country of their colonial pestilence. In December 1991, the Philippine government gave the United States one year to fully withdraw its military presence from our islands. It may have required almost one hundred years and the assistance of our land, our seas, and our forgotten gods, but we had finally taken a step towards the possibility of something resembling true independence.

Toss the remaining chilies and red onion on top of the sisig. Slice a few calamansi, or one lemon, or one lime. Squeeze some onto the sisig.

Mama soon grew tired of making do. Of surviving her childhood, only to have her adulthood be more of the same. Her own children, left without a house or a father. These endless separations and uncertainties. Volcanic eruptions, typhoons, a sleepwalking daughter, an angry toddler.

"I was so scared and lonely," she said to me not long ago. "I hated having to leave our own house. Having to live in that tiny room—my brother's room!—in my mother's house. You, my smart girl, my happy girl, acting up and disobeying, sleepwalking. You had ulcers in your tummy, remember? I wouldn't hear from your dad for months."

One of Papa's aunts convinced Mama to make the leap.

"It will be easy," she had said to my mother during one of her glamorous visits from the US. "Come to the US on a tourist visa, with the kids! And then we can help you find a job at a bank. And then we can petition you for papers, you'll see."

That aunt must not have recognized the privilege she held, having married a white American man. A privilege my mother would never have. As it turns out, that same aunt had, along with other aunts and uncles, allowed my father to languish without help in New York.

"Your dad actually tried to renew his visa before it expired," my mother began. "The uncles and the aunties shamed him for asking for a ride, said he was asking too much. They refused to take him to the embassy in New

York—his brother, his uncles, aunts—and he couldn't afford the trains and buses, didn't even know how to get there. It expired, and no one cared."

Mama summoned her iron Gonzales will and decided to take us to New York.

"It will be fine," she told Papa. "Your auntie said it would. You need your family. We need you."

Crack eggs on top of the sisig, which should be hot enough to cook the whites and yolks.

Nine days before our flight to join Papa in America, on August 4, 1992, Pinatubo erupted again. Perhaps we should have seen it as a sign. That in creation, there is inherently destruction. My mother chose to destroy our life as we knew it. Chose to transform ourselves by fire in America, a land that had benefited, for so long, from the destruction of our islands.

Quickly carry the hot cast-iron pan to the table, where garlic sinangag rice awaits. Place extra slices of calamansi in a small dish.

My sisig brunch is now ready. I lay the cast-iron pan on the table, where the sinangag waits with a cafetière of strong coffee. My fingers, in gloves, sprinkle sliced bird's eye chilies on top of the cracked egg, sizzling atop the finely chopped up pork cheeks, nearly-burnt ears, and belly.

Stir the egg through the sisig. Season with dashes of Maggi, to taste.

I take a spoonful of the crispy, chewy, creamy meat. Put it between my teeth, my tongue swallowing the taste of home soil. Far from our barrios, our volcanic mountains and stormy islands, I cook, so that I may practice swallowing our difficult, undesirable truths, acidic and blood-heavy.

3

Lengua Kare-Kare
(Oxtail, Beef Tongue, and Tripe in Peanut Stew)

1992–1997

SERVES 4

1 pound beef tongue, whole

1 pound cow tripe

1 pound oxtails, prepared by a butcher

*6 cups water to cook oxtails, to be used as base for
    kare-kare stew*

2 cups unroasted, unsalted, skinless peanuts

¼ cup uncooked jasmine rice

2 tablespoons annatto powder

1 can banana hearts

1 head garlic

1 onion

3 Filipino or Chinese eggplants

1 bunch long string beans

4 or 5 pechay

2 or 3 dried bay leaves

1 cheesecloth

At the table:

Steamed rice

Sweet bagoong

Spicy bagoong

I am at the grocery store, and I cannot find the peanuts. The aisles are in no particular order—at least, no sense of order that is familiar to me. This chain seems to have found that shoppers buy taco shells alongside fish sauce. Scraps of entire continents' cuisines are crammed into half an aisle, boxes of nori and packs of egg noodles next to jars of instant curry powder and dried ancho chilies. There is, however, an entire half aisle for British bread, another half aisle for British biscuits.

Another lost turn. There is a man at the end of the aisle, younger than me, thirty-seven maybe, potbellied, his brown forehead and thatch of black hair shining under the store's overhead lights. Next to a pallet, he is unpacking the latest golden oat this, cocoa puffed that, boxes of berry wheat things.

Dad, I almost say.

I ask the man about the peanuts; he looks at me with a half smile. He gestures with a finger for me to follow him.

"Peanuts, miss," he says, with a small nod. His open palm gestures at three rows of many different kinds of peanuts. I thank him too profusely, and this makes him uncomfortable. He walks away, pulls his gloves back on. Unlike my father decades ago, he protects his hands while stocking groceries.

It is the second day of my first foray into making kare-kare from scratch. I am determined to make it the old way, not from a packet of instant mix, or with a jar of extra chunky peanut butter, or ready-made rice flour in a plastic bag. My arms burn, each grinding turn made by the pestle around the mortar a dial up on the pain. The just-roasted peanuts, still hot from the oven, are smearing circles in the mortar's belly, beginning to turn creamy, oils releasing into freshly ground paste. Shove down, around, grind. Shove down, around, grind. Clockwise, then counterclockwise, as if to go back in time. Making the real thing—becoming the real thing—is the most difficult task of all. I have nearly finished the peanut butter when, with an exhausted crack, the mortar splits down the middle, laying its weary halves down on the cold granite in surrender. Next time, I say to myself, use a molcajete.

Place the lengua and tripe inside the pressure cooker. Add fresh water until just covered. Cook for 40 minutes on high pressure.

Kare-kare—ground down, slow-cooked, integrated—demands the full body's attention. In older times, it would have taken more than one person to make it. It would have taken days, and yet it cannot take too long: if the meat falls off the oxtail bones, you would be left with only tripe, the part of the stomach that absorbs food, liquid, acid. And kare-kare cannot be made with tripe alone. In some regions, it is made with beef tongue, which we call lengua, like our South American, Central American, and Caribbean cousins do, all of our tongues shaped by the Spanish. Lengua was once cooked for days to acquiesce. Like our tongues, it must be cooked down to be soft in the mouth, tender enough to speak while we chew, broken down enough to absorb all the seasonings in the stew. Easy to swallow. Easy to understand. Kumusta po, mamsir? Cómo está, ma'am, sir?

Kare-kare requires everything that the Philippines has been, is, and will become. It requires technique from our central region's Indian and Tamil rajahnates' kari dishes. It needs our Mexican cousins' annatto seasoning, which comes from their native achiote tree, carried across the Pacific by Spanish ships. It wants pechay leaves, floppy and green, brought over by our Chinese siblings from the banks of their Yangtze River. It is made complete by plants native to our soil: yieldingly sweet banana hearts; fat, purple eggplant; and green, stringy, long sitaw. Charred over open flame, these culinary remnants of empires are laid into a bubbling, yellow-orange stew of crushed, creamed peanuts, bubbling over in a single pot.

Kare-kare is made unsalted. The beef oxtail and the beef tripe, or what we lovingly call twalya, are softened on gentle heat for hours, too, so that the twalya—a muscular stomach lining resistant to the teeth—can give in, breaking down on the eleventh or twelfth chew. After so much time in its own broth, the oxtails' marrow is turned into gelatinous butter, resting inside bone, waiting to slip out. It slides yieldingly onto the plate, any remaining bits teased out with a fork, sucked out by lips and tongue. We season each spoonful to our taste, right there on our plates and in the bowls of our mouths, for Filipinos eat in a way that the rest of the world should: food heaped by the fork onto the spoon, combinations chosen along the way. Decide, as we load a cube of eggplant, a piece of sitaw, a hunk of banana heart, a pat of rice, a piece of beef, and a slice of tongue onto the spoon: Do we want sweet bagoóng paste, or spicy? Perhaps a pat of both? Bagoóng, a beloved native condiment made of shrimp caught off our shores, gives flavor to rice when there is sometimes nothing else to eat. Should one be lucky enough to eat kare-kare, the rice is kept steamed and plain, so that the kare-kare can, rightfully, be the center of attention.

Kare-kare seasoning packets are ubiquitous in any diasporic Asian supermarket, in every diasporic pantry. Because of this transformation, it is now safe to say that kare-kare, besides it many other cultural influences, is also American. That is: industrialized. Mass-produced. Convenient. Cheap. Portable. This is what happens when a Filipino leaves the Philippines and moves to the United States. Ground down into profitable powder, flattened into an easily readable, unobtrusive paper packet, packed en masse into a box to ship across oceans. Finished in under an hour.

No one knows, for sure, how kare-kare came to be. Like our islands, its origins are lost to unwritten time, claimed and devoured by self-interested parties. The Kapampangans say that they created this dish. That they baptized it with a cute name, "kare-kare," as if to say, "little kare," "something like a kare," "sort of a kare." Still others say that while the Kapampangans may claim to have created kare-kare in its current form, the deeper clue is in the name. *Kare*, as in the old Tamil word *kari*: a spiced sauce, spices, a side dish, black pepper, meat, charcoal, peat, the color black, depending on the sentence around it. The Japanese say "kare." The Indonesians say "kari."

And how did we come to chew and swallow this Tamil word in the first place? Did it arrive on our shores through the trade of our pre-Hispanic city-states, the easternmost trading stop on the ancient Chinese Silk Road? Did it come to us through the Portuguese, who brought indigenous Incan peanuts to their colonies in Goa and elsewhere, or through the Spanish, who landed on our shores in the sixteenth century? Was it the British, who ransacked our harbors for Spanish gold stolen from our land? There are many possible beginnings.

There is an old tale from our Moro sisters and brothers, their Islamic sultanates native to our southern islands long before the Spanish came. A tale of terror and fear, of monsters and haunting. Of people driven into hiding, of monsters hunting them down. In the ancient days of this tale, four hideous beasts stalked the forests and lowlands, destroying villages, devouring humans whole, from skin to bone to blood. Afraid for their lives, the people of these sea-bound islands were forced to hide themselves: they lived underground or in caves, in places where the monsters could not find them. These stories of fear, hiding, and death soon reached Raja Indirapatra, who lived on an island nearby. Upon hearing of these people's fear, of these monsters' bottomless hunger, Raja Indirapatra asked his warrior brother, Raja Sulayman, to slay the beasts. He asked his brother to help free these people forced to live a life of terror and darkness.

"Of course," said Sulayman. "And before I depart, I will plant this tree in your courtyard, brother. As long as I live, so too shall this tree."

With that, the warrior prince set off for Mindanao. After some time, the first monster made itself known to Sulayman. This was the Kurīta, a terrifying beast of the land and sea. Its many limbs stemmed from an enormous body, which needed to swallow large quantities of human flesh each day. Drawing his bolo from his waist, Sulayman slayed the monster, slicing its limbs, belly, and throat into pieces. After binding his wounds to stop the bleeding, Sulayman journeyed to the next mountain.

When the lengua and tripe are done, remove them from the pressure cooker, and throw away the water. Allow the lengua and tripe to cool on a rack.

Of the many imperial monsters who came to terrorize our islands, the British stayed for the shortest amount of time, from 1762 to 1764. During one of their many wars of discontent and greed, they stayed just long enough to raid their Spanish enemies' stores of stolen gold at Fort Santiago in Manila. The British also promised military support to the rebel Diego Silang. On behalf of his people, Silang had, at first, sought out a compromise for self-rule with the Spanish. After the Spanish rejected his attempts, Silang allied himself with the British, who betrayed him as soon as it was advantageous to do so. Silang was soon assassinated by the Spanish; his wife, Gabriela, led the remaining rebels in his name. She was captured and executed in Manila in 1763.

Like everything else in their empire, the British did not do this alone. For this battle, they conscripted the reluctant Madras sepoys. Like us, they were a people trying to slay their own imperial beasts back home. Once they landed on Philippine soil, the Madras soldiers abandoned ranks, for like all of us forced to live in fear and hiding, they understood that the prospect of liberty on foreign soil might be sweeter than tyranny at home. To this day, generations of their offspring live on our islands. It is likely that they brought with them their own home cooking, what we came to know as kari.

With 6 cups of fresh water in the pressure cooker pot, cook the oxtails on high pressure for 30 minutes. When done, let cool, undisturbed. The oxtail water will be used as the base for the stew.

In those early years of self-silencing in America, we did not eat kare-kare, unless it was at a family gathering or some other Filipino party. We did not have the time or the money for such a dish, which some say was made only for the upper classes, the rajahs, dons, and doñas of our past. I do not remember much from these early years in New York, Pennsylvania, and New Jersey, except for the nagging feeling of wanting to go home soon, as if America were an uncle's mabongga, overly long reunion party. Surrounded by love, family, doting grandparents, and friends in my city of birth, I was not afflicted with the colonial longing that devoured Mama and Papa, the belief that our life in Manila was inferior to any life in America. But unlike my parents, I had yet to experience the tyranny of lost dreams, the sense of inferiority that comes with that loss, a sense that is reinforced by the prejudices of the world around them.

Mama, my sister, and I landed in Newark Airport late on the night of August 13, 1992. I remember the deserted arrivals gate echoing with our voices, an announcement from a corridor somewhere. Papa and his cousin, my Tito Marvin, stood apart from the others, their hands in their blue jeans pockets, white Reeboks, T-shirts tucked in. I hung back, suddenly feeling shy. Watched Mama rush forward, my little sister in her arms. Saw Papa consume them both in a big hug, his face in her hair, her face in his neck. They muttered words into each other, words mingled with sniffling. Two and a half years apart.

And then came the screaming. I stepped back a little, saw my sister's tiny face wrinkled into angry sobs. Her fat little hands shoved at Papa's cheeks, her legs kicked against his chest. I ran to her.

"It's OK, it's OK," I said, stepping towards her, trying to soothe her with a stroke of her hair. It was my job to stop her crying, my job to hold her at night after the yayas left. "This is Daddy, Papa, Dada, remember? We say I love you on the phone? I miss you?"

"Ayoko! Ayoko sa'yo!" she screamed at him, her face red, shiny with tears and snot, pushing and kicking at his face, his hands. She really did not want to be anywhere near this stranger she did not recognize, this intruder daring to touch our mother.

My sister was upset, she tells me years later, because she had no idea who he was. For most of her three and a half years of life, she had only said I love you, I miss you to Papa's disembodied voice on the phone. To her, a father was a person who was absent, to be heard but not seen or touched. Not to be trusted. She did not recognize that same voice that was now in front of her, raining kisses upon her head, begging for her to remember who he was. She did not know this man, let alone miss him or love him. Still furious, still kicking, my sister pushed and wriggled herself down to the floor, out of Mama's arms. She scrambled to me, tiny arms reaching out and encircling my side. Her big brown eyes warily sized up the enemy, who was daring to hold Mama's hand. It was only then that Papa saw me.

"Uy. So tall!" he said to me, ruffling my hair. "Still payatot, ha. We'll have to get some meat on those bones."

In that instant, surrounded by my sister, our mother, our father, I was happy. They were all there, with me. Papa was looking at me, standing next to me. If I spoke out loud, he could talk right back. We could talk for as long as we wanted to, instead of for three minutes on an expensive long-distance call. Yet, standing next to this person, I also felt uncertain. This was not the same man. He looked wrong, felt wrong. The corners of his mouth did not stay up as they used to, as if weighed down by a heavy secret. There were now lines on his forehead, a tension on his brow, creases in his cheeks. When he smiled, his eyes did not smile with him. He sounded different, the English softer on his tongue, vowels drawled in that American way. This was not quite my Papa.

Maybe a joke would bring him back from wherever he was hiding.

"Well . . . maybe you can give me some of your taba!" I said, poking at his new potbelly. I had yet to discover that in America, our people ate food meant for fiestas as their everyday meals: kare-kare, dinuguan, pansit, sisig, lumpia, lechon bagnet, afritada, kaldereta. I had yet to learn that in this land of disappearance, food from home was our only way to remind ourselves that we exist. Meals together one of the few places we could speak in our own language, words and flavors freely mingling on tongues. Our way of caring for each other in a land that cared nothing for us.

Papa laughed a little too loudly, patted me on the back. We walked towards baggage claim, Mama and my sister, still crying, following behind. At the baggage carousel, our suitcases and boxes were the only ones left, their sides sagging outwards, tied with rope and lashed with brown tape. They made lonely circles under a cold light, waiting, like me, to be claimed.

Some days or weeks after our arrival, we took a trip from New York to Maryland, a drive of seven hours down something called the I-95. Mama and Papa did not have driver's licenses yet, so an uncle or an aunt drove us. I did not know why we were traveling. It was my first ever American road trip. I was so excited for my newly reconstituted family to be traveling together.

I brought two new paperback books with me: Michael Crichton's *Jurassic Park*, and Stephen King's *It*. I had selected these from a recent trip to an enormous store that had everything from jeans and frying pans and bedsheets to books and bicycles and toys and garden chairs, a store with the word "mart" in its name.

"Here," Papa said, ducking into the car. "For the trip."

"What's this?" I said, taking the plastic bag. Inside were dozens of American snacks. M&M's, peanut and plain. Cheetos. Doritos. Lay's sour cream and onion potato chips. Rold Gold thin salted pretzels. Snickers. Mars bars. Hershey's Kisses, Hershey bars. Reese's peanut butter cups. Herr's salt and vinegar potato chips. Sour Patch Kids. Jawbreakers. Lemon Warheads. And my favorite: Kit Kat bars. Temporary sweetness for a lingering want.

"Uy!" Mama exclaimed from the passenger seat. "That is so much junk! Is this from the gas station?"

"Yes," Papa said, giving me a kiss on the forehead. "It's just a little something. Extra from the store. The guys won't notice." He ducked back out and closed the car door. Stepped back from the car, put his hands in his pocket, gave my scowling sister a little wave (she still refused to touch him). My chest sank.

"You're not coming?" I said, dropping my hands on top of the bag. Why is Papa staying here? Are we being separated again?

"Sorry, anak. I can't really take any time off from the gas station kasi eh."

"How long?" Not this again.

"Maybe two weeks. Be good for your aunties and uncles. Don't embarrass me, OK?"

He stood in the driveway, becoming a blur as tears filled my eyes. Once he had said he would be gone for nine months, and that became two and a half years. Now he was making promises again about time and place. Should I believe him? Would it be two months instead of two weeks? There always seemed to be plans made above my head, plans that only Papa knew and, sometimes, Mama too. Plans that did not include what their children needed or wanted.

Fat drops of tears landed on the plastic bag as we pulled away. Reluctantly, I waved goodbye, and Mama, buckling herself into the passenger seat, did too. I saw Papa's shoulders drop down in relief.

I refused to look out the car window, refused to participate in this charade of a road trip. I refused to look at America, a place where I had no friends, no Lolos or Lolas, no favorite places, no say in what happens each day. I lost myself in the pages of *Jurassic Park*, a story about science and wonder, about bringing back long-ago lost creatures through a remnant of past life. I was only beginning to understand that we were not in America for a visit. That we were not there to see Disneyland, as I'd said to the American man at the US embassy. That we were not going to go back home and take Papa with us.

While the oxtails and broth cool, preheat the oven to 250°F. Place the unsalted peanuts on one tray and the uncooked rice on another tray. Roast both until golden.

We arrived in Maryland tired, out of sorts, and hungry after a day of gasoline station snacks and something called bologna sandwiches, which were actually OK. Mama, my sister, and I were staying in yet another room at yet another relative's house. This time, it was at the house of Uncle George and Aunt Marta, one of Lola Rosing's younger sisters. Next door to this house lived another aunt and her family too. The guest bedroom was large and comfortable, with a wide, wonderful soft bed, its own bathroom, and windows that looked out onto a beautiful yard. They had something called potpourri in the bathroom, which smelled good but also made me sneeze. Their kitchen was beautiful and roomy, overlooking a dining room with a table long enough for what seemed like dozens. There were soft fabrics everywhere, something called carpet on the floor, which had vents that magically blew out cool air on those hot early September days, then warm air when winter began to arrive. These spots became my favorite corners to read. The only thing I found strange was that there was no household help: Papa's auntie cleaned her own house, and sometimes even her white husband would clean, and their son would put dirty dishes in something called a dishwasher. Perhaps, I concluded, the girls and women here had more to do than to find work minding children or cleaning someone's house for low pay, like they did in Manila. It would take me years to learn that women did these things for low pay and no rights in America too.

Weeks passed. Papa did not come to Maryland like he had promised. Mama disappeared every few days to places like Washington, Richmond, and Annapolis, driven to job interviews by the aunties, driven by a secret fear she hid from her children. She interviewed at banks and something called credit unions, interviewed at the Philippine embassy and other institutions. She had a business and economics degree, with honors, from a university older than the United States itself. She had over ten years of experience in banking. Yet each day, Mama would come home from these interviews tired and frustrated. With each day, she withdrew further and further away from me, into a space where I could not reach her. Once, I heard her on the phone with Papa, who was pulling double shifts at the gas station in New York.

"It's the same thing over and over." She sighed. "It's not at all like Auntie said it would be. Today, the interviewer asked me if UST was a real university. He said he'd never heard of it."

Americans, so proud of their imperial power, so ignorant of the people swallowed by their empire.

After a month, it became clear that Mama would not find work in Maryland or in DC. Yes, interviewers would say, we know you have equivalent experience at, what is this bank called again, yes this bank in the Philippines, but it's just not the right fit for this bank. Perhaps try starting at an entry-level job and work your way up. I'm so sorry, said another, but you're overqualified for this entry-level job. Mama's plan was to find a banking job in Maryland and secure an H-1B visa. Papa could then join us from New York, and Mama would petition for the four of us to live in America through her work visa. Mama Sita's Instant Family. Add pulverized dreams to water, and stir.

"I couldn't get an H-1B," Mama told me decades later, "because the US didn't have banking in the list of acceptable work visa jobs for Filipino applicants. I was not a nurse, or a domestic worker, or a doctor, or an engineer, or even a teacher. The lawyer said those were the acceptable jobs for Filipinos. Those were the only ones that qualified Filipinos for a work visa. All we could get was a tourist visa."

When Americans ask "Why don't illegals just apply?"—as if their own ancestors did—I think about this. About how America, a self-proclaimed melting pot of prosperity, still persists in taking away from those in need, allowing some to access its riches while disallowing others. Visa-less entry and easily obtained work visas for any job for those from European or white-coded countries; limits upon limits for others, like us. If we had known about the Manong generations before us, those long-ago Filipino farm workers on the West Coast who fought and died for the right to work in America, known about the angry white men with their bombings and killings of Filipino men and women who were merely trying to live in California, in Oregon, in Washington, about the decades of racialized struggle for Filipinos in America, perhaps we would have been less surprised.

By September, Mama had no job offers and no savings left. No more job interviews to attend, no more job openings to apply for. She and my sister were to return to New York. Mama wanted to be with Papa, while I was to stay with Aunt Marta and Uncle George. Aunt Marta was a teacher at a nearby Catholic school, and my parents were tempted by the free tuition, determined to continue the same kind of private education I had in Manila.

Besides, I was already enrolled for the year. There was a hope that perhaps Mama could try for another job in Maryland some other time.

And this is where any memories of these months become unclear, unspeakable. All that comes back to me now is a deep sadness. Left behind by my parents, oceans away from the life, family, and friends I had loved, I stopped eating. I stopped sleeping. Stopped reading, stopped writing in my journal, letting its key grow dusty. My tongue silent, my body wasting itself. And even though I had scored high in an aptitude exam, moved up from the third to the fourth grade at the beginning of the year, I stopped caring about school. Abandoned my curiosity, for curiosity led to questions, which only led to more confusion. I made no effort with classmates who tried to include the strange, quiet, sulking new girl in the back of the room. Back home, I had been outgoing, friendly, confident. I was voted the class treasurer, had a group of good friends, was the onstage host of school concerts. In America, I was nobody, and I did not care.

Thanksgiving, my first, came and went, a weird event of forced cheer. Aunties asked what I was thankful for, and I could not say. Why did America need an entire holiday to tell themselves to be thankful? How boastful, like the richest man on the street crowing about his stolen wealth for all to hear. What was I supposed to be thankful for? I missed my sister, snuggling up to me before falling asleep, giggling next to me while we watched Disney's *Beauty and the Beast*, cutting off her Barbies' hair while I read my komiks.

I asked for both dark and white meat, in the hopes that one of them would be less dry. I did not understand why cranberry sauce was a cold, firm slice of translucent red disk, still ridged with marks from its tin can. It wobbled on my plate next to the mashed potatoes. I chose to eat the kare-kare and the lechon instead. Someone offered me pumpkin pie. Since that, too, might be a firm, cold disk from a tin can, I said no, thank you. I remember leaving the table early to go back to my room. There, finally alone, away from people who were not the family I knew, wanted, or needed, I did feel thankful for a minute. I don't think anyone noticed my absence.

When I started wetting the bed, I hid my sheets and underwear in the cupboard underneath my bathroom sink. I lied about their whereabouts when asked by Auntie Marta. Don't embarrass me, Papa had said. Sometimes, I would wake up with a scream from a nightmare—that same one again, with the waves drowning my parents, the same one I still have today—and I would feel the hot, stinking urine creeping underneath my back, down around my hips and legs. In the mornings, my pillow would be covered with bits of chewed up hair, some in my mouth, my throat. My fingernails and toenails were bitten down to stubs, a habit I had started while trying to sleep each night. Most nights, sleep would not come until almost dawn. I would go to school like this, hair half-chewed, a depressed, anxious, bed-wetting insomniac at nine years old. During recess, I hid in the library, away from the lonely playground. I fell asleep between the bookcases. My benign engkanto friend—the one who let me sleep while taking my anxious body for a walk each night—did not dare to visit America. The trees were too bare, the nights too cold. They had nowhere to sleep.

Remove the peanuts and rice from the oven and let cool slightly.

One December evening, Aunt Marta and Uncle George handed me the telephone. It was Mama.

"Jill," she said, sounding tired and far away. "Your Tita Celia is driving down to come get you, OK? When school breaks for Christmas."

"OK," I said. I did not feel anything. I had not made friends at this new school. Auntie and Uncle were tired of me. Where would Mama and Papa put me next? We had relatives everywhere. I wondered where Massachusetts was. How about Virginia? Maybe I could go to California, where Disneyland was, the happiest place on earth. Maybe it would be the same old lost feeling in a new lost place.

After a six-hour drive with Tita Celia, I woke up in New York, in the driveway of Auntie Lorna's house. As the second-oldest sister, born just after my Lola Rosing, Auntie Lorna was the de facto matriarch for our extended American family. Her house was a cozy five-bedroom cottage just outside New York City. Over the decades, it had become a sort of safe house, a landing place for family just arriving from our homeland. Papa, Mama, my sister, and I were the latest recipients of Auntie Lorna's kindness. She gave us the spare bedroom on the basement floor, just off the family den. A place to stay and save money until my parents could afford a place for us.

I found myself standing at the top of the stairs that led down to this den, where Papa sat with Tito Melvin and Uncle Roy, who was Lola Rosing's youngest brother. There was a Bulls game on, and they were all fixated on the television. "Jordan to Pippen. Pippen to Grant."

"Hi Papa," I said, just above a whisper. I felt nervous.

Tito Melvin elbowed my father. Papa's eyes flicked towards me, then back to the screen. His jaw tensed. Did he see me? "Oh! Look at that beauty from the top of the key, that's 18 for Michael . . ."

I stood there, at the top of the stairs, frozen. I thought there would be some kind of happy reunion, my father running to the stairs, excited to see me after so long. Tita Celia bumped into me from the hallway, a plate of pansit and a can of Coke in hand.

"Why are you just standing here?" She laughed. "Go on down!"

Papa still would not look at me. I trudged down the stairs, feet weighed by fear and confusion. Sat at the edge of the sofa, next to him.

"O," he said, still fixated on the game. "What were you staring at?" Resentment radiated off his skin in waves.

Huh? "I . . . I don't know," I said. "I guess . . . I thought . . ."

"Ano? I thought, I thought kantot, ha!" he said, using Tagalog slang for "fucking," a coarseness in his voice I had never heard before. He shoved me off the sofa. I stumbled to stand up.

"You're not happy to see me?" he said, still staring at the game. "Sige. Go upstairs. Your Mama will be home from the bakery soon."

Tito Melvin laughed uncomfortably.

"Si Manong Andy naman," he said to my father. "I think you're scaring her."

I walked towards the stairs, numb. I did not hear the rest of the conversation as I climbed, step by step, afraid of this man who had taken the place of my Papa. I must have done something terrible, something unforgivable, for him to be this way. Was it because I wet the bed? Or because of the Bs on my report card? I must have embarrassed him terribly. Closing the door behind me, I turned to the living room to look for my sister, to wait for our mother, to think about what I had done. Ashamed. A failure.

Return to the lengua and tripe, now cool enough to handle. Remove the lengua's skin, then slice into thin 1- or 2-inch pieces. Slice the tripe into pieces of the same size.

"O, Jill!" said an aunt. "Halika, come eat, there's pansit, there's lumpia. Do you eat pinakbet, you like vegetables? There's kare-kare, too, you want? You like sweet bagoóng?"

I hadn't eaten kare-kare since Manila. I ate a bowl of it, two pieces of oxtail and sauce atop steamed white rice, with crispy string beans, hunks of smoky eggplant, and a dollop of bagoóng. Chewed on tripe and beef, chewed on what it was I had done so wrong to shame my father. Still, it was the best meal I'd had since arriving in this land of confusion. Soon, Mama arrived from her shift at the bakery. She needed to start earning and had accepted a job as a part-time cashier. The pay was minimum wage, but she was guaranteed twenty hours a week and could take home any leftover breads and pastries at the end of each shift. The chocolate babkas and garlic bagels she brought home, new to my pandesal, ensaymada, and pan de coco–loving stomach, were my favorites.

I ran to Mama, hugged her through her coat, thin and chilly with January cold. She patted me on the shoulder, wrinkled her nose at my hair.

"Hay nako, you stink. Go take a bath. Do you know how to do that now?"

I hadn't had a yaya for months or a mother for years. Of course I knew how. Head down, looking for my sister, I followed Mama to our basement-level bedroom, just off the den. And this is where my memories go from blurry and faded to black and empty.

"My first memory?" my sister tells me, decades later, when I ask her. "It's of Dad beating the shit out of you in that basement in New York. Like every day."

"What do you mean?" I did not understand. Beatings? Once or twice, maybe. But every day?

"Yeah," my sister said, her sigh crumpling into white noise over our FaceTime call. "Like every day, after he came home from the gas station. It's all I remember. I hated him so much for that."

I closed my eyes to remember. My spirit body and our elders, witnesses to it all, continue to remain silent.

With a very clean grinder, pulverize the now-cooled roasted rice grains into a fine flour. If preferred, do this by hand in a molcajete or a heavy-duty mortar and pestle.

In those first several months of living in Auntie Lorna's house, there was much to learn. I learned that we were no longer comfortably middle class. That we were now poor and homeless, dependent on relatives' goodwill. At school, I learned that I had a funny accent, my English all wrong, too formal and old-fashioned. That I was Asian, lumped together with being Vietnamese, Chinese, Cambodian, Thai, Korean, Japanese. I learned that we were not going back home, and that this was somehow my fault, according to Papa. I learned that Papa was angry with me every day. I never knew what it was I did wrong, and therefore could never fix it. I learned that Mama would keep on receding further and further away from me, her life in America just a continuation of her childhood. That her main goal now was to earn money to feed us and to keep Papa happy. I learned about the reliability of uncertainty and fear, that this was the air, water, and ground for both our inside and outside worlds. I learned that hiding from all of it—monsters at home and out there—was the only solution. I hid inside books and stories I wrote in my diary, inside my schoolwork, in family gatherings where I could feel, with some certainty, that Papa would not hurt me. Books, writing, homework, family gatherings, and food, are all I remember.

I started to call my parents Dad and Mom. Papa and Mama were gone.

"I remember how Dad would just launch into you for no reason," my sister continued, her voice breaking. "You would be, like, just quietly reading a book, or doing your homework, and he would come home from work and throw you across the room, or take off his belt and start hitting you all over. One time, he was beating you up, like really bad, kicking you on the ground and stuff," she said, trying to catch her breath. "And our cousin, Robbie, he was five or six, he was little too—he opened the door to the den where we were, because I was screaming and crying watching you, and you were screaming and crying too . . . and his dad, Uncle Odie, he just pulled Robbie away and closed the door. He said 'Leave them, leave them.' How could the adults do that? How could they let that happen? We were so little and helpless, and Mom was at work, and they were all there, the aunties, everybody, and no one did anything about it. They never did anything about it. No one came to help you."

Silence, stilled tongues. The first and most enduring lesson of America.

Images flicker quietly behind my eyes. "Did he say 'You're not supposed to be here' a lot? You know, in Tagalog?"

"Yeah, stuff like that." She sniffled.

You shouldn't be here.

You're a fucking mistake.

This isn't supposed to be my life.

You're the reason this is all happening.

We should have aborted you.

My body remembers some things, flashes of terror that still send me into spirals, gasping breaths and shaking hands. Should someone clap too loudly next to my ear, or burst into a room in excitement, or appear behind me soundlessly, I descend, my body seizing into automatic panic, heart hammering, tears springing involuntarily. But like the people in that old Moro tale of beasts, hiding, and silence, most of these memories have been driven underground, buried beneath the fear.

We shared that basement bedroom at Auntie Lorna's for one year. The four of us slept on a queen-size mattress on the floor. We laid on it crosswise, so we would all fit. This worked especially well when Dad had night shifts at the gas station. Mom worked double shifts at the bakery, sometimes on weekends for time and a half pay.

I developed a disorder that no doctor ever treated me for: encopresis, a condition in children that can be caused by stress, anxiety, a turbulent home life. For days, I could not poop. But on those days, small liquid amounts would leak into my underwear, usually just after getting home from school, before Dad would come home from a shift at the Shell station. A telling omen of the terror that seized my body. I could not let him see my soiled underwear, for this made him so very angry. He hated disorder or dirtiness of any kind: shoes in the wrong place, a shirt folded into the wrong shelf, hands unwashed after playing outside. At least I'd stopped wetting the bed.

I decided that the best way to avoid Dad's violent rage would be to throw away the poop-stained underwear. I snuck to the edge of Auntie Lorna's backyard, just before it melted into a small patch of woods, and threw the dirty evidence away there, amid shrubs and weeds. Walked back into the house, thinking I had gotten away with it. Safe for one more day.

Hours later, I found myself screaming, crawling away on the floor, begging Dad to please stop, *I'm sorry po*, I screamed while being dragged by my hair towards the toilet bowl. Apparently, Auntie Prudie, one of my Lola Rosing's siblings, had seen me at the edge of the woods. She had laughingly told my father about it, as if it were just a funny anecdote: Your weird little tomboy daughter threw her dirty panties into a bush. As if she didn't hear him beating me every day.

Dad kicked me into the base of the toilet bowl, and before I could crawl away, another kick threw me backward into the hard porcelain, my neck hitting the bowl's squared edge. He yanked my hair, pulled me up, and dunked my face into the shallow bowl. Cold, the faint taste of chlorine and maybe piss. Pulled up, dunked again.

"You want to be filthy? You want to be disgusting? Yan, drink this!"

When I came to, I was curled up in the shower stall, cold needles of water stabbing at me from above. Papa was gone. I stayed there, sobbing quietly, the uncles' and aunties' voices and footsteps upstairs, carrying on as normal.

Minutes, hours, half a day later maybe, Mama came home from her shift at the bakery. She jumped when she saw me there, her ten-year-old daughter, bloody, clothes torn, half passed out under the shower. Without a question or a word, she washed me. Gently rinsed the blood from my matted hair, cleaned my soiled bottom, which had relieved itself sometime during the beating. Pulled pajamas over my limp arms and legs, checking for breaks, apologizing when I yelped in pain at my left ankle, which remains vulnerable to this day, prone to turning over, weak at the slightest unevenness of pavement or soil. Fed me mushroom soup from a can, warmed, though I had trouble swallowing with a swollen tongue. She took the next day off to stay by my side. I remember my sister insisting on sitting next to me, warm, protective, scowling.

This is the only time Mama cared for me after one of Dad's rages. Her tongue had not yet learned to ask me, "Have you thought about what you did to make him angry?" Perhaps this time, she was afraid that he might hurt me enough to require the hospital, where the police might be alerted. The last thing we wanted, we were often told, was for the police to know about us. We could not renew our visas. We could be immediately deported. Perhaps she was afraid he might kill me, and that would definitely attract police attention. Silenced tongues as safety, even as my flesh bled and bones broke. I often wished that he would just do it, already: kill me, or at least hurt me enough to need the hospital, where maybe a nice nurse could adopt me, or, if I was lucky, a doctor. Who was the scarier monster? Papa, or the American immigration system?

In a molcajete or a heavy-duty mortar and pestle, grind the still-warm roasted peanuts in circles, until a paste is made. This can be smooth or rough. In case more peanut butter is needed at the seasoning stage, keep a jar handy.

It was strange, beginning in a new school for the second time in a year. This one was a public school, my first, after a lifetime of private Catholic education. Someone introduced me to Sara, a nice white girl my age who lived across the street. She was my first friend in America. She had rosy, pale skin, blue veins showing on either corner of her mouth and under her eyes. Her light brown hair was fine and long, and her eyes were a light brown to match, mesmerizing when the low winter sun shone through them. It was January, so she wore a purple knit hat, a striped magenta scarf, and a puffy jacket with colorful triangles of turquoise, violet, pink, and streaks of neon yellow. For fun, she had orange gloves, which flashed as she grabbed the straps of her Lisa Frank backpack. Next to her, I felt shabby, with my 1980s hand-me-down outfit. I wore a cousin's old jeans and a ratty boy's sweater, a puffy maroon corduroy hand-me-down coat with a white chevron in the back, too-big dark blue driving gloves, used, from an auntie, and a checkered gray scarf Papa used to wear to work. I had an L.L.Bean backpack in olive green, embroidered with a forgotten relative's initials. I smelled like mothballs and the back of an aunt's musty closet.

Sara didn't seem to notice this difference between us. She chatted with me about television shows she loved, and books she liked, and her latest crushes as we walked to school each day. It would take me a few more weeks to realize, but when she talked about the boys she liked, I felt a twinge of possessiveness, a twist of jealousy. I hoped she didn't notice, and to compensate, I tried not to look at her as much. She was very pretty and was so nice to me. I was secretly smitten. I did not have crushes often—the last one was Lucky, the boy next door, in Manila. A crush felt nice to have. A hopeful feeling, one I hadn't had in almost a year.

On the first day of my new school, I stepped into the unfamiliar fourth-grade homeroom. Everyone wearing whatever they wanted, no uniforms. Dad's words echoing in my head: if anyone asks, you were born in California. My parents were terrified, believing children like me to be disallowed from state-funded schools. Ignorant of the fact that undocumented children were given the right to a free basic education back in 1982.

"What's your real name?" one boy asked.

"Jill," I said, hunching down into my right-armed desk, which was all wrong for me, a leftie. I drew spirals at the corner of my notebook. I used to draw suns and stars, back home.

"No, no, your Philippinese name. Is it Ching Chong?"

"Or Ching Chang, because you're a girl?"

"What do you mean you're not Chinese? Isn't the Philippines the same thing?" He and his friends laughed at me. One of them pawed inside my backpack.

"No dude, I think it's next to Puerto Rico. Cómo está?" He snickered.

"Ew, what are you reading?" said another boy, looking through my backpack, pulling out Auntie Lorna's copy of Patricia Cornwell's *Postmortem.*

Something about America pulled me towards death and danger, the macabre and the unknown, away from my Manila favorites like *Sweet Valley High* and *The Baby-Sitters Club.* Those books of sunlit friendships, suburban comfort, warmth, and loyalty, I had decided, were lies. America was nothing like Jessica and Elizabeth's sunlit California world, nothing like Claudia and Mallory's suburban neighborhood of idyll and easy resolution. America was the taste of blood, the bruising of beaten flesh. The cold of an unheated room, the kick of a father's booted foot. The indifference of a country to those who come to its shores in need. America was the news I saw on the television: Rodney King, Brandon Teena, the LA race riots, murdered women and missing children as entertainment on *Unsolved Mysteries* and *Law & Order,* the first World Trade Center bombings, the Waco standoff. A kare-kare of tongues silenced by death.

"Hey," said a tall girl with hazel eyes, bronze skin, and long, curly golden-brown hair down her back, hands on her hips. She had a sharp chin and full lips, a face crowned by baby curls. Her proud bearing seemed to quiet the boys cackling around me and my L.L.Bean hand-me-down backpack. "Leave her alone."

"Or what, Linda?" said one of the boys.

"Or you'll find out," she said, leaning towards him, tilting her head left and right as she spoke. He cowered.

"Come sit with us," she said to me, snatching my Patricia Cornwell book and my backpack. "And you're all morons. The Philippines is in Asia, in the Pacific Ocean? And she's Filipino, not Philippinese, and it's not Chinese. I'm from Puerto Rico, which is in the Caribbean."

Linda turned to me then, her face softer. She introduced me to a corner of girls in class, girls separate from the white girls in the opposite corner of the room, who were nice enough, polite and remote, but never asked me to sit with them. There was Farah, a Black girl whose family came from a place called Haiti. There was Trish, a lighter-skinned Black girl who later told me that her father was Jamaican and her mother Dominican. And Carla, who was Filipino. Her family was from Cebu, though she was born here. I liked them all instantly, because back home in Manila, I was once like Linda and these girls here in New York. Quick to act, to say my thoughts as they came to me. Warm, raucous, loyal. Unafraid of monsters. A tongue that lived to speak.

In those few months at that school, with those new friends, I slowly learned to quietly call upon my old, braver self. Remembered how I once pushed back against bullies from the all-boys' Catholic school across the street from my all-girls' school in Manila, regular trips to the principal's office, Papa's delight at my fighting spirit. Remembered how I once saved friends from playground bullies too. Good trouble, Papa called it.

"Never let the bullies win," he used to say to me in those years in Manila. More than once, he picked me up from the principal's office, the corner of his lip fighting a smile while we were both lectured by Sister Mary Something-or-Other on the proper comportment of good little Catholic girls. Me sitting proud on his shoulders, suspended from school for three days for kicking a bully in his crotch, my reward a trip to the park and a big cone of cheese ice cream. Papa so proud of me, then, in a way he never would be again.

In a glass or a bowl, soak the crushed annatto in a cup of water. Let this turn a deep red-orange.

The old Moro tale teaches us how to survive and defeat the beasts of our fears, real and imagined. As Sulayman waited, the second monster, the Tarabūsaw, revealed itself. It breathed in his ear, hot breath that stank of rotting flesh and blood. Sulayman spun around to face the beast, whose body was similar to that of a man's but larger, as tall as the tallest trees in the forest. There was a long struggle, with the Tarabūsaw wielding trees, tree branches, rocks, and boulders, hurling them upon Sulayman's head, his body. Eventually, the warrior prince began to find his footing, and the battle turned. Sprinting up a high boulder, Sulayman found an opening and jumped. His bolo in his right hand, he landed on the Tarabūsaw's shoulder and, with a mighty shout, pierced the beast's hide, where its heart was. When he pulled out the bolo, Sulayman jumped down to the ground, and was bathed in the monster's blood.

In its dying throes, the Tarabūsaw vowed: "If I am to die, then you shall die with me." And Sulayman was crushed under the Tarabūsaw's body.

Far away, back in the palaces, Raja Indirapatra looked up. He saw that the tree planted by his warrior brother had wilted and died, and he ran to it in sorrow, and wept. After some time, Indirapatra was able to stand, and he vowed to complete Sulayman's work, to exact revenge for his brother's death. He journeyed to the edge of the forest, where the Tarabūsaw's enormous body lay. Beneath a limb, he found his brother's bones and sword. Overcome by the sight, Indirapatra fell to his knees and wept once more.

Finely mince the garlic and finely chop the onion. Slice the eggplant crosswise into circles, cut the string beans into 2- to 3-inch pieces, and slice the pechay leaves off their base. Open and drain the can of banana hearts.

Our Tarabūsaw was a country called Spain, which once ruled much of the world and, like all empires do, believed that it could grow and rule forever. Spain was consumed by its hunger for gold, for its kings and queens were greedy and threw the entire nation into debt. To cover this debt, Spain extracted wealth from swaths of continents, gold and silver wrung from the soil by slaves both native and imported. To justify their theft, they claimed to spread Catholicism, and this is what they brought to our islands, which did not need their help or their rigid notions of God or country. The Spanish tormented our land for hundreds of years, and our ancestors hid, changing themselves so that they might be allowed to live. In 1571, the conquistadores finally defeated Rajah Sulayman III, the last native ruler of the city-state then known as Maynila (not to be confused with the Raja Sulayman of our old Moro tale). Like his fellow warriors, chiefs, sultans, and rajahs across the islands—for we were not one nation, then, but many different tribes, nations, and city-states of different faiths and traditions—Rajah Sulayman III had battled fiercely against the invasion and died doing so.

These greedy, starving white men turned Maynila—a bustling city-state of communities, lilies, and mangroves, the easternmost stop of the ancient Chinese Silk Road—into Manila, a paved fortress of obedience, stone, and gunpowder. They crushed the last remaining Muslim people of this ancient Muslim city, turning it into a base for Christian missionaries and for trade with its colonies across the Pacific. Century by century, these frailes, nego-ciantes, and conquistadores broke down our resistance, so that not only did we pray their prayers, but we also wore their clothes, sang their songs, tried to climb their caste ladders, and cooked our food with their ingredients. We disappeared, hiding ourselves from ourselves, too afraid to admit that we were doing so. Our voices and histories, songs and traditions, were buried underground, trampled over by boots and sandals, built upon with churches, forts, and prisons. Our mouths sealed with our own blood, tongues silenced, not speaking unless spoken to.

Two ingredients from our time with the Spanish beasts made their way into our pots of kare-kare. Peanuts, crushed and ground into paste, were smeared into the oxtail broth. Achiote seeds, also known as annatto seeds, are native to our siblings in Mexico. This became a staple, dried and crushed into powder. It is used to give the kare-kare sauce a deep rust color, an al-most undetectable but unmissable depth of flavor, a woodlike, earthy note to anchor the taste of the peanuts. We use this in many of our recipes, and it is what makes our form of kari particularly ours alone.

In a large pot on the stove, gently sauté the minced garlic until golden, the onion until translucent.

Back in our old Moro tale, Raja Indirapatra was still deep in grief next to his brother's body. He looked up and saw a jar of water next to his feet, a jar that had not been there before. Indirapatra knew that it was placed there by the gods. He poured this water upon Sulayman's limbs, thinking it might consecrate his brother's remains. Instead, Sulayman's flesh returned to life.

"I live, brother," he said, standing up, as Indirapatra embraced him with joy. "I was merely resting and waiting for your return."

Indirapatra sent his brother home to rest, for he understood that this was a sign from the gods that he alone should complete this journey. He traveled to the land of the third beast: the dreadful, seven-headed Pah. Legend says that should one head of the Pah be cut off, another would grow in its place. But Raja Indirapatra knew what to do. As the Pah lunged towards him, he made a great leap in the air. His double-edged kris sword, the Juru Pakal, slashed as he flew towards the beast. In one long, sharp strike, Indirapatra cut off all seven of the Pah's heads, for that is the only way to kill this particular monster. As he landed, unharmed, on his feet, Raja Indirapatra thanked the Juru Pakal, which has a mind of its own. The Juru Pakal had decided to fight on the righteous side of the young prince.

Having slain the beasts that terrorized the islands of Mindanao, Raja Indirapatra and his brother, Raja Sulayman, restored peace over the land. Slowly, the people who had lived for so long in fear, hidden underground and in caves, began to emerge. At first, they were only a few. By month's end, they came out of the dark by the thousands, then the tens of thousands, for they were now a people who could live in the light.

Skim the fatty scum from the surface of the oxtail broth.

In the summer of 1994, tongues silenced, bodies undocumented, wishing to hide from other Filipinos and their silent judgments, my family moved to Shillington, a rural town west of Philadelphia. An old friend of Mom's from her Philippine banking days had called to say *Come work here*. Dad and Mom had had enough of living in a damp basement room in Auntie Lorna's house, as kind as it was of her to let us live there. Besides, Dad had started too many fights with his uncles and oldest brother.

In Shillington, they found a small, two-bedroom apartment in the Governor Mifflin Apartments, an affordable housing complex, a unit on the second floor. It was no big marble house, but after almost a year in a cramped single basement room, this apartment felt like the American dream.

Mom's friend, Tita Alice, helped both my mother and father to apply to Redner's, the grocery store down the road from the apartments. Tita Alice was a kind, friendly woman whose fridge and kitchen always seemed to be stocked with more treats and homemade food than ours. She and Mom had known each other as colleagues in the Philippine National Bank. Now, they were colleagues again, pulling shifts scanning groceries at the checkout line together.

"That was so hard," Mom told me recently. "My feet were killing me, my back was killing me. We didn't have insurance, so I had that undiagnosed thyroid disorder. I was so skinny, remember?"

At that job, my mother saw glimpses that she would later understand to be signs that America was not quite as advertised. That this land did not believe its own myths of self-determination and prosperity, not even for its own white people.

"I checked out groceries for so many white people on food stamps. Food stamps! Unable to afford food? In the US? I would never have believed it if anyone had said that to me in the Philippines."

"Yeah," I said. "I had classmates who had free lunch at school too." I thought of the reams of squatter lean-tos on my way to Catholic private school in Manila. The bone-skinny toddlers and children begging for food at our school jeepney's window. What was the point of living in the center of empire, the leader of the free world, as they called themselves, if they couldn't even feed their own?

"I said to one customer, wow, you must have a big dog!" Mom continued. "I was scanning cans and cans of just dog food. And she said, 'Oh, this isn't for a dog. This is for me. It's cheaper than our food,' she said."

Dad worked at Redner's, too, as a night-shift stock clerk, assigned with restocking the cereal aisle while the store was closed. Mom had gotten lucky with an error from the Immigration and Naturalization Service: she received a clean Social Security card, one that did not say "Not Valid for Employment," like mine did, like my sister's did. Dad did not have a number at all, having spent his first year in America with no guidance from his relatives. So that he could work and pay taxes through his paycheck, he used my sister's Social Security number. With his meticulous, detailed, architect-trained hands, he doctored photocopies of our cards until the "Not Valid for Employment" disappeared, and the photocopy looked like any other photocopy of a Social Security card. He submitted this to the grocery store's manager, claiming that the originals were locked away in a safety deposit box. Mama Sita's Instant Legal, Tax-Paying Immigrant.

Our college-educated, white-collar parents became minimum-wage grocery store workers, making rent, utilities, and the car payment each month, buying the food they could afford from Aldi, from clearance racks with produce and meats expiring today or tomorrow. During the week, we feasted on cans of SpaghettiOs or Chef Boyardee for lunch. Dinner was frozen microwavable instant Salisbury steak and gravy, or turkey slices with mashed potatoes, or beef lasagna. Years later, when Mom was diagnosed with breast cancer and Dad with diabetes, both suffering from heart disease, it was not hard to understand why.

Filipino food like kare-kare or palabok was a rarity, encountered only at Tita Alice's apartment or at her sister Cathy's townhouse. Unlike us, Tita Alice and her sister were legal immigrants, marrying nice Filipino husbands with papers and decent jobs. At their weekend get-togethers, our small community of three Filipino families sat in a circle, eating at a Chinese buffet after Sunday Mass, or feasting on Filipino food. A tiny speck of diaspora in an almost all-white small town, eating food from home behind closed doors, celebrating life.

Transfer the oxtails to a bowl and set aside. Pour the golden broth into the large pot with the garlic and onion.

Next, in 1898, America, the seven-headed beast, came to rule our islands. Their largest, most fearsome head, the military, killed between 250,000 and 1 million Filipinos, many of them civilian noncombatants, between 1899 and 1902. Their schoolteachers, with their well-meaning condescension, arrived and taught us savages how to speak and write in their language, as if we had no spoken or written language of our own, no oral literary tradition of our own, more ancient, formidable, and mythic than their folk songs, country tales, and imperial myths. Their missionaries infiltrated into my father's people's Cordillera mountains, turning people with generations of indigenous animist connection to the soil, trees, water, and sky into people of Protestant Christian false piety. Their administrators descended upon Manila, that long-ago beaten ground, and insisted that we build institutions like theirs, with classed prejudice and gatekept aspirations like theirs, though perhaps three centuries of the Spanish made this easy. They built universities, schools, governmental agencies and departments, all with the aim of mimicking the "American way of life," the way of exclusion, denial, and capitalist striving. Their cooks and farmers came to our islands, deeming our ancient ways of homegrown, bahay kubo sustenance farming and seasonal eating to be inferior and unhealthy. They taught us to eat their canned corn, their tins of Spam, their hot dogs and powdered cow's milk, their Ovaltine and Tang, their Heinz ketchup and processed Kraft cheese. Their writers and artists beckoned to us from their land of amber waves of grain, awarding scholarships so that they could teach us to only see, feel, and create the way they did, and to us, this was exciting, for the Spanish, with their caste system, made assimilation nearly impossible.

To the Spanish, we had been merely resources from which to extract wealth. At least the Americans allowed us to pretend as if we were part of their new commonwealth, right? Their capitalists, those robber barons of industry, came to our islands, saw the resources to be plundered—still plentiful even after three centuries of Spanish extraction. They saw the land to be stolen and put under bankers' usurious lock and key. They taught us that the only way to grow (that favorite capitalist word) was through industry, both in body and in infrastructure.

This is a long-winded way to say that kare-kare as we know it today— 5 x 6-inch packets of instant-mix powder—is a manifestation of that American destiny. An industrialized waste of an ancient, slow-cooked recipe, stirred hurriedly into tepid water by frazzled Nanays and Inas, Ates, Titas, and Lolas, to make pots of kare-kare in thirty minutes, not thirty hours, because everyone has to clock into the hospital, factory, or office early the next morning, and rice takes long enough as it is. No one has the time for grinding peanuts or for passing down time-honored traditions. Our traditions were newly labeled; dirty Filipinos cooking dirty food. Our kitchens were called dirty, too, an abjected room kept outside, away from the American-made Westinghouse, the imported Frigidaire (or as my grandmother called it, the prigider).

Add the bay leaves to the pot. Keep the heat on medium to medium-high.

In Shillington, I had become both my sister's nanny and the kitchen maid, staff my parents were used to having and did not know how to do without. I was only ten, eleven, twelve, thirteen. I reveled in this time spent with my sister, five and a half years younger than me, imbued with a quiet, deep energy that brimmed either with hate or with love, depending on the day, depending on how far away Dad was, how long ago his latest rage had been. Afternoons with her dozens of stuffed toys arranged like students in a classroom, our shared bedroom scattered with books, notebooks, and a dry-erase board. Me teaching her the alphabet, her numbers. How to read, write, add, subtract. Puppet shows with her toys, her giggles and squeals of delight my reward. Mimicry, survival. The bending of the tongue inward, an American accent our greatest disguise. I learned, and taught her, how to hide in plain speak.

After school, I stood on a stool to wash dirty plates, swept the kitchen floor and vacuumed the apartment's beige wall-to-wall carpet. I spent entire sunny afternoons with Mom or Dad, watched, on tiptoe, as clothes tumbled in a coin-operated machine at the laundromat down the street, at a strip mall. Went home to help put everything away while *Law & Order* blared in the background, a show I put on even today, mistaking copaganda for comfort. And if I fucked anything up—a kitchen sink drain, unemptied, or a puddle on the floor, unmopped, then I could expect a beating from my father. Some beatings left marks on my body that could not be covered by clothes, bruising welts that were raised, red, and hot, hammered into the backs of my small, thin thighs, criscrossing my back, arms, and shoulders too. When classmates and teachers asked me if I was OK, if I wanted to see the guidance counselor, asked where the marks came from, I bit my tongue, kept silent.

Sometimes I made up a story. Stories are easier than the truth when your entire existence is a lie.

Over summer vacations, my tongue learned how to sound American. The English that was my first language was a preserved, out-of-date, American colonial version from decades before, local culture lagging behind empire before the days of the internet. I said things like "foodstuffs," "perhaps," and "May I sharpen my pencil please, ma'am?" English is often the first, second, or third tongue for Filipinos—the first for me and my sister, second for my mother, and third for my father. Our newspapers, government documents, advertisements, and radio and television shows are all in American English.

Yet, to Americans, I sounded like a damned foreigner from the islands. State tests indicated that, at eleven, I wrote, spoke, and read at college level. A true product of colonial mimetic aspiration. Ever the class weirdo, I spent each summer vacation alone, silent, friendless. I roamed the Governor Mifflin Apartments' parking lots, the asphalt of Colonial Drive shimmering with afternoon summer heat. I read my library books outside, on small, mounded patches of lawn, shaded by the gray-beige buildings that loomed in perpendicular arrangements, clumps of affordable, low-income despair, families crammed and housed in the hopes of keeping our unhappiness at bay. In the hopes that the working class might stay silent as the beast of inequality ravaged, and continues to ravage, the United States.

I talked, sang, whispered, and read to myself in the contemporary American tongue. I softened my lengua, my language acquiescing to the pressures of immigrant life. Lowered my voice into my chest, crushed vowels together, smoothed my consonants. My tongue the pestle, the bowl of my mouth beneath, the mortar. Sometimes, in front of the bathroom mirror, I practiced getting the facial expressions right, the hand gestures just so, tilting my head left and right, shrugging in the insouciant way my American classmates did, the kind of attitude that earned a slap from Mom every now and then. Imaginary conversations, jokes, newly discovered phrases and words. *Totally. No way. You got it. Phony. What a loser. Such a dork. Hey Jill, what's up?* I would ask myself in the mirror. *What were you up to this summer? Where were you at?* Like kare-kare, I enfolded these new influences into myself, my body and mind a stirred pot of its own code-switched, assimilated, differently accented ingredients.

Gently strain the annatto seed water into another cup. Put the annatto seeds into a cheesecloth. Knot the top.

When the Spanish arrived with their achiote seeds, how long did it take for saffron to be forgotten as an essential part of kare-kare? Did anyone notice, or miss, the spices that vanished, along with our islands' connection to trade from Indian lands?

"What happened? Your accent's gone," said Tanya, a friend I made reluctantly, the only one willing to talk to the weird new girl. This school in Pennsylvania was my third new school in less than two years.

"Really?" I said, reveling in my newfound ability to shorten the long "e" in the middle, to push the "l" to the middle of my palate, rather than on the tip of my tongue. Rillee. Rilly. Rully. The Tagalog-accented pronunciation, equal emphasis on each syllable, ree-lee, was to be reserved only for moments of incredulity. *Reelee? You've gotta be kidding me!* This accent was a full workout for the tongue, a small muscle tasked with lifting an entire identity.

Tanya and I had bonded over our shared friendlessness. Mostly, I did not want to get to know anyone. I was probably going to move again anyway. And no one wanted to get to know me, the moody Philippinesian girl or whatever, the one with the sarcastic attitude problem. Not Ingrid, the flaxen-haired, icy beauty who was most definitely not interested in girls, or Dean, the handsome, doe-eyed, brown-haired boy who sat across from me for all of the fifth grade. And I did not want to get to know myself, this tongue-tied, lonely nobody who felt like she could fall in love with anybody, and therefore avoided everybody. It took me years to begin to make friends. I was too shy, yet spiky and mean; too strange, off-putting and eager to please, all at once. Bullied by the popular girls, shunned by the less-popular girls, a cafeteria table and gym class liability. And sometimes, my Filipino accent slipped out, a spasm from my tongue, the hardest working muscle in my body.

"Wund? What's a 'wund'?" a girl named Liz once said to me, at lunch. "It's 'wound,' loser."

The other girls laughed, except for one, who felt sorry enough for me to keep talking to me.

Liz was a tormentor in the same alphabetical surname grouping as me, mocking me in every class we had together until I was moved up to advanced classes, leaving her behind. I began to skip lunch to sneak into the library, picking out books to read, memorizing how to pronounce words, pretending to be too busy, too cool, to bother with a clique. How dull. As if! This country, I discovered, was about being a quick study—its oldest tradition. Fake it till you make it. Mama Sita's Instant American.

Chewing and swallowing so many microwave TV dinners, each bite changed my body, cell by cell, tissue by tissue, forming a new tongue, new vocal folds. They say it takes seven years for your body to completely replace every cell; my body, softened by shock, by pressure, needed only five. My American language education was hours on the couch watching the nightly news and my roster of creepy television shows: *Tales from the Crypt, Twin Peaks, Unsolved Mysteries* blaring on the fat, heavy, wood-encased 1970s cathode-ray television. Dad and Mom had salvaged it from a garage sale somewhere outside Wyomissing, the wood faded in places, knobs with labels long rubbed off, and an antenna that refused to stay in place. We had to stand up to change the channel, or turn up the volume, or turn it off and on. Constant vigilance, much like maintaining an American accent.

Pour the annatto water into the broth. Place the knotted cheesecloth of annatto seeds into the broth. Stir.

After six months or so as a checkout clerk at Redner's, Mom found a job listing in the newspaper. A local branch of National Penn Bank needed a teller. At the interview, she quelled her nerves, bracing herself for the inevitable.

"Well, Ana May, it actually looks like you're a bit overqualified for this teller position."

"I see. OK, I understand." Mom began to stand up, smoothed down her skirt and jacket.

"Wait," the interviewer said, gesturing for her to sit down. "We actually have a management trainee program that runs twice a year, and I think you have the right amount of experience for it, and certainly good grades from your bachelor's degree. Would you consider joining this program? You would be paid $40,000 a year."

Mom's head spun. Management? Training? $40,000 a year? More than what she and Dad earned all together at Redner's?

Mom excelled at the program. Stood up for herself when a fellow trainee, a white man, tried to take credit for her ideas during a group exercise. Her old fighting spirit from years under the Marcos regime remained undiminished. Three months into the six-month management trainee program, the bank offered my mother a permanent position at their branch in the nearby town of Temple. She was to become an assistant manager to the branch, and her pay would start at $45,000, with a guaranteed raise and bonus at the end of each year, full medical and dental, and paid holiday time off.

"We did it, baby!" Dad sang into our tiny living room that night, one of the moments of happiness I can remember. He had picked up my mother in his arms, spun her around in a circle. I danced around them, tooting on my kazoo, happy to be happy with my family. On the couch, my sister smiled grimly, cautious and vigilant. Waited for the monster to put our mother back down on the floor without hurting her.

It did not take long for my little sister, possessed with the ability to see through everyone, to be right. I doubt that Dad truly knew what he was doing, but as Mom took home paychecks that were twice the size of his, he began to devour her confidence, her sense of self-worth, her self-regard.

"You don't know how to manage our finances," he would say to her. "I'll do them." He took control of her money, gave her no access to it for the next thirty years.

"You have no idea what you're doing," he would scoff. "I'll take care of the kids." He took control of her children, undermined her in front of us, made Mom even weaker, even more dependent on his approval.

"Go ahead and try to divorce me," he would taunt her. "Or call the cops. See how quickly you get sent home." He used our undocumented status as a threat, so that we would never report him or leave him. We adjusted to all of this as normal, swallowed it as a truth we could never tell. A monster we could never slay, for he would kill us in revenge, like that ancient Tarabūsaw.

Kapampangans say that kari-kari, as they once called it, was sold in huts that they called kariyan. We now know these kari huts as karinderiya, where we now buy more than just this dish. Karinderiya, turo-turos, street hawkers: it is understandable how my parents, growing up with such riches around them on the streets of food-loving Manila, under its balete trees, and inside air-conditioned shopping centers, never learned how to cook.

If they wanted to give the maids a day of rest, there was good, homemade food everywhere in the city. In America, the microwave became my parents' best culinary aid.

Over medium-low heat, stir the fresh-made peanut butter into the broth. Add the ready-made peanut butter, if necessary.

As they began to earn more, our parents began to cook Filipino food. Kare-kare appeared on our dining table, green beans filling in for sitaw, and other vegetables depending on what was available at grocery stores and our local Asian mini-mart, which was where Mama bought the paper packets of instant Mama Sita's Kare-Kare Mix. She was so proud of her pots of kare, which she thoughtfully improved with big spoonfuls of extra-chunky peanut butter from a jar. It is rare, in America, for the Filipino home cook to grind rice flour and peanuts from scratch for kare-kare. The land of industry, production, and year-on-year growth does not allow for such indulgences.

Our Pennsylvanian kare-kare never contained banana hearts. A ruinous omission. The banana tree, some say, is a gift from an engkanto, or encanto, which is what the Spanish called the enchanted spirits who lived in our forests, rivers, caves, mountains, and seas. They can bring good luck or great loss, sorrow or joy, healing or pain. Some engkantos choose to occupy human bodies, draining them of life and energy or infusing them with tremendous love and power. Other engkantos choose to take on the human form, though this transformation is only temporary. If we had banana hearts in our Mama Sita's kare-kare, an engkanto might have gifted us with the return of Papa and Mama. Instead, our own hearts drifted further away from home as our stay in America turned into years, one budget microwaveable frozen TV dinner and instant powdered Filipino shortcut at a time. It was also in those first two years that Mom and Dad met Mr. Sison, a slick Filipino American immigration attorney. A monster of the worst kind, the kind who preyed on his own people for profit.

Our parents often visited this Mr. Sison at his office in Manhattan. They would take the three-hour drive to see him, sheafs of papers in a folder, a checkbook in Mom's purse, a Rubbermaid cooler full of snacks for me and my sister if we came along. After each visit, their shoulders less hopeful than before, the family checking account emptied into Mr. Sison's, we drove back home to Pennsylvania, hours of flat highway at dusk.

"Is it fixed now?" I asked after one of those trips to Manhattan. Perhaps our fourth, or fifth.

My father, seething, drinking water by the kitchen sink, did not answer.

"Dad? Is it fi—"

In response, Papa flung the glass into the sink. It shattered everywhere, shards cutting into his arm, skittering across the apartment's linoleum floor. By then, I had been in America long enough to know that there would be no maid to clean up the sharp, glinting mess. I knelt down, broom and dustpan in hand, and swept quickly, carefully.

Years later, Papa would tell me that over the course of two and a half years, Mr. Sison took thousands of dollars from my parents, wasting the two years we had to obtain worker and family visas, filing motions and paperwork that did nothing. To this day, we cannot be sure if Mr. Sison ever submitted anything to the INS on our behalf. I have since been told that there is no such record in the government's system. Perhaps it was due to the INS's disorganization and neglect, perhaps Mr. Sison's duplicity. Perhaps both.

"And then he said there was nothing he could do. That maybe—" Dad choked on his words, hiding his tears behind hands roughened by years of manual labor. "That maybe your Mama and I should go back home, or move to Canada as a last resort. That family members could adopt you and your sister, so that at least you could be legal and petition us in twenty years. Twenty years." The only remaining pathway out of our cave of hiding was long, winding, and uncertain.

Our real survival began then, in Shillington, Pennsylvania. Dad, with no visa, no Social Security number, continued his night shifts just down the road. There were boxes to be punched open by his angry, ungloved fist, splitting the skin at the knuckles. Rows of cereal to be stacked, pallets to haul in, fast and heavy, injuring his back, his hips. A self-administered punishment, a heart broken by his own pride, or shame at what he had become. Mom, accidentally almost legal, Social Security card and driver's license in her pocket, became our roof, our walls, our breadwinner. The bank gave her two promotions, which would eventually become many. From bakery checkout girl to local bank regional manager in five years flat. Mama Sita's Instant Breadwinner.

We soon moved out of Colonial Drive and onto Community Drive, to a slightly nicer apartment complex across town called Shillington Commons. The new place was twice the size: an end-unit townhouse with a front yard and a small patch of backyard. There was an upstairs and a downstairs, with two bedrooms, each bigger than our old apartment's bedrooms. A set of stairs bisected the floor plan: two flights, with a landing in between. A landing I would come to know well. A landing my face landed upon, often. I would learn how to roll safely down these stairs, like a Hollywood stuntman, whenever Dad pushed me down them in his latest rage. Learned how to lie to the dentists who fixed my broken teeth, the pediatrician who relocated my shoulder, the teachers who saw my bruises. Mama Sita's Instantly Fine.

Add the rice flour to the peanut-oxtail broth until it thickens to a stew, clinging to the back of a spoon.

Like any good kare-kare, we took time to remake ourselves. We crushed our spirit into paste, hopes ground to powder, realities enfolded into our bodies, tongues speaking in accents we had to learn quickly as a cloak of invisibility. We absorbed being called Ching-Chong on the street, in the park, at the store. Absorbed being stared at by a restaurant full of white people, then being seated in the very back, by the bathrooms. Absorbed notes in the church parking lot left on the windshield shouting GO BACK WHERE YOU CAME FROM STOP TAKING OUR JOBS. Absorbed being called Connie Chung, or Jackie Chan, or Long Duk Dong to my face by white classmates. We absorbed it all like the tuwalya in the kare-kare, that stomach lining that can take corrosive acid and anything else it encounters. America, after all, thrives on efficiency in all things.

While Mama earned her promotions, and Papa battered boxes open, and I mastered how to sound and act like an American, my sister, a quiet, simmering cauldron brimming with the same resentments as me, packed her backpack each morning to run away from home. Underneath her extra sweater, she would stuff a few packs of instant oatmeal, next to her books, along with some clothes.

"I didn't have a plan," she told me recently. "I just wanted to leave, to get away from Dad. I didn't even think he would notice, or Mom would notice.

You might, but I figured you'd understand. I thought I could live in the woods behind the school."

One afternoon, she finally found the nerve to execute her plan. She walked out during her first-grade homeroom period, down the hallway, and through one of the side double doors. She marched down the back road behind the school, towards the wooded area between the building and one of the main roads in town. Walked towards freedom.

We might have lost her forever had Tita Alice not spotted her, having just dropped off her son at school that morning.

"Tita Alice drove over to me and asked what I was doing, was I not feeling good or whatever. I just said yeah. And then I spent the day at her house. I didn't try to run away again after that."

Perhaps Tita Alice knew better than to tell them about it. Her silence was our protection. I hate that I could not protect my own sister, even if I was only a child myself. That I was too scared, trying too hard to survive, to see her unhappiness.

Heat a frying pan or a stovetop grill. Brush lightly with oil. Grill the eggplant, string beans, banana hearts, and pechay, brushing with oil and turning to cook evenly.

In my solitude, my silenced tongue continued to find refuge in words, in the multiplicity of their meanings over time, in meanings lost and found in their translation. My tongue, the only thing I had control over in this new life. I marveled over how there are words in Tagalog that do not exist in English, and vice versa. We might say "kasamahan," for example, meaning "to be with," "to be together" in a social context, or "to have unity" in a more political conversation, or "to be close to" in kinship or in love. Its closest English translation is the word "community," meaning "to make common, general, public." Between these two words, togetherness as defined by spirit and heart is lost, replaced by Western materiality as defined by rigid law.

At school, I somehow started doing well at something called a spelling bee, words turned into competition, that most American of capitalist pastimes. In the fifth grade, I lost to a girl named Laura in the grade-level spelling bee. Nerves and the word *kindergarten*, where children go to learn words, to make friends, to become comfortable in a new place, and then return to the safety of home. A word that meant nothing to me.

In the sixth grade, I lost in the school district-level spelling bee. Sloppiness and the word *antediluvian*, The time before the biblical flood. The time before the tidal waves that swallowed my parents every night in my recurring dream. Before we were drowning in fear, clinging to rocks between two unforgiving oceans, a cruel past and an impossible present.

In the seventh grade, I lost in the county-level spelling bee. I cannot remember the word I misspelled, but I remember the pressure from my father in the year that followed. In the eighth grade, in exchange for my diligent spelling preparation—he convinced me to quit the track team, to miss friends' birthday parties, to stay at my desk for so long I developed hip pain—Dad bought me a boom box, stacks of cassette tapes, and the Merriam-Webster dictionary.

"Jill," the track coach said to me one afternoon, after school. "It wasn't your choice, was it?"

I held my tongue, said nothing.

"I know you didn't want to quit the team," she continued, concern in her eyes. "Do you want me to talk to your parents? It doesn't have to be one or the other. You could be a scholar-athlete in college someday, you know. You have so much potential. I can help you get there."

I only remember trying not to cry, tongue still silent, walking away from her.

Dad made me sit at my desk seven days a week, swallowing words, contorting my tongue into letters spelling words whose meanings I learned down to their origins. On the wall in front of me, Dad had taped a letter-sized piece of paper. On it, he had written DOWN PAYMENT in his square, perfectly proportioned architect's handwriting, a little house drawn under the words.

"What you should do is spell every word in here and record it on a tape, then listen to that tape every day. You should be making new tapes every week. There's a $5,000 prize if you win the nationals. We could buy a house." This was the beginning of my father's transformation, into seeing me as a site of extraction. I was fourteen.

Each day, for six months, I stared at the sign he had handwritten and taped above my desk, flapping to my breath in front of the boom box, recording words, spelling them off the dictionary. I didn't know what a "down payment" was, exactly, but I knew it meant a house. A house meant a mortgage, maybe two. A double mortgage meant a lawyer, Dad said. A new lawyer meant we could try again for legalization.

I opened the dictionary to the most recent word. I pressed record.

"Deficient. D-E-F-I-C-I-E-N-T. Deficit. D-E-F-I-C-I-T. Defied. D-E-F-I-E-D."

In the eighth grade, I won the grade-level, then the school-level, then the county-level spelling bees, sick with the flu throughout, probably from stress. My name and face were in the local newspapers, a picture of me smiling while receiving a hug from my beautiful but tired-looking mother. I was advancing to the nationals, a kid with no papers but all the right answers. Dad, unwilling to let me write my own answers to the newspaper reporter's follow-up questions, wrote out my own personality for me. Hobbies: running, writing, reading news magazines and the newspaper. Career goals: doctor. Something about enjoying studying word etymologies. This did not help me win any cool points at school, but I didn't mind. Dad was nice to me for once, bringing up snacks and meals while I studied for nationals. Pages flipping, cassettes recording, tongue folding, enfolding, unfolding new words.

Add the lengua and oxtails to the pot. Lay the grilled vegetables on top, or plated to the side.

I lost in the 1997 Scripps Howard National Spelling Bee just before the final rounds, which were televised on ESPN. The winner was Rebecca Sealfon, a brilliant and jubilant champion from Brooklyn who was completely herself, buoyant and leaping, joyful in her win. I envied this selfhood of hers, this confidence she had despite other contestants' jeers, the loving family that surrounded her afterward while my father refused to speak to me, let alone comfort me.

"There shouldn't be a bee, even though I won," Rebecca said in an interview just after her win, "because many children are in grief."

My losing word was *shillibeer*, a horse-drawn carriage for a hearse bearing a dead body to a funeral or a burial. The death of our chance at legalization. My consolation prize was a fifty-dollar US bond certificate, which Dad kept and still has, a full-sized Merriam-Webster dictionary, and my parents' silent treatment on the long car ride home from Washington, DC. There would be no house, no second mortgage, no lawyer, no legalization for us. I had failed to secure our down payment. I accepted the blame, which is the duty of a firstborn. I compressed the guilt into its condensed essence, ground it down to a fine powder, and sealed it into my heart. Flattened its bulk into a packet. A shelf life of decades. Mama Sita's Filial Piety.

I wonder what it means, that these national spelling bees are so often won by immigrant kids, immigrants' kids, or immigrants' grandkids. A competition for whose tongues and minds have assimilated the most, absorbed culture into our stomach linings, our bloodstreams. Who among us has most successfully parroted the empire's tongue in the hopes of acceptance? I wonder if any of us eventually ever do find a place to belong that doesn't ask so much of us.

Serve the kare-kare hot, with steamed rice. Offer sweet and spicy bagoóng in bowls. Serve family style.

The wind gusts outside while I stir the kare-kare, its bronze peanut sauce coating the sides of the pot. I pour myself a fat, round glass of pinot noir, while the pechay, eggplant, and green beans char on the stovetop grill in front of me, their steam rising to meet my cheeks, fogging my glass. It is a privilege to have time, money, and resources to make kare-kare from scratch. Today, it has come to this: me, an immigrant nobody, honoring myself with an ancient dish for royalty. Roasted rice and charbroiled peanuts, ground down by my own hands, an effort I am willing to make so that I may know my own worth.

At the table, I dip the ladle into the tureen, scoop out the largest hunk of oxtail. I drape it, alongside the pechay, the eggplant, and the banana heart, on top of my rice and dollop of bagoóng. I go back in for a generous helping of peanut sauce, a big, dripping ladle from the shared pot, textured with the ground remnants of my own suffering.

4

Sinigang na Hipon at Isda sa Sampalok
(Prawns and Fish in Soured Tamarind Broth)

1997–1999

SERVES 6-8

Jasmine rice, steamed (at least 10 cups when cooked)
10 large to extra-large prawns, unpeeled, with heads
1½ pounds boned milkfish belly
10 yard-long beans
8 ounces water spinach
2 white radishes (Philippine labanos or Japanese daikon)
2 medium onions
2 red or green finger chilies
1 or 2 fish heads in knotted cheesecloth
1½ to 2 cups tamarind paste
¼ cup Filipino patis
At the table:
Filipino patis
Halved calamansi fruits or calamansi juice

I dip my hand into the bag of floppy, long-stemmed water spinach leaves, which I remember as kang kong. The decision to make this sinigang was a spontaneous one, prompted by a visit to the local Asian grocery store.

They happened to have a shipment of these leaves just in, fresh from Thailand.

Kang kong leaves rinsed and drained, I scoop two sticky tablespoons out of the jar of tamarind paste, the last of it. Plop the spoonfuls into the broth, using a finger to smear off the last remains. I ladle some broth into the jar, swirl the paste off the glass, and pour it all into the pot.

"OK," I say to myself, licking the earthy, tamarind tartness off my finger, sourness fading halfway down my throat. "Let's put the prawns back in."

In a pot, wash the uncooked rice to be cooked with the sinigang. Reserve 3 quarts of this milky, starchy rice water, which we call hugas bigas, for the sinigang. Cook the rice in clear water as normal.

Sinigang dares you. Its sourness taunts the tongue into confusion: Do you hate it, wish to spit it out? Do you like it enough to have another spoonful? Or, like me as a child, love it enough to drink from the bowl, draining it empty, chin dripping broth, raising the bowl up to Lola to ladle in another helping? The sourness squeezes the cheeks, puckers the base of the tongue. Floods the basin of the mouth with acid, gentle salt. Lets us know that we are alive. We sour the broth using any acidic fruit or vegetable. On our islands, there is calamansi, kamias, green mango, guava, kandis, tamarind, piña. Out here, in the diaspora, there is lemon, lime, yuzu, strawberry, green apple, rhubarb. We seek out this sourness to remind ourselves that there is more to the tongue than the sweet or savory. To remind ourselves that life is best lived with a hit of acidity, some struggle before the reward. Filipino dishes almost always contain this element of unavoidable sourness, a lip-smacking embrace of life's inevitabilities: the calamansi squeezed over sisig, the cane vinegar that makes up half of our adobo's silky confit, the chilied pinakurat vinegar in which we swirl a crispy piece of salty lechon skin. There are Filipino dishes that are even bitter—ampalaya sautéed with shrimp, bell pepper, red onion, and egg. But I am not yet wise enough to savor the bitter.

There is no one way to make sinigang. Like us, this dish is nimble, made in any season or climate, with any variable set of ingredients and any amount of money in your wallet. I choose to make this sinigang not with pork, my childhood favorite, but with king prawns and milkfish, which I grew up to

know as bangus. A pot that honors our sea-born beginnings, our fluidly gen-
dered selves. The Philippines is a collection of islands, of people born, raised,
and buried surrounded by the flowing energy of water. In mountains, plains,
and valleys never too far from the embrace of any sea, from trade with neigh-
boring islands and thalassic kingdoms. We pluck treasures from the water,
because it is the most generous wilderness we know. Because our seas and
rivers have been willing to yield what the land often only begrudgingly gives.
Perhaps we love sinigang because we understand suffering best. Whether it
was from our own sultans and tribal leaders, or from the Spanish governors
and priests, we seek out the acid, the sour note, because we know that with
great suffering, there must surely someday come great satisfaction.

*Using kitchen scissors, gently devein the prawns, keeping the shells
and heads intact.*

Lolo Pedring once told me the story of a boy who dove too deep into the
sea. One sunny afternoon, this teenage boy and his two friends decided to
make one of their regular after-school swims a little more interesting.

"O, ito na," the boy said, standing at the edge of the rocks. "Whoever dives
the deepest and stays underwater the longest wins."

The three boys took off their school uniforms and dove in. Heads tucked
into arms outstretched, hands meeting in a perfect V. Legs together, feet
pointed, fin-like. They entered the water all at the same time, three little
splashes against the big ocean. A deep, thick tapestry of blues, greens, and
grays, woven out of water by the great Aman Sinaya herself, daughter of
earth mother Gaea, sister of sky god Bathala and of goddess Amihan, she of
the north wind that brings about all change. Splash, splash, splash, barely a
mark amid the white-topped crashing waves.

The boys resurfaced. First, the tallest one with the lanky limbs, then the
darkest one, with the kayumanggi skin. But the boy who started it all, the
one who came up with the contest, did not resurface. The other two waited
for their friend to come back up. They laughed and rested, floating, bellies
up, basking in Aman Sinaya's ocean hands, under Bathala's burning gaze.

"Uy," said the one with the kayumanggi skin, after another minute. "San
na yun? He's taking too long."

"Ah, alam mo naman what he's like," laughed the lanky one. "Always showing off. Probably swam to the other side of the island. Probably sitting on a rock, pretending he's underwater all this time."

A few minutes passed. The two boys began to worry. They treaded water and shouted their friend's name into the air. The wind—a northern one, stirred by Amihan's hand—began to blow, carrying their voices away. Pushing clouds over the sun. The boys began to shiver. They decided to get help. Swimming back towards the rocks, they put on their clothes, leaving their friend's belongings pinned under a heavy stone, in case he did surface after all, annoyed that they left him behind. The two boys ran all the way back to the village, their feet leaving wet marks on the stony dirt road.

All afternoon and into dusk, the strongest women and men of the village swam, searching for the missing boy. They dove beneath rocks and between caverns, swam over the edge of the coral shelf, around the rim of the island itself. They swam next to dolphin pods, hoping they might share a secret, or a sighting. They cautiously dove close to the local, sharp-toothed barracudas, gingerly asked if they'd seen anything (snarl, they had not). They searched the mangroved edges of the island, where the brackish water leads inland to the river's mouth. Others searched behind and beneath the waterfalls. Some villagers gathered at the island's peak, wailing and sending prayers to the gods above. Still others jumped on their bangka, the ones used for fishing. They rowed out to the farthest edge of their known waters, scanning the blue, blue, blue. They saw nothing. A deep curtain of darkest ocean had been drawn, keeping them from finding the missing boy.

Meanwhile, far beyond the land, in the near-black depths of the sea, the missing boy awakened. He opened his eyes, as if from a deep sleep, his breath bubbling up around his face. Up above, so far above, the distant surface of the water shimmered, fingers of light waving hello from way up there. He could not believe what was down here. That he was here, at all. He held out his hands in front of his face, looked down at his body. No wounds, no pains. Felt his head, his heart, beating. Breathed in, breathed out with ease. More bubbles. Alive. He was lying on a bed of seaweed, a thousand soft cushions. He looked around at the endless depths of blue, looked up, saw swaying colorful ocean flora, fauna all around. Was he dreaming? How did he end up so deep undersea? He looked around and felt unafraid. He noticed his own lack of fear and wondered at it.

Then, from the depths, a beautiful young woman appeared. She drifted towards him, a smile on her face, her curved figure accentuated by a long, elegant tail over twice the length of her torso. Except for this tail, she looked like someone he might have known from school. Her hair, the color of deepest night ocean, was afloat in what seemed to be water, but what felt, to the boy, like air, which he could inhale, exhale. Magic. The boy knew this was a sirena. His Lola often told him about such stories—of beautiful women and men with heads, arms, and torsos like humans, but with long, beautiful tails like fish. Of their vast oceanic kingdoms deep beyond the reach of any human. He sat up on the bed, alert, curious.

"Hello," the sirena said to him, a gentle smile on her face. "You are finally here."

"Finally?" the boy said, his teenage voice cracking a little.

"Yes, finally. I have waited many years for you. The one who would come from the land above to become my king." She went on to explain that she was the future queen of the ocean's realms, that this land, vaster than any island, than any mountain, belonged to her family.

The boy shook his head. "I ended up here by accident. I think I swam too far off the edge of the corals. I must have fainted."

"Don't worry," the sirena-princess said. "I will be by your side and show you the way. You will come to love the treasures of this ocean world."

She sat next to the boy, and he let her hold his hand. One, two, three, four, five more sirena appeared, men and women, each bearing a tray of oceanic delicacies.

"Eat," the princess said, "so that you can grow strong and explore this world with me."

The boy shook his head, refused. He remembered his mother's warnings, that these sirena are tempting, wily, and difficult to resist. That they will do anything to lure humans, those never-content creatures roaming the land, into water. He remembered that his mother said to never accept food from them, lest he be lost forever.

"You live here, now," the sirena soothed him. "You must forget all that is on land. You will be my consort when I come to inherit these realms from my mother. We will answer to no one but Aman Sinaya herself."

On land, the villagers' search continued towards the edges of the night.

As the god Bathala darkened the sky, the villagers had no choice but to go back home, to tell the boy's family that they, too, had found nothing. The village began to prepare for their ceremonies of mourning. The boy had dived too deep into the unknown. They had lost another child to the sea.

Check that the milkfish steaks are fully boned. Remove any bones found.

Of the many places I missed from home, the gentle seas of my childhood called to me the most. Mythical in the way that we like to remember our pasts, personal and national. I longed for my childhood's magical, timeless weeks by the sea, those air-suspended days between Christmas and New Year's spent sleeping in beach huts, meters away from lapping waves. Time and light, equatorial and generous, seemed to refract and soften in those days, flitting through palm fronds, warming the black-brown Zambales sand, glinting off waves, toasting my skin. I played in the water, a cousin's slightly too big hand-me-down swimsuit hanging down off my toddler body. Jellyfish, stingless and tiny, cupped in my palms. Fresh coconut, drunk out of husks hacked open by kind men with large forearms and sharp itaks to match. Papa—before he was lost to the sea and became Dad—gently feeding me fruit, cradling a glass of milk as I drank from it. Building an architecturally scaled sand castle for me, laughing as I poured seawater all over it when he was done. Spit-roasted fish and octopus, just-caught prawns stewed in coconut gata. The silence of sunset, as if everyone understood that the sea and the dusk were for a communal moment of peace. For a thank-you to Dios and Mother Mary, to Bathala and Aman Sinaya. And at night, the melodic choruses of pulutans scattered around the village, across the beach with its rows of vacation huts: titos and titas, lolos and lolas, moms and dads, singing Elvis, Frank, Nat, Aretha, Carole, Pilita, Sharon, Gary.

This appreciation for beauty despite hardship, for the skies and sunsets despite the storms they bring, must be another reason we love sinigang. The sourness may be almost too much to bear, but the flavors that follow, and the craving for more that follows that—it is worth the acidic pinch in the back of the jaw. Our country, the second-lowest emitter of greenhouse gas worldwide, is regularly cracked in half by typhoons that grow more harsh and deadly each year. Yet, we live, starting over, again and again. We wait for the next year's storms, for water to reclaim what was just rebuilt. We sip the broth of sinigang to remember that to eat, to live, is not just to enjoy.

In America, in search of the sea, we drove a few hours each summer to beaches in New Jersey, the next state over. Puberty was self-consciousness in my new body, unsure of its first-ever two-piece swimsuit. The water was cold and brown, its waves tall, violent, and pounding, careless in how they threw our bodies down beneath the water's surface, as if wishing to kill us all. The sand was white, a novelty at first. The beach was crowded, noisy: families with tents, boom boxes, coolers full of bottles of beer and sticky soda. I hated the boardwalks, all those loud arcades and sports bars, aggressively drunk Americans with orange tans stumbling out of them. Painfully sugared saltwater taffy, thickly battered fried food that tasted only of oil and salt. Big bass rattling windows, throbbing from nightclubs into the warm air. The acidic wail of sirens. In those summers of rented beach cottages, we split rooms with Tita Alice and her children. All of us kept awake by Dad, his drunk anguish barely muffled by thin walls.

"Mahal na mahal kita! Don't you understand how much I love you?"

My sister and I burrowed deeper into the twin bed we shared, facing each other, eyes pinched shut. Mama must have caught him looking at other women, again. Maybe she was asking him about an auntie's offhand remark. *Andy had a girlfriend on the ship.* Worn down by his 2 a.m. tirade, Mom's voice, pleading, begging him to stop.

"Forget it, tigil na, Andy. Let's go to sleep, please let me sleep."

Dad would be on his best behavior in the following days, humbled. His usual touchy anger, so omnipresent, pushed under the surface by the presence of Tita Alice, her husband, and their kids. In those afternoons, he would gaze out over the Atlantic, lost in the depths of memory. Who were these sirenas of his? How long did it take him to realize that their promises were lies? That their promises of love and riches were nothing more than a myth? That once he ate of the cornucopia of America, he would be lost in its depths forever?

Filipinos have dived too deep into these amber waves of grain for decades. We have fought for the right to life, liberty, and the pursuit of happiness for generations. Year after sour year, Filipinos sought the right to work and be paid fairly, to savor the earned rewards of their labor. Larry Itliong. Philip Vera Cruz. Chris Mensalves. Pete Velasco. Silme Domingo. Gene Viernes. Countless unnamed others, many killed in the fight to live in America. Has it been worth it, these decades of submersion in the acidic broth of America? This diving too deep into waters that seek to change us so that we are no longer ourselves, that seek only to use us until we drown?

Prepare the vegetables. Cut the yard-long beans into 3- to 4-inch pieces. Cut the thickest stems off the water spinach.

Weeks passed for the boy who dove too deep. The beautiful sirena hardly left his side, insistent that they get to know one another. There was only one problem: he still refused to eat.

"Why will you not eat?" the sirena asked, pressing a tray of food towards him.

The boy remained quiet. He looked up, to where the daylight played amid the corals. Thought of his mother's cooking, the fresh vegetables growing around their humble bahay kubo: malunggay, sili, okra, kang kong, mangga, kamatis, kamias among his favorites. This undersea place was beautiful, unlike any other place he'd ever been on land. The realm this sirena would rule over—the wealth and power he would have as her consort—unimaginable. Could he see himself here for the rest of his life?

Slice the radishes into thin disks. Cut the onions into halves, then quarters. Wash the chilies clean.

In the depths of these souring years, school became my safe harbor. I threw myself into my studies, excellence as a lifeline, a means of survival. I stayed late at the library, wrote extra-credit book reports, stayed behind for tutoring I didn't need. A way of escaping Dad, who often did not sleep in the daytime hours between his night shifts at the grocery store. His lack of sleep had, over the years, worsened his depression, made him overly sensitive, quick to take offense at everything. Angrier, even more violent. The weeks between the end of marching band and the start of concert band, or between the end of swim team season and the start of track and field season, were unbearable. I filled in the gaps of time by joining other clubs. If it was after school, I was there. Sometimes I made up activities, staying in the library instead to do my homework.

My friend Jane convinced me to try out for the student newspaper. I went, eager to do anything I could to stay away from home. To say to my parents that this was necessary, so that I could put it on my college applications, because that was what they talked to me about the most: college. A future. A good paying job. Helping them someday.

Mr. Stanley, the adviser for the student newspaper, asked each of us to write either a pitch or a prospective article for the following issue. Jane immediately knew what to write about: the upcoming 1998 presidential primaries. She loved current events and politics, civil rights, feminism. Another friend of ours, Lisa, cared about school issues—Title IX funding allocation for girls' sports versus the seemingly limitless funding for boys' football alone, cutbacks in cafeteria staffing, library shortages, improvements to the snow day announcement system. They, along with the other writers-to-be, seemed to be so much more involved in the world, so much more knowledgeable, passionate. One proclaimed that she wanted to only do movie reviews and new album releases. Another said he was excited to cover student activities: government, sports, applying for colleges, proms, homecoming. Someone else said she was interested in photography, in designing the layouts, the typesetting and typefaces.

Where did these interests of theirs come from, and why was I so behind? What did I care about, besides making it through each day alive, possibly unscathed, maybe just an insult or two from my father? Besides avoiding detection, arrest, and deportation by the government? I had no idea.

"What do you want to change?" Lisa asked me as we walked out of the meeting.

"Or what do you worry about?" added Jane. "That's where I start."

Should I go home? I thought to myself. *Will Dad be awake?*

I stayed late after school for a week to prepare for the school paper pitch. Diving deep into the research, I cast about for books in the library, using a microfiche to search through newspaper articles. And when those resources lacked more current information, the librarian helped me search this new thing called the internet.

My submission included not just a trial article but also a pitch for a series of articles focused on climate change, its emerging effects and future possibilities for our world. The first article was on desertification. The next would be on deforestation. Then the melting of the polar ice caps, then the hole in the ozone layer, then a final piece tying them all together. I interviewed my biology teacher and my geography teacher, getting a quote from each of them. If I did a good job on this prospective series, maybe I could be a section editor. Of a section I'd created!

The next day, just before English Lit, Mr. Stanley stopped me in the hallway. Asked me to step into his classroom. My stomach flipped. Was this it? Was he going to make me a section editor this soon?

"So I've read your, uh, piece that you submitted," he said. "It's a good piece. And you handed in a pitch, too, ambitious."

My mind raced. This was it! What do I call my section? *Our Planet*? *Climate Crisis*? Or simply, poetically: *Rising*?

Mr. Stanley picked up my article and its accompanying series pitch off the stack of other submissions. Licked a finger, flipped through the pages.

"You didn't write this, did you?"

I stared. "S-sorry. What?"

"Who wrote this? Your mom?" He snorted, tossed my article down on his desk.

"Excuse me?"

"I mean there's no way you wrote this. You're new here, right?"

"Um, not really. I've been a student here for—"

"No, that's not what I meant." He sneered, and I understood his meaning.

"First of all," I said, face hot, body trembling, "my first language is English. I wrote this at the library, at the computer lab."

A snort. "Why would you write at the computer lab?"

"We don't have a computer at home. Do you want the librarians to verify? They helped me with my research."

The smirk had slid off Mr. Stanley's face by then. Proof. The last thing he wanted.

"Sure," he sighed, after a pause. "Fine."

"What?"

"I was going to report this for plagiarism," he said. "But I guess I'll have to take your word for it."

He waved his hand in my direction. Dismissed.

Pour 2 quarts of the rice water—the hugas bigas—into the pot. The rice starches will slightly thicken the broth and absorb overly fishy flavors. Save the remaining quart for later, in case it is needed.

I found care and support from other teachers, from friends. There was Geetika, Indian American, one of the smartest students in our year, friendly, warm, and fun; our close friends Naurah and Namrah, twin Pakistani American girls. We were four of a handful of students of color in our year, our bond natural and instant. The four of us drawn to each other, alien creatures swimming in a sea of white. I received encouragement from English teachers who appreciated my writing, art teachers who submitted my work to shows, track coaches who pushed me to run multiple events. I found a belief in myself outside of home, one that my father could not touch, no matter how much he hurt me.

"I think the only reason you and I are still alive," my sister said recently, "is because of all those adults at school who made us feel like we were worth something."

Eventually, Dad found ways to insert himself into my school life, into the only happy part of my new life in America. To pull me down with him, his sorrow clinging on to me, deadweight. To remind me that no matter how well I did in any class, sport, club, or activity, I was still drowning. Still worthless.

One afternoon in May 1998, at a track meet, my relay team won the final race, the 4 x 400. I ran the lead leg just after we also won the 4 x 100, where I ran the third leg. Our team won, earning us a spot in the county championships. I spotted my sister, my mother, and my father just beyond the bleachers. Felt a glimmer of joy. The first and only time they attended any of my sporting events.

I ran to them, a smile on my face.

"Hi! Hi!" I said to my family. So happy to see them. "We won, did you see?"

Dad looked around, motioned for me to come closer. His hand came out of his pocket, swung back. Slapped me, hard, across the face.

"Punyeta ka," he said. "You were supposed to be home an hour ago to watch your sister. Your mother and I have an appointment."

I'm sorry, my sister's eyes seemed to say.

Not your fault, I shook my head, reached for her hand.

What appointment? An immigration lawyer? Another one? How much money were they going to waste? There were no roads to legality anymore: not work visas, not family sponsorship, not asylum. I understood, that afternoon, what Dad's message really was: there was no running away from our reality, no matter how fast or excellent I was.

When the water begins to boil, add the onions as well as the cheesecloth bag of fish heads, for flavor. Let simmer for 10 minutes.

At the end of each track practice, I walked straight home, alone, not bothering to shower and change in the locker room. It had become too confusing in there. All of those changing bodies, all of us girls turning into sirens, longer legs, fuller hips and breasts, everyone so beautiful and different. It felt natural to find them beautiful, my attraction to them instinctive. The shame that immediately followed felt natural too. This shame soured my adolescence, girls and boys beginning to pair off with each other, as if on Noah's ark. As if it were the only way to stay alive at sea. I was strange and alien, the odd bisexual out.

Once, I spent hours inside the walk-in closet I shared with my sister. I was hiding from Dad, dizzy after he had slammed the back of my head against a wall. He had found my old yearbooks going back to the fourth grade, the ones where I had drawn hearts around everyone I had a crush on. Girls and boys, boys and girls. This boy, for his cute dimples and big brown eyes. That girl, for her gorgeous curly hair and feline face. This one, for his sense of humor. That one, for the way she laughed when I told jokes.

Mom found me hiding among my hangers of skirts and pants, shirts and dresses.

"Come on, let's go," she said, using her new American accent on me.

"No," I said, fresh tears welling up, thickening my throat. *Something's wrong with you,* Dad had said. *You'd better go to confession this weekend. It is a sin!* he had shouted, his palm finding the underside of my jaw.

"Jill, your dad will be awake soon. Come down. I made pork sinigang, your favorite," she said.

"No."

She seemed to soften. Walked over to me, crouched on the floor next to me.

"He probably isn't mad anymore," she started. "What happened?"

"No."

"You know, all he usually wants is an apology. You just need to think of what you did. Can you do that? Think of what you did to make him angry?"

I said nothing. I stayed inside that walk-in closet until Dad left for his night shift. Mom made up an excuse for me: a headache, a stomachache, a heavy period, which never failed to sufficiently disgust my father. She brought up a bowl of sinigang after he left. Eating alone at my desk, I let my tears salt the bowl of sour broth. Resigned to this world where I did not belong. I resolved to play straight. Boys only.

But boys were also forbidden by my father.

I had asked for permission to go to the school's annual Sadie Hawkins dance, the one where girls got to ask boys to be their dates. There was a boy I thought I might ask, though he seemed to be as far out of my reach as the girl I would have asked, if I could. I also thought that asking a boy, and letting my father know that I wanted to ask a boy, would allow us both to forget the sinful yearbook incident.

"Ask a boy? What would you want to do that for?" he had said with a laugh. "So that you can what? Become a teen mother? Sadie Hawkins. Mga Amerikano."

The boy might have said yes, had I asked. We had been circling each other for two years, almost three, never exchanging a word. Ryan was a year older, a junior while I was a sophomore at Governor Mifflin High School. His friends were the most popular kids in school, different from my circle of brown girls. I was a marching band nerd who played the flute in formation at halftime and finished fourth at the 100-meter hurdles at best. He was the star quarterback, the star point guard, the star first baseman. None of this mattered, to me. He was smart, shy, and gentle. And unlike all of the other boys in school, he actually saw me.

Every day, we said a silent hello, passing each other by in the hallway. We settled into an unspoken agreement: on a bathroom break, he would walk past my Spanish class, where I sat in full view of the door from the hallway. A nod. A smile. I would do the same later in the day, during his calculus class. At Sunday Mass, we'd exchange furtive glances across the church during Communion, hands clasped in prayer.

"Is that boy looking at you again?" Dad would whisper, annoyed.

"What boy?" I would whisper back. My sister, giggling next to me. Making kissing noises till I tickled her beneath her joined hands.

The hallway routine titillated my friends.

"So," Nina would ask. "Is he ever going to say a word to you?"

I could only look at her, smile a little. She would never know that she was the star quarterback's biggest competition. Ryan may have spent each day walking past me and saying wordless hellos, but Nina was with me for two or three classes each day. And not only did she actually talk to me, she was also one of my few friends, one of my closest friends. We shared the same favorite Bath & Body Works scents (sweet pea, plumeria, freesia), the same favorite bands and songs (Dave Matthews Band, "Crush"), the same favorite place to shop (Delia*s, though I owned only three pieces from the catalog's clearance section). We both loved Daria on MTV, daydreamed of getting Lilith Fair tickets over the summer. She had wild, curly long hair the color of honey and eyes that changed from hazel to blue to green depending on the seasons. We did track together. I hung back during warm-ups to be by her side.

But the longer the daily hallway-and-classroom greeting routine continued with Ryan, the more distant Nina became. As she listened to my daily stories of hallway smiles and classroom walk-bys, as she accompanied me to his basketball games—where he sometimes looked at me with a smile and a nod after scoring—she began to like him too. Slowly, she pulled away from me. Perhaps she resented that he paid attention to me, felt that I was undeserving. As someone who had a crush on her myself, I couldn't blame her for this resentment. In this secret love triangle that only I knew about, none of this mattered. They were both too good, too beautiful for me. If anything, they deserved each other.

Another year of the hallway routine passed. I began to understand that Ryan's diffidence wasn't out of shyness. It was out of shame. He never did more than say hello, because perhaps he could never admit that he liked me.

A girl one year younger, skin the wrong color, and from a poor part of town. I was no sirena. I tempted scorn, not desire.

In the way high schools tend to be, his friends found out that I liked him. In Honors Chemistry, I heard their snickers behind me:

"She likes Ryan? That's hilarious."

"I heard he likes her too, though."

"How? Isn't she Mexican or something?"

I sank into my seat, finally feeling the shame Ryan must have felt about me all of this time. Me, an odd creature from a foreign land, trying to become someone she was not, telling lies about who she was and where she was from. I began to understand that to be in America meant to be alone. That there would be no sirena waiting for me to join their world, feeding me their food so that I might be with them, forever. I could never be what the boys or girls of this realm wanted.

Add the prawns—still in their shells—to the broth. Let cook for 3 minutes, until they change color.

Deep undersea, as his mother, father, and brothers wept tears of mourning for him, the boy remained, continued to ponder his dilemma. He slept most of the day, waking up only to see the final rays of light sweeping the surface of the sea far above. The trays of food, the best the realm had to offer, brought in by sirenas, went untouched. Watching him as he refused to eat yet again, the princess-heir sirena visited his bedside, concern on her face.

"My dear friend, the boy who should be my king," she said, "you must make a decision at dawn: Will you eat of our food, and become my consort? Or will you refuse to swallow a single bite, and return home?"

The boy looked at her, this beautiful creature the same age as he, the kind of beauty that, on land, would have brought in suitors from barangays and probinsyas from all over. He looked around and saw the abundance and joy of her subjects. Life could be so easy, here. He could be happy, here. All he had to do was eat the realm's food. To become someone he was not.

"All right," he said, turning towards her. "I will keep some of this food with me. At dawn, I will make my decision."

The sirena drifted away to let him be. He stayed awake: Was it worth changing himself just to belong? To be loved? To prosper?

Using a slotted spoon, scoop out the cooked prawns. Place in a bowl— they will be returned to the pot as a final step.

As 1998 drifted into 1999, months lapped over each other, waves of barely survived time. Life in America continued to sour. I recall less of these years, as if my mind has sunken them to the darkest parts of the ocean, lost forever. I was sixteen, new to the realization that America itself—not just our immigration status—was the real danger, citizen or not. That this realm, this place that we thought was so full of promise, was nowhere near as good or as safe or as exceptional as it claimed to be. These were the years of the Unabomber, of the Olympic Park bombing in Atlanta, of the Oklahoma City bombing, of the Columbine school shootings in Colorado, of New York City police brutalizing Abner Louima and gunning down Amadou Diallo, the murders of James Byrd and Matthew Shepard. Guns and bombs, state violence and apathy. A girl from school, a track team acquaintance, left our school and fled in the middle of the night to Seattle with her mother, a civil servant and advocate for racial and religious rights and fair housing. They were being terrorized at work and at home by the local Ku Klux Klan and its Grand Dragon, a member of the American Nazi Party.

Danger was everywhere, no longer just at home. Was this why America called itself the home of the brave?

In those years, my mother's bank branch was robbed. A masked man held her at gunpoint, his handgun nozzle cold and sharp on her temple. The safe was emptied as she knelt on the floor and sobbed for her life. She refused to go to the police station, to describe the thieves, to take the witness stand at their trials when they were finally caught. She was afraid of the police and did not want to be inside a precinct. She was more afraid of being found out and deported than she was of the thieves' retribution. Fear and anxiety. The acid and salt of our drowned lives.

I had begun imagining my university years on the horizon, a lighthouse beaming from a distant coast. Lolo Pedring wrote to me from Manila, asking if I wanted to keep my place in the University of the Philippines, Diliman, where he had fully paid my tuition almost as soon as I was born. It sounded wonderful, and after seven years away, the thought of going back home—where I had friends who liked me and family who didn't hurt me—was enticing.

"You can't do that," Dad said. "If you leave here, you won't be able to come back."

"Why?" I asked. "Can't I just apply to visit again, like before?"

Dad pounded the dining table with his fist. He stood up, his legs throwing the dining chair back against the wall. Stalked upstairs. He slept for a few hours before work. He never answered my question.

In early spring, our tenth-grade World Cultures teacher, Mr. Kostzewa, made an exciting announcement. I loved Mr. K, as many of us called him. He was kind, interesting, worldly, and engaged, less interested in befriending the popular kids like some of the other teachers were. He knew, upon finding out where I was born, to ask me if I spoke Tagalog, and encouraged me to continue doing so.

"Some news, folks," he began, walking towards the front of the classroom. "I've just confirmed our annual trip to New York City!"

To my surprise, Dad signed the permission slip without his usual barrage of questions. He had begun to soften towards me recently. I sensed danger but did not allow myself to wonder why.

Add 1½ cups of tamarind paste as well as the string beans and chilies to the pot. Stir. Let simmer for 10 minutes.

My classmates, Mr. Kostzewa, and I boarded a large, air-conditioned chartered coach bus at six in the morning in front of the high school. A bus full of sleepy but excited sixteen-year-olds, headphones and Discmans in hand for some, a library copy of Michael Crichton's *Sphere* for me. I had finished reading it the night before but needed to submerge myself into it again, to come up for air with new discoveries. A story of humans diving to the deepest sea to investigate an alien life-form, only to resurface having learned new secrets about themselves. The bus trip passed this way, the low hum of early-morning chatter becoming quieter after an hour, as the roads brightened and became wider, grayer, flatter.

It is impossible to ignore New York City once its towers rise above the horizon. Once inside it, the feeling is one of submersion, of being swallowed by a sea of noise, hunger, power. But as the coach bus rolled uptown towards West Fifty-Third Street, I felt a slow, heavy jolt of energy surge through my body. Felt myself awaken, as if, rather than being submerged, I was emerging from a deep hibernation. I zipped *Sphere* into my backpack. Stared out and up at the buildings. Watched the fingers of sunlight dance between streets.

Our first stop was at the Museum of Modern Art, an imposing rectangle of modernist granite and glass. While everyone immediately entered the building, some eager to see the gift shop, other more sophisticated classmates excited for the Mirós and the Picassos, I stood outside and looked up. Dad, once an architect, would have had so much to say to me about this, back when he was still Papa. Look at the volumes, the way they sit together. See the negative space. Watch the interplay of the textures. Rural Pennsylvania was not exactly the kind of place for grand, deliberate architecture. It was a place of landlocked practicality: barns, churches, town halls. Schools, banks, grocery stores. Baseball fields, football fields, farmland, cow pastures.

Inside, the art was a portal, each sculpture and painting a sirena of its own. Nina had disappeared to join the other, cooler girls, the ones who did not want to be seen with me. I had learned long ago not to care too much about the sting of rejection from white friends, who often saw me, perhaps subconsciously, sometimes deliberately and to their own benefit, as a step below their white friends. At some point in those seven years in America, I had learned to enjoy solitude. To find more strength and energy in being alone. Trying to become someone I was not, to swim in alien waters, had already become too tiring by then.

After all of the paintings and sculptures—art I had seen only in textbooks—we walked to Lincoln Center for lunch and a show. Our school had bought tickets to watch Plácido Domingo in a rehearsal for *I Pagliacci*. The seats were in the Family Circle, highest up and farthest away from the stage, but it didn't matter to us.

"Can you believe we're going to see Plácido freaking Domingo?" whispered one girl, always so proud of her Italian immigrant ancestry in a way that I envied. My Filipino heritage, despite being a part of the United States' colonial expansion, was not one that was enshrined in the metropole's shiny buildings, like my classmate's Italian heritage was. I mashed at the buttons next to the screen in front of me, so that I could read the opera's Italian translated into English.

The theater darkened, the thick curtains swooping upward, a hush falling over all of us, our faces lit by the stage below. The orchestra's music rose, as if from deep underwater, filling the room, raising my skin into bumps. As I looked down at the broad sweep of stage, Plácido Domingo appeared, this man I had only ever seen on television. He opened his mouth, a small dot from where I was sitting, and began to sing. The air changed as the sound waves reached us, feelings turned into vibrating particles, filling my eyes with tears. I had never listened to real opera before. There, alone, happy to have escaped my father for the day, I found myself able to see, hear, and feel the world around me. It was in that cavernous theater at the Metropolitan Opera House that I first began to understand how much of the world I had shut off. That I had been forced to shut off to survive. Sealed off from everything around us, our existence out of control, unable to make contact with the land we had been born in, raised in, and known.

It was just nearing dusk when our class stepped outside, all of us hushed with awe. I walked ahead, across the courtyard and towards the street, where the coach bus waited to take us home. Stood there, alone, on the sidewalk of West Sixty-Fifth Street. Closed my eyes. For the first time in years, I could hear. Smell the air. Feel the whoosh of cars and people and the wind on my skin. I opened my eyes. Looked up, around, across. Saw the glowing street lights, turning on against the darkening sky. The blur of people rushing past, places to go, things to do. I did not feel any fear. I noticed this lack of fear. Wondered at it.

There, as people strode past me, as Mr. Kostzewa shouted my name, called for me to board the bus already, I finally understood. New York was a place where I could feel alive, not drowning, not drowned. My body, born and raised in Manila, the most densely populated city on earth, must have needed this kind of urban frenzy in the air, that particular vibration that moves only through cities, through people who match its frequencies. For seven years, I had disappeared beneath the surface, hiding, hidden by my parents, by their fear of being found, of being sent back home. No wonder I felt like that boy underwater. In rural Pennsylvania, I had been wasting away, trying to become something I was not. Here, like in Manila, no one cared what I was or was not, where I was from or where I was going. I could just be, alone, yet held in its energy. Separate, but part of a singular, resonant mass.

I stepped onto the bus. Someday, I would live here.

Add the milkfish and radishes. Let simmer for 10 minutes.

After that trip to Manhattan, the sour tides turned on life once again. One Saturday afternoon in late May 1999, our parents sat us down in the dining room. Mom had found a new job, they said. They had bought a house. We would be moving to New Jersey at the end of June. I was sixteen. This would be my fourth new school in six years.

"N-no," I said. "What about my high school?" My last two years, just before college.

"Come on, you'll adjust," Dad said, smirking.

Perhaps Dad thought I was like him or his brothers, able to absorb multiple moves, no real friends, no real place to call home. Perhaps he knew that I couldn't, and wished to, consciously or not, inflict the same kind of sourness upon me that he had had to experience. Perhaps he just didn't care.

"Here's the thing," Mom said. "You know how I got lucky with a social security number, and your dad didn't get one? Your Dad's boss is starting to ask questions about his social. We *have* to move."

"Be excited!" Dad said, teetering between glee and rage. "We have a house! Four bedrooms, two bathrooms, with a garage! Your mom did this! With her hard work and her bonus money. Imagine that! No papers, but we have a house! Wait till they hear about this back home."

The family meeting ended. My sister and I went up the stairs to our bedroom, both of us silent. She climbed up to her top bunk, rustled around a bit. I climbed into my bottom bunk.

"What the fuck," I said.

"Yeah," she sighed.

Seven years of finally learning how to drown myself in this new world, only to be cut loose and set adrift, again. I cried myself into a long nap. My sister and I, the children of two people constantly choosing the wrong road, doubling down on their mistakes, diving into waters beyond their depths.

Taste the broth. Remove the cheesecloth of fish heads. Add more tam-arind to taste. Add the fish sauce.

At dawn, the princess-heir sirena returned to the boy's side.

"Have you decided what you would like to do?"

The sirena and the boy swam side by side, fingers interlaced. They swam up, towards the colorful edge of the coral reef. He looked down, towards the depths where he had lived for what was only a few days, but felt like years. He could not see anything. The deep curtain of darkest ocean had once again been drawn. The two of them surfaced.

"Here are two roads," she said to him. "That is the road to your village. This is the road to what could be our kingdom. You must decide. The road to your village is familiar, but it is rocky, long, and narrow, a path of difficulty that will bring you back home to what you know: a life of much struggle. If you join me, we can rule this oceanic kingdom together."

The boy finally spoke.

"My dear friend, I thank you," he began. "I am grateful to you for saving me. For flattering me with your offer of marriage. I am not like you, and will never be like you. I must go back home, where I belong without having to try."

He turned away from her, took a deep breath and swam towards home. Moved fast, with purpose, for the first time in what seemed like years.

He chose a life of suffering as himself over a life of ease as someone else.

Turn off the heat. Add the kang kong to the pot, gently stirring in. Cover the pot and let sit for 5 to 8 minutes.

"OK, pull it down with all your weight!" Dad said, laughing. I jumped, grabbed the moving truck door's metal handle. Hung from it for a second, before it rolled down to a close.

It was five in the morning. We were scheduled to leave in the afternoon. Dad and I had spent three weeks packing up the rented townhouse on Community Drive, just the two of us. He brought home boxes from work, the thick-walled, squat ones that carried six-packs of gallon jugs of spring water. My job was to reinforce the boxes' seams with packing tape, then to seal each packed box shut, labeling it. Despite my secret heartbreak at having to leave yet another school, yet another group of friends, I did my best to hide it, playing the cheerful, eager assistant. It seemed to work, and we were almost Jill and Papa again.

Still, I was angry. "I don't get it, Mom," I said on one of our last trips to the grocery store. "You both keep saying we're in this country for a better life, but you both just keep ruining mine." The complaint of a self-centered teenager, but a valid one.

"This is a better life, Jill," she answered. "We've always wanted a house, and this job pays me more. You have to make a sacrifice so that our family can make it. Life here is hard."

"Did it ever occur to you that life is hard because of the bad decisions you and Dad keep making?"

She gripped the steering wheel, jaw twitching.

"That's enough."

Add the previously cooked prawns, still shell-on, to the pot.

We pulled away from Pennsylvania in a caravan of two. Mom and my sister in the family car, Dad and I in the thirty-five-foot-long rented Penske truck.

As Dad turned up the music in the truck, I rolled down the window, looking one last time at the school I had come to know and begrudgingly appreciate. To the friends, almost-friends, and first loves. To the snatches of belonging I was able to claim for myself. If I had to say goodbye to this place, I would have willingly left only if it meant returning to Manila, to the last place I belonged. Instead, my parents chose to continue dive deeper into the unknown.

"Goodbye," I whispered out the window. To Geetika, Naurah, and Namrah, the four of us black-haired and brown-skinned girls in a sea of white, the only three who understood me. To the track ringing the football field, where I ran, freely, for two hours a day. To the school buildings just beyond, where I discovered a love for writing and art and just enough of myself to hold on to.

Serve the sinigang with the freshly steamed rice. Keep a bowl of fish sauce and a bowl of calamansi juice at the table.

I slurp sinigang broth from the prawn's head, just as my father once taught me. I crunch a crispy string bean between my teeth, follow it with a spoonful of broth. The sourness hits the back and sides of my mouth. I swallow as my mouth fills with saliva, begging for more. Thoughts of Philippine beaches, of clear seawater and sand below, swim in front of me. Of a house just off the beach, thatched roof and woven rattan walls, the winds of Amihan clearing off storm clouds from the night before, the rustle of banana and palm leaves bringing in the scent of bougainvillea and the sea. I add a bit of milkfish to my spoon. Submerge it into the broth. Sip from the spoon in one go, letting the sour finally turn into the savory.

5

Dinuguan na Baboy
(Pork in Blood Stew)

1999–2007

SERVES 6

10 to 12 ounces pork blood, fresh or frozen (thawed)
1 cup vinegar
1 pound pork shoulder or belly
1 pound pork cheeks, ears, and/or offal
1 head garlic
1 onion
2-inch piece ginger
1 tablespoon vegetable oil
2 tablespoons fish sauce
3 or 4 green finger chilies
Sea salt
3 dried bay leaves
1 tablespoon brown sugar
Ground black pepper
1 cup water
At the table:
Steamed rice or puto

Dinuguan makes utang ng loob digestible. It is a precolonial dish of blood. Thicker than water, darker than love.

This pot of blood stew is just for me. I set down the bowl of just-chopped pork belly and offal, cheek and ear cut down to uniform squares and cubes. Stir the pig's blood, let it fuse with the cane vinegar. Raw, the blood is opaque, near-black. Traces of red drag at its edges. Oxygenated plasma and hemoglobin clings to porcelain. Seeks life where only sterility remains.

I have not had moontide blood for many years. For years, I bled for my family. Gave myself up in the hopes that we might be brought back to life. That I might be loved, in return.

Pour the pig's blood into a bowl.

The Philippines is a never-clotted wound of freedom. Segregated by empires, we have fought each other for centuries. We seek to free ourselves of the West's entitled destiny, the kind still manifested upon us today by the Americans. It runs through our veins. We judge and class each other by how well we have assimilated into empire. We fight, fail, bleed, fight again. We owe each other this fight. It is our utang ng loob sa isa't isa. *Utang*, debt. *Ng*, of. *Loob*, inside.

Giving to one's parents is a common immigrant act of love, an expected Filipino pillar of survival, nothing to brag about. My sister, my only true flesh and blood, says I owe nothing. That I have given enough, that I must now live for myself. My guilt is a product of our history, our culture. Filial piety, familial debt. Relatives expecting from each other what the state owes them but will never give. This does not lessen the feeling that I have failed my family.

Stir 2 tablespoons of the vinegar into the bowl of blood. Let this rest, covered, in the refrigerator.

This dish is born of ancient need, of the Filipino desire to waste nothing. Before the Americans arrived with their industrialized food, eating animal flesh was for special occasions only, a treasured norm of culture and care. A way of honoring the animal's blood sacrifice.

Parents often lie to children about dinuguan. Sometimes, children believe them. This pot of blackened blood and pork, green chilies peeking through its surface, is served with steamed rice on the side.

"Ano ito?" my sister used to say, a toddler wanting to know what she was about to put into her mouth.

"It's chocolate meat!" said her nanny. She airplaned a spoonful towards my sister's mouth. Our mother, at the other end of the table, ate her dinner, indifferent.

Eventually, my sister opened her mouth, chewed. Her chin smeared with black blood, bits of rice cornering her lips.

"No chocolate!" she would spit, half-chewed meat and rice falling out onto her plate.

"I wish they'd just said what it was," my sister said, decades later. "It was the lie I hated. That was not Hershey's!"

Chop the pork shoulder or belly into 1-inch cubes. Keep cold and covered in the refrigerator.

"We can't risk Dad getting caught," Mom explained, my father crying behind her. It was August 1999 and we were in Jackson, New Jersey. The four of us on their bed in the new house.

"He can't work anymore without a social. We need your help."

My sister, only ten years old, watched this unfold, worried. Looked at me, the sacrificial pig.

"Do I use my own Social Security number?" I asked. Was this part of their plan when they moved us here? Put the sixteen-year-old to work immediately?

"You'd work part-time," Dad said. "Any extra money you earn, we'll put into a higher-interest savings account. For your college."

"Sure," I said. I believed him, chocolate for blood. This was family, right? Sacrifice. By being a dutiful firstborn, I could repay my utang ng loob. Debts incurred by being born.

Dad found the photocopy of my Social Security card, the one he made, I would learn years later, with the "NOT VALID FOR EMPLOYMENT" erased. I applied for jobs at the mall and found a job as a bookseller.

"Remember," said Dad. "Your SS card is in a safety deposit box, tell them."

Half-shifts after school on Tuesdays, Thursdays, and Fridays; full shifts on weekends. My paychecks covered groceries, utilities, my parents' credit cards. At school, I pretended to be saving up for a car too.

After school, Dad or Mom would pick me up in the family car to drive me to work. I spent most of my time reading, doing homework at the cashwrap. Mom worked a second job across the road, at a leather goods store at the mall. Her eyes bagged with dark circles, exhausted. Mom took her body, and gave it up for Dad.

Dad bought a piano so that he could, he said, practice his music for a return to the cruise ship, or perhaps to find work as a musician in New York. Instead, he slept all day. Not playing much music, not looking for work. Other jobs were too menial, he said. Though he was at home all day, he left every-thing, including household tasks, to me and Mom. Women's work. My sister, only ten, was spared for a few more years. After sleeping the entire day, he shuffled out of the bedroom, sulking, then declared Mom's cooking inedible. Returned to the bedroom until she went to him, pleading. Sometimes, they fought for hours.

"Why don't we leave him?" I said. She was crying while driving us to our weekend shifts.

"And what?" she said. "Just throw him away?"

"So you'll throw us away instead?"

She didn't respond. I wonder if Mom knew that his avoidance of work was deliberate, not just a symptom of depression. That millions of us, despite being undocumented, found work, paid taxes, and weren't arrested. Dad said he couldn't work because he had no Social Security number. Years had passed since undocumented immigrants could legally obtain a tax identification number, allowing us to work and pay taxes. If there was one thing the govern-ment did not miss, it was the chance to bleed taxes out of everyone, citizens or not. Dad, an avid reader of everything, constantly collected information on immigration, citizenship, taxes, and loopholes. I am convinced that he knew. He had despised working since their early years in Manila, when Mom teased him for his rich boy allowance, his stays in expensive hotels with girlfriends, shopping sprees, and fancy dinners. Mom and I did not have to shoulder all of the financial burden.

They once said, in the Philippines, that beautiful women were to be avoided, not to be trusted. They might be mangkukulam, casting spells to get revenge, to get their way. Or an aswang, ready to pounce at nightfall. Maybe a manananggal, viscera suckers waiting for the right moment to lure you in with their beauty before they consume your blood, your insides. The hysteria around manananggal rose alongside the number of Filipinos converted into Catholicism.

Catholicism infested Dad's veins as time passed, his notions of goodness and obedience conflated with control and abuse. He was not religious when I was small: when I was conceived, he tried to pressure Mom into an abortion. As I grew into adolescence, he became preoccupied with hiding my lengthening limbs, my blossoming chest. Stopped hugging me after my period began. My shorts were too short, my bra straps showing. He drove us to confession, though he never stepped into the wooden box.

At Sunday Masses in church, we chanted. *The blood of Christ.*

And the Father asked us to give up our sins and said:

> *Take this, all of you, and drink from it:*
> *This is the cup of my blood,*
> *The blood of the new and everlasting covenant.*
> *It will be shed for you and for all*
> *So that your sins may be forgiven.*

The last two years of high school were forgettable, passing through my veins like a spoonful of vinegar. I was afraid of the new school, so much bigger and wealthier than my old one. At least there were Black and Brown students, two other Filipinos in my class alone.

Finely dice the offal, if using.

It is said that dinuguan, one of our most indigenous recipes, has much in common with a dish the Spartans ate before battle. They, too, made a pork meat and blood stew with vinegar, a dish they called melas zomos, black soup. They ate this dish as a kind of talisman, a ritual meal to help strengthen their resolve to kill. In 1896, our revolutionaries, too, felt this resolve, encouraged by correspondence and collaboration with other antico-lonial and anti-imperial movements among our pan-Asian siblings. Felt the shared rising of resistance in our blood. Andrés Bonifacio, one of the found-ers of our Katipunan resistance, saw an opening. He saw how the Spaniards' punitive arrests of hundreds of our people—many innocent, yet imprisoned and executed—could rouse the uprising. He gathered thousands more revo-lutionaries against the weakening Spanish. In coordinated attacks, some led by Bonifacio, others by his deputy, Emilio Aguinaldo, they captured colonizer strongholds, one after another.

I, too, felt the stirrings of separation, rising, in my blood. My body was becoming a problem. I hated unwanted attention from boys at school, felt violated every day. My body was a separate creature from me, something that elicited responses from others that I could not control. In 1999, when we could still fly domestic, my mother, my sister, and I flew west, to the place where Filipinos have gone, for more than one hundred years, to be digested by the state. We stayed with Tita Christy, one of Mom's relatives.

One afternoon, while I played with my sister by their pool, I heard her husband, Tito Lenny, say:

"What a body. Like a Victoria's Secret model."

And later,

"If I were her dad, I'd put her in a chastity belt and lock her up."

For the rest of that visit, I avoided him.

The manananggal—an ancient, legendary, viscera-sucking monster—can take several forms. In human form, they are very beautiful, most tempting to men, who cannot help themselves. They are usually women, single, childless, living alone or with other manananggal. Hiding, removed from society, re-viled by all. They have deep, dark armpits. Their eyes have a shifting, indirect gaze. Their presence is preceded by flocks of ikik birds screaming into the skies. Their favorite food is dinuguan.

During full moons, they strip naked, cover their torsos in coconut oil mixed with pig dung. They stiffen their hair into wings, though some sprout wings from their shoulder blades. They wriggle themselves, twist, tearing into two. They free themselves of their bottom halves—hips, wombs, legs, and feet stay behind. Their eyes enlarge to bulging to see in the dark, their ears lengthen to hear everything. Their tongues become mosquito-like, a sucking proboscis. They fly into the night, just their top halves, tits out and wings flapping, intestines dangling like ribbons. Free of their domestic prisons, searching for their lifeblood, their joy. Manananggal, root word *tanggal*, to remove. They who separate from themselves.

They land on rooftops. Their snouts sniff for blood and guts. Their tongues snake out of their lips, grow long like string, slithering into roof crevices, between walls, beneath floorboards. They love fluids, phlegm, blood. They eat the ill, the tuberculotic, the very pregnant. Those who fail to hang garlic and peppers in windows and doorways are the easiest to access. They sip and swallow through the belly button. Lungs, hearts, intestines. Fetuses, placentas. Amniotic juices. Secrets, wishes, dreams.

Spanish missionaries found the equal power in some of our tribes and kingdoms aberrant. Found some of our women and men abhorrent—genders fluid, transient, all of us not she or he, but siya. They took away the powers of our women healers and leaders by degrading them, weaponizing old tales of the manananggal, the mangkukulam, the aswang, to divide us. They took advantage of ancient prejudices and inequalities already present, and we believed their lies. The missionaries said, *These women are not healers or mediums or leaders. They are creatures of death who will not aid you in birth or in illness. Whores who will steal your men, drink your blood, eat your insides, swallow your babies. Witches who will pluck a hair from your pillow, curse you, kill you as you dream.*

When the Americans came in 1898, all a-swagger with their Manifest Destiny, we believed them, also when they said they would help free us from the Spanish. Look at what we have done for Cuba, they said, and then killed hundreds of thousands of us. This American history of conquest and colonization in Asia was not in my eleventh-grade Honors US history class. I didn't care about grades the way my higher-achieving classmates did. What was the point? I was an undocumented immigrant riding on the underbelly of society's goodwill. I was never going to college, at least not in this country. My classmates accumulated their 4.0s, earned Honors Society appointments, studied with their SAT tutors. They collected their activities and leadership roles curated for college applications, for med school, law school, grad school, business school. I cared only about two things: not getting deported, and Dad not hurting me. Still, I earned university-level credits in a handful of college-level AP classes.

Mr. Darton and Mr. Linehan were my history and English teachers for two years, at Honors and AP level. They became my champions. Like my teachers in Pennsylvania, they had a radar for students like me.

"Damatac, get in here," Mr. Darton yelled from his desk one afternoon.

"Mistress of Sonnet Analysis, Supreme Essayist of *Macbeth*, do join us!" boomed Mr. Linehan.

I thought I was in trouble. That they had somehow found out that I was undocumented. Instead, Mr. Darton and Mr. Linehan made me an offer: they would be my references for something new called the Gates Scholarship. I took the application as they spoke and lied about filling it out, said my thanks. I stuffed the paper into my backpack and went outside, where Mom was waiting to drive me to work.

At work, I skimmed the form. In fine print, it said: *Eligibility for US citizens and legal residents only.*

A few weeks later, I earned a near-perfect score on the verbal portion of the SATs. A decent score in math. I took the test mostly to prove to myself that I could.

"You can't apply for this," Mom said, holding the Gates application aloft.

Dad slipped on his reading glasses. "Says for US citizens and legal residents only."

"Can't I try? They might not even ask."

"Jill," Mom said. "No."

I cried myself to sleep for a few nights. My future was separating itself from my life. My parents had filled my head with dreams of a career in law, maybe medicine. How was I meant to get there?

Something in me persisted. My teachers' belief in me had seeped into my blood. At work, I perused the College Admissions book section. Searched for universities that fit my SATs, GPA, and possible majors. And not too expensive, either, because I would have to work my way through college. Back then, undocumented immigrants did not qualify for any forms of public funding: in-state tuition, loans, scholarships, or grants. Private universities were too expensive.

I applied anyway, convinced Mom to secretly pay the application fees. Weeks later, some acceptance letters arrived. Early decisions, rolling decisions.

My father intercepted the envelopes. Furious. He tore the envelopes in half, ripping a thumbnail as he did so. He lit the papers on fire the same way he burned junk mail and credit card bills; watching, I sobbed, helpless, part of my hair burned. He destroyed the paper trail of our lives so that we might never be found. To keep us safe, he said.

The university letterheads curled in on themselves, burning to black the drops of blood from Dad's torn fingernail. UC this, CUNY that, U of there. I never mentioned college to anyone again.

I grew to love my bookselling job. I became a manananggal of books, sucking up words and worlds. Drank up knowledge until it was time to go back home and be a compliant daughter with no ambitions. I made friends with the backroom guys at the bookstore. Asked them to set aside the stripped books they threw out, replaced by newer editions. Publishers only needed the covers with bar codes to calculate profits and losses. After each shift, I found the discarded books in clear bags by the back door. Post-its on them that said JILLY. Publishers' trash, an undocumented immigrant's treasure. This would be my free college education, I decided.

One morning, Mr. Darton pulled me aside. I was more relaxed by then. No papers, no college. Nothing to try for. If I worked full time at the bookstore after graduating, maybe I'd get to be a section manager. I could still write. It was all I wanted to do.

"What do you know about Kentucky?" he said.

"Why?"

"Berea College. Top liberal arts college in the South. Full scholarships, like Cooper Union. Great humanities program. Eligibility doesn't say anything about citizenship or what have you."

I had lied to him when I failed to apply for the Gates. Something about being legally under my mother's work visa but not qualifying for scholarships, loans, or grants.

"You can still make the application deadline, kid."

I sighed. "Fine."

I was admitted to Berea College with a full academic scholarship. Dad, unable to deny the power of free money, did not stop me, though he was unhappy about the loss of my income. When the college confirmed that I was eligible for their private scholarship despite being undocumented, he only grimaced while Mom said nothing. My sister cheered. Perhaps my parents consoled themselves with the thought that someday, after graduating, I could support them through a higher-paying job.

At graduation, Mr. Darton shouted "BEREA!" as I received my diploma. He seemed to know more about me than I had ever revealed. He was more proud of me than my own parents were.

Dice the onion. Mince the garlic and ginger.

In Kentucky, I felt free, safe from home. I became a jubilant monster, released from her heavy lower half, wings flapping, screaming free into the air. I snuck into and out of men's and women's dorms, out of the rooms and cars of good Christian girls and nice mama's boys. I was becoming myself, reveling in this newfound ability to be fully in charge of my body, my desires, my needs.

At Berea, tuition was free for all; we owed only room and board. From 2001 to 2002, this cost approximately $2,500 per term, or $5,000 per year. Most students paid through federal grants or loans; because I was undocumented and ineligible, my parents paid the first term. In return, we were expected to work part-time on campus. I took morning shifts at the cafeteria, cycling across campus from 5 a.m. swim practice to chop vegetables in the kitchen before class. I felt like I had a future.

One sunny September morning, finished with a kitchen shift, I unlocked my bike, happy. I was excited about an essay for a class called "Power and Prejudice."

"Ay, Yank," said a boy walking past. "You seen the TV yet? They hit the Twin Towers."

"What?"

Mom was supposed to be in Manhattan for work training. I sped back to Pearson Hall, sprinted to my room. Every thirty minutes, I dialed, desperate. *We're sorry, you have reached a number that has been disconnected or is no longer in service.* There was another crashed plane reported in Virginia, another in Pennsylvania. The towers crumbled, soundless and unreal onscreen. Would there be more? Where was my mother?

I spent all night and the next day dialing. The *We're sorry* message had been replaced by a busy signal. Anxiety boiled in my veins.

Finally, on the night of September 12, my call went through.

"Why are you crying?" Dad demanded.

He handed the phone to my mother, who hadn't made it to Manhattan on the eleventh after all. The phone was busy because she had been on the phone to Manila since the dawn of the twelfth. Her father, my Lolo Baldo, had died suddenly in Manila. A heart attack.

Lolo Baldo was the first of my grandparents to leave this plane. A kind, gentle man who drove me to school in an ancient VW Beetle, where he kept Rabbit candies just for his grandchildren. After a long day at work, he made late-night beef tapa to share with me. He patiently stood behind me in the dark late at night all those years ago, waiting for me to sleepwalk back to bed. He so loved his dearest daughter, my mother. He sobbed unceasingly the night before we left for America.

I skipped classes for a week, hid my grief from my new friends. I cried alone, at the edge of the woods. A sorrow taller than any tower, a pain that eclipsed America's.

We could not go to Lolo Baldo's funeral. To leave America's borders would mean deportation, a ban. Mom couldn't go home to honor her father, couldn't kneel for his last rites. She couldn't embrace his coffin, to say salamat, Papang, for all you did for us, for all you gave to me. Couldn't embrace her mother, brothers, and sister, the first family to whom she gave herself, and with whom she shares her flesh, blood, and utang ng loob.

I was not privy to my mother's pain, and I was overwhelmed by my own. They say that genetically inherited major depression tends to manifest itself in late adolescence and early adulthood. That the inability to produce happiness in the blood is passed on through blood also. That this can be triggered by a big life event: a move, a change in circumstances, by sudden trauma, or a sudden cessation of it. I'm not sure if there was anything I could have done by the time my genetic inheritance came for me in February 2002, the month I turned nineteen.

For entire days, I slept through classes and swim practice, sat in the dark, cried. Went back to sleep. Ate other girls' food from the communal fridge, because I couldn't find the strength to walk ten minutes to the cafeteria. Unwashed, I stank. Alone in my dorm room, I dimly thought of Dad, back home in New Jersey, staggering out of bed for two or three hours, angry at being awake, going back to sleep, staying in the dark for days. I'd inherited his body and his mind, illnesses for me to pass on someday too. Like my father, I was helpless against the determination of blood.

Why bother with classes, anyway? I asked myself. No one would hire me after graduating. I might as well do what undocumented immigrants like me do: clean, pick, care, pack, haul, build, mow, deliver. Get paid under the table, sneak back home in the dark.

I stopped returning my parents' calls, ignored Mom's emails. I failed my papers and exams. Continued to skip class. My grades plummeted. The mental health of students—the idea that blood, hormones, and neurotransmitters were responsible for our success or our failure—was not particularly prioritized back then. Once, I tried a nurse's visit: she sent me home with a sick note.

Winter turned into spring. I skipped more classes, skipped an academic intervention arranged by a counselor. One morning in March, I walked back from a boyfriend's dorm, needing a shower and the oblivion of sleep. Ahead, a friend waved at me.

"Jill! Your parents. They're here. Ohmygod. Your room is upside down."

I hadn't spoken to my parents in weeks. Running up to the fourth floor, hoping the RAs wouldn't see my father there, an invader of an all-female dorm. Reached my room. My desk and clothes drawers were yanked open, birth control pills out on my desk. Bed unmade and pillows thrown aside. Clothes everywhere. Boxes under the bed, emptied. I turned around. Mom stood in the doorway.

"We're here to take you home. You're going to withdraw."

Dad parked the van in an empty parking lot on the campus perimeter, the four of us crammed into a rented van, my skin, nerves, and heart on edge, feet ready to run. Dad declared my failure and said that there was no option but to bring me back home.

"You can go back to work, make yourself useful."

The *no, fuck you*, that flew out of my mouth was immediately followed by Dad's slap-punch-head-slam. I forced myself out, sprinted across the black asphalt and up a brambled hill. RAs kept my parents from entering Pearson Hall while I cowered inside, my forehead bleeding. Someone shouted at them: *You should be ashamed of yourselves.*

I was nineteen, officially an adult, able to decide my own fate.

Put on a pot of rice to cook, or buy fresh puto from a local bakery.

Despite being an independent, sovereign nation, the Philippines has long been stymied from deciding its own fate. Perhaps the reason dinuguan—ancient, precolonial—persists in today's karinderyas and kusinas is because it is the closest thing we have to indigeneity, to the land's origins as ours, and no one else's. So much of what is indigenous to the Philippines has been destroyed, overwritten in the blood of battle and occupation. Not even the Americans' industrial foods, tinned, boxed, jarred, could displace dinuguan, which cannot be reduced to a packet of flavored powder or a canned stew to heat in the microwave. They have, of course, succeeded in erasing much of everything else. When they first blasted their way into Manila Bay in 1898, the Americans saw disorder and opportunity. There was a struggle for power within the Katipunan resistance, leaders betraying each other, Filipino blood spilled by Filipino hands. The old Spanish empire was nearing its end, limb after colonial limb consumed by debts, land sold or ceded to the United States. With each expansionist acquisition—the Louisiana Purchase, Florida, the Texas Annexation, California, Oregon, all of it stolen Native American lands—America sought to become an empire, itself. They had just recently acquired the American West. A self-proclaimed destiny, manifested through battle and occupation. The Americans took our blood and guts and threw it into their imperial melting pot.

A month after Mom and Dad tried to take me home, I was still at Berea. My parents did not pay that term's bill, but I was still convinced that I could find a way to remain enrolled. A letter from the college arrived with a deadline for payment. I called the financial services office to confess: I was an undocumented immigrant, my father was a physically violent abuser, I had to stay, please. That I needed their help and guidance in paying off that term's room and board, that I would go back to class, fix myself. Were there any other forms of financial support or loans available for students like me? Was there some way of paying in installments? Maybe increasing my hours at the cafeteria?

The woman I spoke with said she would get back to me.

I sat alone in my dorm room, alone in the early April dusk, unwanted. The swimmer I was dating had just broken up with me. The girls had gone to a party. Three weeks to come up with the money for this term's room and board, and then what? I had less than fifty dollars, gifts from aunties for my nineteenth birthday. What a loser. I couldn't even make it through one year of college.

There, in a corner, was my roommate's bottle of Wild Turkey. I twisted the top open. Sniffed. My mouth flooded with saliva; my throat retched. I tipped the bourbon into my mouth, swallowed throatfuls, felt it flood my stomach, my blood. A headache grew at the base of my skull.

I staggered to my desk, opened a drawer. Pulled out the bottle of acetaminophen. This was it. I had no money, no family, no papers, no home, no choice. One pill, drink. A second pill, drink. I swallowed a third pill, a fourth and fifth, tears and snot, more bourbon, a sixth. Sobbed on my knees, keeled into my bed. I tipped fistfuls of pills, cascading, little pill sounds spilling into my palm. Filled my mouth with the rest, their small poisoned sweetness crowding my teeth, pressing back into my palate. A choked cough. More bourbon.

I lay down. Let the poison flood my liver, my blood. The room swirled, darkened. Sounds, silenced. I closed my eyes. So sleepy and tired. Relaxed, for the first time in months. Ready. I let my spirit separate, blood screaming for freedom.

When some girls at the dorm found me in bed, my eyes were slightly open, blank. I must have been watching, separated from my physical half, from above. An ambulance screamed through campus, a tube rammed into my throat, liquid charcoal poured into my belly. A doctor appeared by my bedside.

"It's a miracle you survived that," the doctor said. "Another hour, and you would've been—"

He snapped his fingers, pulled back his chin as he stood.

Later, at a compulsory session, the college psychologist told me to look into a mirror and say *I love you* ten times.

You stupid bitch. I glared at the monster that reflected back at me, the one that feasted on my brain, my heart, my blood. *Just let me fucking go.*

Another letter arrived from the college finance office. No advice or solutions given—I still owed them money. A second letter followed. Given my poor academic performance, it said, I was expelled, with two weeks to vacate my room. They did not notify my parents about my suicide attempt or my expulsion.

I called Tita Christy, the relative who lived out west, the one we had visited two years before. She decided that I could stay at her house while I recovered. Find a job. Maybe earn enough to live on my own. Luckily, my student ID was enough to let me board the plane, as long as I was still a minor. I pretended to be seventeen.

Tita Christy was not someone I knew well. A devout Catholic, she seemed more shocked about my use of birth control than she was about my attempt on my own life. I did not know her husband, Tito Lenny, at all. He existed on the periphery of my childhood memories, a cold, negative presence in family gatherings. He had mostly ignored me until two years before, when he had made his comments about my body.

The weeks passed. May, June, and July, months of healing peace. Sun every day, each day warmer and more blossomed than the one before. I can get better here, I thought to myself. I think the sun is helping.

I soon tired of the slow, hot afternoons, which stretched out, aimless and long. I was bored. I had nothing to do but chores, which Tita Christy asked of me in lieu of money. I cleaned the bathrooms, dusted and vacuumed the entire house twice a week, did two rounds of dishes every day. Scrubbed the kitchen, skimmed their in-ground swimming pool. Swept the gardens, watered the plants. Fed and walked the dog. I ran for miles in the heat, letting the flat suburbia rush by. The runs helped soothe my growing restlessness and anxiety.

After one late July run, I flicked off my sweaty top, my sneakers. In a sports bra and running shorts, I walked across the house's cool tiled floors to the backyard, where the pool waited in half-shade. I sat at its edge. Dropped my legs in. Breathed out the heat coursing through my veins.

"You running around in that?" a voice said. I jumped. Tito Lenny. No one was supposed to be home. I slouched, tried to hide myself.

He looked me up and down, raised an eyebrow, went back into the house.

Heat a wide pot deep enough to hold the blood stew.

Tita Christy took me to the nearest branch of the Philippine Embassy. I coordinated with my uncles back home to help me renew my expired passport—the first step towards attempting to apply for some kind of legal status, if it was still possible for me. She knew it was futile, but I could at least have some form of valid, unexpired identification. My parents were too afraid and did not cooperate when we asked for my birth certificate or my expired passport.

"We'll say it's lost," Tita Christy said. In a way, it was.

Tita Christy encouraged me to apply to community college. Maybe it was out of kindness, but I suspected that it was also to get me out of the house. Her daughter was beginning to resent my presence, dropping dirty dishes and used glasses in the sink right after I had washed up, or walking her dirty shoes across the gleaming, wet tiled floor I had just swept and mopped. She allowed her high school friends to peek into my bedroom window, made jokes about her crazy, suicidal, college dropout cousin.

"Since you're not a virgin anymore, Ate," she leered one afternoon, "do you think you could sleep with my friend? Do him a favor so he's not a virgin anymore?"

By this time, I was struggling to sleep. Late one night, not wishing to disturb Auntie, another relative staying with Tita Christy, I trudged into the living room, my beloved copy of *The Count of Monte Cristo* in hand. I was surprised to see Tito Lenny there, on the sofa.

"Just finished a movie," he said, standing up, as if he was about to leave. "*Mulholland Drive*. Seen it?"

"No." I did not look at him. Sat at the far end of the sofa.

He moved towards me. "Hey. Have you ever kissed a girl?"

I moved to an armchair. He continued to talk, even though I showed no interest. He came over, crouched next to me.

"How about *American Beauty*?" A lewd half-smile crept over his face.

"No." I squirmed away. Panic in my belly.

"Oh come on, don't be like that," he said. He reached over, placed a hand on my thigh. I jerked my leg away, upwards, curled myself into a ball.

"Don't you like that?" he continued. He began to stroke my left shin, up and down, up and down. I tried to pull my leg away.

"No."

He lurched forward, his face shaped into a kiss. Just in time, I jolted up, away from the armchair.

"Where you going?" he said. I could feel his eyes on my body as I half-ran away, back to the room Auntie and I shared. The one next door to the room he shared with Tita Christy.

I stared at the ceiling, hated myself for being there. This was my fault. My fault for being a loser. A failure. A queer. A slut. I stayed up all night, panicking. I could not go home to my parents, back to Dad's violence, his rage and despair. I just had to be patient, wait it out until I had my passport, until I could get a job and live on my own, a manananggal removed from society.

Trauma, I am told, is the remover of memory, of innocence. There is not much that I remember from my time at Tita Christy's. This is what I do remember:

I remember: waking up the next morning to see Tito Lenny in the bedroom I shared with Auntie. He lay on the top part of the futon bed where Auntie slept, above the pull-out, where I slept. He reached out his hand to touch my waist, laughed when I stood up, begged him to go away, and no one heard me, because I was alone. The next day, I told Auntie about what happened. The touching. The attempted kiss. Should I tell Tita?

"I always knew he was a pig," she said. "Don't tell your Tita Christy. Just get your passport first."

I remember: a family party in late July, when I became dizzy, some kind of substance in my drink leaching into my blood. And when I hid in the dark, just beyond the pool, to try to shake it off, he found me. Put his lips and his hands on me, knowing I would be too drugged to resist. Thin-lipped, dry, old, disgusting. I told Auntie everything, trusted that she would do something about it, be my ally when we went to tell Tita Christy. Auntie and Tita would help me, wouldn't they?

I remember: August, when Tito Lenny began taking more days off work, knowing I would be alone. One morning, I returned from another run, cut short from the heat of late summer, my face red, temples throbbing. I sat on the couch, to breathe, eyes closed. Drank water, stretched my calves against the coffee table.

"Hello," Tito Lenny said, appearing from behind a door. He sat next to me on the couch. Lunged. Pushed himself on top of me.

I remember: how he covered my mouth with his, thin, dry lips on mine. His sour breath. My stomach contracted. I could not scream. He pinned my arms above my head with his hands, pinned my legs beneath his legs. And then, quickly, he was inside me, my shorts pushed aside. One, two, three thrusts.

I remember: two more times, even though I did my best to always be with Auntie, to never be alone. Each a sneak attack, once in a guest room while I was vacuuming the house, and another time in the garage after I had watered the plants. Garage remotes stashed in his pocket, hands clamped over my mouth. My body split into two by terror. I watched myself from above, helpless. Mouth open in a silent scream.

I remember: the rapes were not screaming-fighting-back-calling-out-for-help-shouting-no!-expectant-of-others'-aid kinds of rapes. They were silent-defeated-I-have-nowhere-else-to-go-if-I-say-no-how-will-I-survive kinds of rapes.

My therapist calls the watching-from-above "dissociation." I thought it was the manananggal inside me, tempting men to commit acts of rape and sexual violence. My upper half watched, and as I looked down on myself, I only had one thought: *Hold on. You need your passport. Hold on.*

With the pot heated, add vegetable oil. Let the oil grow hot.

After I finally received my Philippine passport, Tita Christy found out about her husband and the leg touching incident. His attempted kiss in the bedroom. Auntie, after instructing me to not tell anyone, had betrayed my confidence and shared everything she knew. She told Tita Christy that she had seen Tito Lenny skulking around the house, that she thought we might be having an affair.

"You aren't a virgin anymore, right?" Auntie shrugged when I asked her about what she said. "That's what whores do, isn't it?"

I begged Tita Christy to believe me.

"Auntie had convinced me to stay quiet. I wanted to tell you."

She had walked away without saying anything. I knew, then, that I could never say how much else had happened. Tita Christy did not speak to me for a few days, unsure of where her allegiance should be: her husband, of whom she'd always had suspicions? Or her niece, mentally unstable, fragile, suicidal, who had always been a good girl? She encouraged me to spend a few days with one of my new friends, a nice guy named Eric, the son of a family friend. She hadn't seemed angry when I left. Tito Lenny was nowhere to be found.

Eric picked me up, let me crash on his couch. Using the last of a long-distance calling card, I called my father's father, Lolo Pedring, in Manila. I had remembered the full tuition scholarship he had paid for me when I was born, allowing me to attend the University of the Philippines. Dad had not wanted me to go, but I still wanted to. I could go home to the Philippines tomorrow. Start again. Perhaps even be free.

"I want you to think about it. The scholarship is here for you, but you would be banned from the US if you left now," Lolo said, sadness in his voice. "Won't you go home to your parents first? Square things with them?"

A few days later I took a pregnancy test. It was positive. It was Tito Lenny's, no one else's.

I called his cell phone from a pay phone outside Eric's apartment.

"Gosh," Tito Lenny had smirked. "You're all just so fertile, aren't you?"

"It's $400 for the abortion pill, po," I said, like a robot. "I would also like some money for the bus or a cab to Planned Parenthood."

I came back to their house to pick up the cash. Tita Christy was at the front door, tear-streaked, furious. She was throwing my bags, my things, out of her house and onto her driveway. She had caught Tito Lenny sneaking the money out of their bedroom.

"Please," I had sobbed. "I wanted to tell you what he did, Tita. She told me not to!" I pointed at Auntie, who went back inside the house. Tita Christy demanded that I tell her what the money was for. I froze. She still didn't know? I backed away. Said I didn't know anything about any money.

"I told that TV producer that you're a dirty little illegal," she sneered. "Get the fuck out or I'll get you deported."

A local Filipino American news network had wanted to hire me as a local reporter. He had spotted me at a charity fashion show Tita Christy and her friends had produced. The job would have helped me save up for my own place. Or at least save up for a one-way flight back to Manila. The job offer was rescinded the next day; the producer refused my calls. What do we of shared blood owe each other, or expect of each other? In our shared inheritance, what obligations arise? There must be more to this idea of family than shared blood.

Stories abound of manananggal who are discovered and betrayed by their loved ones. And in these stories, the manananggal is destroyed, an evil creature who tempts men, eats babies, and must be punished. Salt and ash sprinkled on their separated lower halves by their families and loved ones, making it impossible to reattach. Doomed to death, their upper bodies left with nowhere to go, entrails dangling, wings flapping. Unable to return to themselves, suffering a slow, desiccating death. Sometimes, exceptions are made for these monsters. They are given a chance to stay alive. In exchange: banishment.

Lowering the heat to medium, add the garlic, onion, and ginger. Fry until the garlic is light gold, the onion soft.

I returned to New Jersey thirty pounds heavier, my body and face showing what I was hiding inside my belly, which was still contracting. My parents didn't seem to notice; Mom only said that I looked fat. I had swallowed the first of the two RU-486 pills the day before the flight, just as the Planned Parenthood nurse had instructed. I would swallow the second in secret, in my parents' house. For five days, I bled, alone and in pain. Heavy flows of thick, fleshy blood spilling out of me. One particularly large chunk swirled in the toilet, a mass of blood and tissue. Relief and horror seized my stomach.

I should have gone back to the Planned Parenthood clinic for a follow-up, or to my own doctor. Since I had flown cross-country, did not drive, and had no health insurance, I just let the blood pass and hoped against sepsis.

For weeks, my mother's extended family descended into arguments, sides taken, blame assigned over the touching of a leg and a waist, the accusations of an affair. They didn't know the entire truth, the disgusting, rotting truth of what Tito Lenny had done, of the pregnancy, the abortion. A bloodthirsty family, ready to kill me for the little they did know. It was my fault for wearing shorts, for wearing dresses in the summer heat, for wearing a sleeveless top, Tita Christy said. Mom flew to out to talk to Tita Christy; they argued only about themselves. About how bad all of this made them look. Dad only cared about how I had told Tita Christy about his joblessness, his violence. Confidences I had shared in the hopes that Tita would help me.

"Jill," my mother said, her voice distant on the phone. "Your Tita Christy is here next to me. Please, can you be honest and tell us what happened?"

I tried to say it. To say the word "rape" out loud. To describe how Tito Lenny did it. How he stalked, trapped, and raped me. How I was relying on them for a passport. How I needed them to be a safe harbor from my parents. And now, I was back under my father's roof, my body bleeding. All that came out was sobs. My sobs, and Tita Christy's voice on the other line. Taunting, cruel.

"You're a little bitch. You're a little whore. You're a little bitch. You're a little whore!" Over and over, she shouted over my attempts to speak, until I hung up the phone.

To this day, like many rapists, Tito Lenny insists that what happened was consensual. Most of Mom's extended family believed Tita Christy when she spread—perhaps continues to spread—his lies. Whether she believes him or not, these lies serve to make herself look innocent, blameless, the true victim. They all believe that it was me who started it, that there was an affair instead of a series of violent assaults. Cousins, aunts, and uncles will not speak to me, some forbidden by her to speak to me, sometimes in exchange for money, gifts, and visits to her new home.

It is difficult to say whether betrayal is a trait that runs in Filipino blood, or if it is learned from outsiders who have betrayed us. Perhaps it is an adjustment that we each make to eke some benefit, some advantage, from circumstances that deny us of any agency, any equality. This is one of the many legacies of colonialism, of hegemony. We are forced to destroy each other, to spill each other's blood, consume each other's insides, in the hopes that we may survive.

Like so much else in Filipino cuisine, there is no one true way to make dinuguan. Regional variations abound: in Nueva Ecija, the souring agent is not vinegar, but sampalok or kamias fruits, and the dish is called tinumis; Bicolanos call theirs tinutungang dinuguan, coconut milk and laurel leaves stirred into hot, blackening blood. In Ilocos, where my father is from, it is called dinardaraan; the Waray call it rugodugo. As a nation of islands, divisions are more than natural: it is in our terroir. Under pressure, the Katipunan resistance soon began to crack along divisions and disagreements, too, faction against faction, each convinced they knew the true path toward building a nation. Instead of remaining loyal to each other—bound by utang ng loob, by kapwa—the Katipunan split into two. Hunted by the Spanish, Bonifacio went into hiding, joined by his loyalists. Aguinaldo, his treacherous deputy, saw this as an opportunity to gather power. He sought out an alliance with the Americans, who saw the Filipinos as temporarily useful for weakening the Spanish. Before he ordered the deaths of his comrades—of Bonifacio and, some allege, of Diego Luna as well—did Aguinaldo prepare a pot of dinuguan to empower himself, like the ancient Spartans did before battle?

Fry the pork cubes and chopped offal until gently browned. Add the fish sauce and cook for 1 to 2 minutes.

The next five years bled into one another, a dissociative blur of isolation, violence, and random jobs. I worked as a telemarketer, selling dubious car warranties to unsuspecting elderly in far-off states like Iowa, Minnesota, Ohio, Wyoming. I didn't last long, fired after nine months for insubordination. I quit that job, then quit three more like it over the years.

Dad still wasn't working. He had stopped sleeping for days on end, his depression and violent mood swings pulsating through the house. It worsened when his father, my Lolo Pedring, died. They were not close and spoke only sporadically.

Lolo Pedring, my grandfather, greatest champion, and best friend, was in a jeepney on the way to the hospital, doubled over in pain as he hemorrhaged black blood all over the dirty aluminum floor. He was killed by his stubborn refusal to stop taking arthritis medication, which had punctured ulcers in his stomach, in his intestines. Lolo was forced to choose between bone or blood, between pain or death, and he chose, one painkiller swallowed after another. He visited me in my sleep on the night he died, walked with me through Loyola Cemetery in the dreamscape of the night. The autumn leaves of my suburban New Jersey street blended with the green of a rainy Manila. There were no words on his final visit. Only a feeling of comfort. Of his unwavering belief in me. Of his love.

It is in you, my grandfather had said, touching the top of my head, then my heart. His last words would haunt me for the rest of my years in my father's house, even as I lay awake, wishing to die. His words would follow me across oceans, decades later. He still visits, sometimes. Reminds me.

"Why you?" Dad asked, days after Lolo's death. "What is *in you*?" His gaze on me, jealous, disbelieving.

Mom found a new job for me, a personal assistant role to a Filipino named Manny. I was paid in cash, under the table. Manny called himself a freelance consultant. His job was to find people in the Philippines who were looking for work in America, linking them to Filipino American employment agencies in New York who farmed them out to nursing homes. He brought in people from all over the Philippines, many of them from the countryside. Some barely spoke English, many didn't speak Tagalog at all. These agencies paid Manny his cut of their cut of the Filipino workers' wages—fat envelopes of cash that he stuffed into his fake designer bag.

Pour in the remaining vinegar. Stir.

After not hearing from Manny for three days, I visited one of the employment agencies in Midtown, where I often spent entire days waiting for him to call with my next errand. I played Chinese checkers with waiting workers-to-be. The agency's owner, Tita Nancy, greeted me.

"Anak. Manny is gone. You don't have a job anymore."

The IRS or the FBI or some other federal agency had been looking for Manny. He fled the United States seemingly overnight, without telling anyone. The workers he claimed to represent turned out to have been trafficked, tricked into giving him money to set them up in New York for nursing jobs that did not exist. As they waited for work, they became undocumented. Manny was suspected of embezzling funds from Filipino job-seekers, employment agencies, and small-time investors, like my parents, who had given him $5,000, believing his business to be legitimate. He is back home now, in the Philippines, occasionally surfacing online in glamorous photos of fundraiser galas.

While stirring the pork and offal, slowly pour in the blood.

I began another part-time job, again through my mother's connections with the Filipino medical community.

"You would help with billing, but you would also cover the front desk," said Emmanuel, the office manager and the husband of Dr. Gutierrez. They were both Filipino, both my mother's friends.

Mom had ascended to an important regional position at the bank. Her job was to sign up new business accounts, to take care of their business banking needs. No one would ever believe that my mother or our family was undocumented. Not with this prominent job and her regional title.

"If you get good enough at medical billing," Dad said, "maybe you can start a business. You could make up to $80,000 a year, maybe more if you pick up business from your mom's doctor friends. Of course, you'd have to pay us back what you owe us, maybe start paying rent."

What did I owe them? What rent? I'd been giving them all of my money since 1999, except for the eleven months I spent in college and out west. What happened to keeping my money in a high-interest savings account for college?

Dad allowed me to take one class per semester at Ocean County Community College. He required that I pay for each class by working additional hours, that the classes not interfere with my shifts at work. Some of the night classes turned out to be in person, held at my old high school. I dreaded the possibility of running into anyone I knew. Convinced myself that it wouldn't happen.

"Jill?" Mr. Darton said, walking past a classroom one night. "What the hell are you doing here?"

I froze, as if caught committing a crime. I was still in my work uniform: cheap medical scrubs. I stood, thinking I could talk to him out in the hallway. Instead, I cried on his shoulder, overcome by shame, regret, and fear.

"Kid. What happened?" He pulled away, hands on my shoulders, eyes wet. Worried. "You're supposed to be graduating college soon. Aren't you?"

"I'll email you, Mr. D. Class is starting."

I never did email Mr. Darton. He died of cancer several months later.

Years flowed by, work, study, paychecks, repeat. I felt myself disappear. Dr. Gutierrez, out of pity, saw me for free, diagnosed me with depression, anxiety, and ADHD. I was uninsured and could not afford medication, but she gave me free samples from time to time. My body, stressed and afraid, broke out in hives and eczema regularly, my lips or eyelids bloating suddenly some mornings. Tiny symptoms of a monstrous unhappiness that could have sprouted wings, split itself in half, and flown freely. I tried to overdose two more times.

The morning of my second attempt in the summer of 2005, a trash can full of vomit by my bedside, an empty container of pills, my father came in.

"Clean that up. Your shift starts in an hour."

Mom, on my third attempt in spring 2006, me sprawled across my bed, vomit on my pillow: "Please don't do this to me. Don't leave me here with him."

That winter, Dad used Mom's and my money to buy two luxury cars, like-new: a Lexus IS 350 and a Toyota Land Cruiser. I thought about Berea College, the $5,000 annual room and board. Was this the college money he promised to save for me?

"I know what you're thinking," he said to me, seeing me look out the living room window at the two vehicles below. "Your mother and I have sacrificed enough. It's our turn."

Everything I had given was still not enough to repay my utang ng loob. A debt of the soul no unity, no kapwa, could ever pay. I turned twenty-four. My friends got their first postcollege job promotions, their own apartments. I couldn't even deposit my own paychecks into my bank account. I never saw a single bank statement, all of them intercepted by my father. In those years of sacrifice, my only consolation was that my sister was not being made to suffer the same fate. Not yet.

Add the whole chilies to the pot.

Internalized colonial oppression and shame is a part of our blood, our inheritance. It colors everything we do, from how we eat—calling dinuguan "chocolate meat," warning white friends and loved ones about the blood, as if European cuisine did not also use blood in their recipes—to how the Philippines became independent. Aguinaldo, seemingly having internalized Spanish and American oppression, declared himself the first president of the

Philippine Republic. Unelected, of course. If Aguinaldo felt that he owed his fellow Filipinos and his fellow revolutionaries anything, democracy was not one of them.

Still, nothing Aguinaldo did mattered. Six months later, in the Treaty of Paris, Spain ceded Puerto Rico and Guam to the United States, who paid $20 million in exchange for the Philippine Islands. The American government went on to claim to know nothing about self-elected President Aguinaldo, denied knowing him despite their secret messages of support for the Katipunan. In betraying and oppressing his countrymen for power, Aguinaldo was betrayed, in return.

Season the blood with salt, to taste.

One September evening, 2007, Mom picked me up after my shift at Dr. Gutierrez's office.

"Jill," she said, jaw tense, her hands gripping the steering wheel. "Your Dad found everything. Why is there cash under your bed? And job printouts? And this Craigslist?"

Fuck. My plans. For months I had been sneaking $200 from my paycheck, spurred with anger from Dad's luxury car shopping spree. Emmanuel, the office manager, had agreed to give me this small amount in cash every month, though he found this request strange. I had begun searching for jobs in New York, determined to find something that paid more than $6.25 an hour. My plan was to find a job and to leave my parents' house immediately, using my saved cash as deposit for a rented room.

I dropped my duffel bag at the front door. Ran upstairs, where my mattress was flipped upside down. All drawers, open. My job and apartment printouts, spread out on my dresser. The $1,400 in cash was gone. And then: Dad's hands, my head pulled back, slammed against my bedroom's doorframe. My mother, screaming, walking away from us, down the hallway, closing doors and windows so the neighbors wouldn't hear. My sister hid in her room. She had just graduated from high school that summer; my plan had been to hang on long enough until she left home for college.

I let him beat me: wanted him to, so that I would not lose my will to leave. There, on the floor of the upstairs hallway, I let him kick me all over my spine, my legs, my stomach, my jaw. I wanted to taste blood, to feel each blow on my flesh. I swallowed my blood, strengthened myself on it.

I stood up, like nothing had happened. He froze, surprised.

"No more," I whispered, blood trickling between my teeth, out of the corners of my mouth. Down my temple, ribboning down my neck. I stared at him, at his shock. Was he cowering? I was nearly his height, lean and muscled from running. He knew my strength—he had marveled at it over the years, though he shouldn't have been surprised. I was, after all, his flesh and blood.

"You are not going to touch me anymore." I stepped past him, into the hallway. He shoved me.

"Is that what you need to feel powerful?" I shouted, over my mother's screams. *Jill, stop it, tama na, both of you!*

"You think you can make it? In New York?" He stepped closer to me. "You think you have a shot? Go ahead! You'll fail and come back like you always do. You failure."

"I am not a failure," I sobbed. "I've never needed your help. You were the one who needed mine."

The fury on his face. His spit that landed on my cheeks, my eyes. His palms shot out towards me, shoved squarely at my chest. I took a backwards tumble down the stairs, rolled, sprang back up at the bottom. Took my cell phone out of my pocket. Texted Jenny, a good friend who lived nearby. PLS COME GET ME. I grabbed my still-unpacked duffel bag by the front door, the one full of sundresses and swimsuits from a secret trip to see Dean, that long-ago boy from the fifth grade, now my secret boyfriend.

Dad had disappeared, then reappeared at the top of the stairs, a kitchen knife in his hand. My sister burst into view. Terror in her eyes.

"GO, Jill!" she screamed, sobbing. "Go! Please go!"

I looked at her one more time, this sister that I loved with all of my blood and bones. I flung the front door open, and ran, the fastest I had ever been, and will ever be. The early September air was cool on my blood-wet face. Jenny's car was at the end of the street.

"What the fuck happened?" Jenny mashed her foot down on the gas, sped away from my parents' house. All I had was a duffel bag and a mouth full of blood. But I was free.

Let the pot simmer, uncovered, until the blood thickens, reduced. Do not stir.

Some versions of dinuguan contain offal, hearts and livers and intestines dotting the black stew, a reminder of our endurance, defiance, and creativity despite want and death. There is an understanding, in this dish and in others, that life, from its beginning to its end, is a sacrifice. Blood from wars of occupation is packed into our earth, fortified with iron from the bodies of our men, women, and children. In 1901, in the red midst of what Americans call the Philippine-American War, Aguinaldo was captured. Under duress, the former self-elected president swore allegiance to the United States. But the Philippine War for Independence raged on beyond this one man's narcissism. Filipino liberation forces fought for four more years, from the northern Cordillera mountains to the Muslim south. In retaliation, Americans captured and imprisoned Filipino fighters in concentration camps. Some American accounts claim no more than 42,000 Filipino casualties, but these claims are chocolate for blood. Modern scholarship estimates deaths of 200,000 to 500,000 Filipino deaths by American hands from 1899 to 1902, an intermingling of causes ranging from US military campaigns to American industrial agricultural interventions, which worsened poverty, hunger, and epidemics during the war.

Add the brown sugar while stirring. Let simmer for 10 to 15 minutes, until the blood thickens. Season with salt and pepper, to finish.

I crashed at Jenny's house for three weeks, a manananggal who will never return. My parents were afraid of what Jenny's family knew, and stayed away. I had just enough money: $200 or so, cash I had earned from singing at a wedding over the summer, stashed away in the duffel bag I had grabbed that night. I knew that I could not stay at Jenny's for much longer. Through Friendster, I saw that my cousin Matty, the only son of my dad's oldest brother, had just moved into an apartment in Queens for his med school residency.

I texted him for help. Memories of riding little bicycles together with our Lolo Pedring flashed behind my eyes, where our past lives. How differently our lives had turned out.

Matty texted back immediately. *It's OK, Jill, stay here na lang.*

I met Mom at the New Jersey Transit park and ride. She gave me some clothes from home. We fought.

"I want my money back, Mom," I said. "I want my $24,000 a year times the past four years, plus the $16,000 a year times the two years in high school."

"I don't know what you mean."

"You cashed all of my paychecks straight into your checking account, Mom. With your own two hands."

"I don't know what you're talking about!" Chocolate for blood.

I leapt out of her Lexus. Ran towards the bus, end destination Port Authority, New York. I gave the driver my ticket and found a window seat just behind him, where I felt safest. I watched my mother drive away. I can do this. After nine years as my family's blood sacrifice, I was finally free. Screaming towards the future, severed in half. Despite the pain and the fear, I knew, then, that I would not die, could not die, from a permanent separation such as this.

Serve hot, with steamed rice or puto, or both.

The dinuguan is ready. Its texture depends on what you prefer. I like a blood stew that is moderate in its consistency. Not too watery, so that it slips through the kernels of rice and pieces of meat. Not so thick that it coagulates in the mouth, soaking up all the moisture on your tongue, your upper palate. I like it silky. Fatty. Buttery, almost.

I close my eyes, send a spirit message to my family. Blood of my blood, flesh of my flesh, I never meant to leave you behind.

6

Spamsilog
(Fried Garlic Rice, Egg, and Spam)

2007–2011

SERVES 2

> 2 cups uncooked rice
> 1 head garlic
> 1 tablespoon vegetable oil
> 1 can Spam
> 4 eggs
> At the table:
> Atchara
> Banana ketchup
> Pinakurat
> Patis
> Coffee
> Tang

It's past noon on the kind of lazy Saturday that reminds me of being a kid. Of being sixteen, my mother opening my bedroom door just after 10 a.m., a big smile appling her cheeks.

"Mantika! Gising na, tanghali na!" Her nickname for me, Mantika, sticky grease. The kind that clings to the pan, or in my instance, to the bed. "Wake up, it's midday."

"It's not midday," my sister, even stickier grease, would grumble at the dining table. "It's not even eleven yet."

When I try to recall good family memories from America, it is easy to do, because they are so few and therefore prominent. Late breakfasts cooked up by Mom, the most tired and reluctant of cooks. Cheerful on a Saturday, the one day of freedom she had from endless work. Dad, the most self-pitying and reluctant of workers, refusing to work every day. While Mom cooked, he chose a CD to put on while we ate. Toto, Bobby Caldwell, George Benson, Chick Corea, the Carpenters. She often made a silog: tapsilog, tosilog, longsilog.

This morning, in my own kitchen, I am making Spamsilog. I am also remembering breakfasts of a different kind: twenty-five, alone, broke, and broken, eating air and drinking water to last me until dinner. How a can of salted, preservative-laden canned pork, now considered junk in the United States, was aluminum-clad American treasure during my Manila childhood. How Spam—brought to our islands by GIs as wartime rations—gave Filipinos a bit of joy during those post-dictator years, while killing them at the same time. How I could barely afford this deadly form of canned survival in those early years in New York.

Spamsilog, and any silog, is the kind of breakfast almost no one can turn down. It contains everything we need to start our day: garlicky rice, a fried egg, some kind of meat, fish, or protein, with a puckery sour, crunchy atchara of ribbony shredded carrots and papaya on the side. Dash the eggs with sweet banana ketchup, maybe some spicy-sour Pinakurat on the fried Spam. Add sriracha sauce, or chili crisp, or some Lady's Choice Sandwich Spread. Have another helping, drain a second cup of coffee.

Silog is food for hard work. Hard work, Americans taught Filipinos, can achieve everything they have in America. As a colony, as a post-colony, Filipinos have learned from America that if they work hard, they can prove their own worth. America says that work is salvation. America says, without irony, that work makes one free.

The day before you plan to make Spamsilog, rinse the rice and drain.

Silog is a portmanteau and a portal. This word allows a glimpse into our colonized past, the way we embrace the junk our oppressors feed us, then turn it into something uniquely ours, to be chewed, savored, swallowed. *Silog* is a word descended from *tapsi*, itself another combination of words: *tapa*—thinly sliced beef marinated in soy, vinegar, and sugar—and *singangag*, day-old rice often fried with minced garlic. Tapa and sinangag. Tap-si. Tapsi. In the 1980s, a woman named Vivian del Rosario eventually turned the word tapsi into tapsilog, adding an egg—itlog—to the meat and rice. Tap-si-log. She sold it as an affordable breakfast, as a hangover cure, a source of joy, in the midst of dictatorship, from her restaurant in Marikina. The same neighborhood as the big marble house Papa helped build. The one I so loved as a child.

Silog can be combined with anything, a flexibility that is so much like ours. Add longanisa: longsilog. Add fried bangus: bangsilog. Add tosino: tosilog. And these days, there is seitansilog and toksilog, vegetarian nods to our pre-colonial past, when we didn't see the consumption of meat as a sign of wealth and health, but of sacrifice and rare celebration, a ritual that recognizes the hard-earned value of life. We add to silog whatever is needed to make it work, whatever is needed to survive. Jobs, industries, occupations, indignities. Add Spam: chew the lie of the American dream. Confuse the taste of fear and survival with the taste of hope and desire.

Repeat the rinsing of the rice until the water runs clear.

On that New Jersey Transit bus in autumn 2007, final destination Port Authority, Manhattan, I thought about the conversation I had just had with my mother. How she denied admitting what she and my father had taken from me. It is crushing, the way our most intimate relationships reproduce the abuse of empire. Maybe, I thought, as the bus pulled into Port Authority, I had been too harsh on Mom. After all, my mother was also a victim of my father's anger. Of his control.

It was eleven o'clock at night as I walked through the deserted station, kiosks and shops closed till the morning. Rows of men and women sleeping in corners on the station floor. My own fate not too far from theirs, half-full duffel bag in hand, no job, no home. All of us, at one time or another, in search of a better life, now gathered here, abandoned in what we had grown up to believe was the center of the universe. I thought of my mother, choosing to protect her husband instead of her children. Of her choice to believe in their past instead of our future.

I decided I had not been too harsh at all.

Place the cleaned rice in the cooking pot. Place a middle finger so that it is perpendicular to the surface of the rice. Fill the pot with water until it reaches the first line of your middle finger.

My cousin Matty had prepared his couch for me to sleep on, though I didn't make it to his apartment right away. A spasm of shame and terror had overcome me, led to a few nights at an emergency overnight homeless shelter somewhere in lower Manhattan. I gave a fake name, afraid of America and my father tracking me down. Lost on the subway, I ended up in the Bronx instead of Queens. By the time I arrived at Matty's doorstep, a one-bedroom, third-floor walk-up apartment in Kew Gardens, it was late at night. My stomach rumbled. I had eaten nothing but a few bags of potato chips and a garlic bagel, spread over the course of three days.

"Sorry I'm so late," I said to my cousin. My resolve had wavered just before I left the shelter, mind echoing with Dad's last words to me as I ran out of their house forever.

"I'm used to being up all the time naman. Barely sleeping," he said, waving me in. He had just started his med school residency at Jamaica Hospital, nearby. "You hungry? I can microwave Vienna sausages and rice."

I nodded in gratitude. A feast. Like Thanksgiving. My cousin and I had a can each, spoonfuls of rice and salty processed meat in companionable silence. The children of two brothers who, like their fathers before them, had believed in the American dream. Only one of us lived in a nightmare.

Let the rice cook until steamed, with no water remaining in the pot.

The United States is a young country, but it is not one without its own mythology, its own pantheon of gods, its own creatures and monsters. Much like how the Romans adopted Greek myths, America embraced its British predecessors' stories and beliefs. Set these beasts and spirits, gods and creatures loose upon an unsuspecting land, that broad, stolen expanse of amber waves of profitable grain.

Most prominent among these beasts is the favorite of the gods, particularly the gods of Democracy, Meritocracy, and Exceptionalism, the three ruling deities of the American pantheon. This beast has a bottomless appetite and thirst, and it is set upon the world at the behest of these gods. It seeks to grow endlessly, swallowing everything in its rapaciousness: land, rivers, seas, forests, crops, animals, air, the core of the earth. People from other lands, entrapped as slaves. Other lands, entrapped as colonies.

This beast reveals itself to us as an economic system, which we call capitalism. This beast, however, is far greater, much older. It lives inside our souls, an omnipresent engkanto that can most closely be defined as greed. The gods of the United States unleashes this monster whenever it sees fit, though this monster—once the servant of Britain, that previous, now-withered empire across the Atlantic—ultimately serves nothing and no one but itself.

When the beast arrived upon our islands—not its first visit, for it once stayed on our lands for almost four hundred years, under a different master—it brought with it many gifts from the Americans. Vienna sausages. Canned corn. Powdered milk. Tang orange drink mix. Spam. These gifts of packaged food were processed at American canneries, buildings standing on stolen land and filled with poor workers, workers of color, workers from other lands, some from the Philippines. Spam, that most treasured of exported American canned goods, was created as a way of selling off pork shoulder, a cut that Americans did not know how to cook, and therefore did not buy. Stuffed into GIs' rucksacks during the Second World War, these rectangular cans tumbled onto our islands. Our damaged collective psyche, taught for generations to believe in our supposed culinary inferiority, awaited with hunger-dried open mouths.

There is a photograph of me from 1987, one year after the dictator and his family had fled to Guam, then Hawaii, in an American Air Force plane. Sweaty, clutching Bruno, my favorite stuffed bulldog toy, sitting on top of a balikbayan box. Balikbayan, another postcolonial portmanteau, another portal glimpsing the ways we have been scattered, as a whole and as ourselves. Balik, to return. Bayan, country. If only returning to one's country were that easy. Fill a box three feet wide and three feet tall with American processed food, chocolates, hand-me-down clothes, cheap colognes and perfumes from the strip mall drugstore. Lash it with layers of duct tape. Label it with enormous letters in Magic Marker. Tie it shut with thick rope, all the better to carry it with, all the harder to break into. Send it home, safe and sound on a cargo ship manned by men from your home country.

Did the Marcoses enjoy Spamsilog once they landed? Hawaii: another postcolonial place making do with junk from the mainland empire. They, too, have their own version of Spam, eggs, and rice for breakfast.

In those post-dictator years, the 1980s and 1990s, the economy a barren wreck, we looked forward to these balikbayan boxes from America. Clothes outgrown by cousins in Virginia, Maryland, and New York, books passed on for us to enjoy. Shoes by K-Swiss, Reebok, and, if an auntie really likes you, maybe even Nike. T-shirts with words like HARD ROCK CAFE and NEWPORT NEWS, VA on them. Bottles of Johnny Walker and Chivas Regal for the Titos, bags of Hershey's Kisses and Kit Kat bars for the kids. Canisters of Ovaltine and Milo, boxes of Kellogg's Frosted Flakes and Coco Pops. And, most precious of all, cans of Spam and Vienna sausages with our names written on the label, so that no one household takes too many. We have been independent from the United States for decades, but are still dependent in so many ways.

Once the rice has finished cooking, remove from the heat. Allow it to cool to room temperature.

I found a job in New York within my first week, photocopied Social Security card in hand. On Craigslist, the job listing said that applicants did not need a college degree, with a pay range of $15,000 to $40,000 a year in the first year. The job was to sell ad space for a Spanish-language newspaper based in Herald Square. No paid time off, no paid sick days, no health or dental, as usual. I was hired on the spot, but I think they hired just about anyone. Bodies to fill seats. A numbers game.

"You get paid a guaranteed draw for three months, but after the ramp-up period, you should have a pipeline of sales. You'll have to earn back what you're paid out of the draw. Do you get it?"

The job was dull and slow. I called businesses blindly, most of them hanging up on me. Nail salons, hair salons, restaurants. I finally got my first sale three weeks into the job. An ad placement for a barber shop. Just as I was closing, the head of sales pulled up a chair next to me.

"Give me the phone."

I handed the receiver over. He closed the sale.

"Good work, rookie. We'll split the commission on that one."

"But . . . I didn't ask for your help."

"Come on. You should be glad I closed for you."

The next few sales went this way. I would be closing, and he would appear. Each time, he claimed half the commission. He said it was normal for new hires to get help with closing. He didn't try it with the other new hires, though. Only me. I was too afraid to complain.

My first paycheck arrived: $1,000 and change after tax and the halved commission. I deposited this at a bank branch near the office. My mother, who had access to the system through her bank job, had recently changed my student bank account to a regular checking account, the one small favor she did for me after I left home two months before.

I gave myself a budget of forty dollars for two weeks of groceries, replenished my cousin's pantry whenever I could afford it. The rest of it would go towards a place of my own, someday. And maybe, one or two years on, towards a class or two at CUNY, maybe Hunter College or Brooklyn College for English Lit. One semester at a time. From my calculations, it would take anywhere from six to ten more years for a bachelor's degree. Though rules for undocumented immigrant students were slowly beginning to change, I did not qualify for any substantial scholarships or aid, not after having failed out of Berea. I would have to pay out of my own pocket.

I began looking for a new job on Craigslist each night, scrolling through endless blue links on Matty's laptop. I did not sleep more than four hours each night, my old engkanto friend sitting on my shoulder, urging me to keep going. I saved the jobs that specifically mentioned "freelance," which meant not being asked for papers. Next to the keyboard often sat a small bowl of instant ramen. I split the packet of ramen in half, carefully doled out half of the seasoning. Saved the rest for the next evening's dinner.

One afternoon, I went to a job interview during my lunch break, when, like breakfast, I usually filled my stomach with air. Its Craigslist subject line said something about helping the environment and fundraising for an environmentally focused nonprofit organization. Their office was by Penn Station and across from Madison Square Garden, in the Hotel Pennsylvania. A building that was once one of the largest in the world, an expression of the wealth of the Pennsylvania Railroad, a company that was also once one of the largest in the world, industry jauntily crisscrossing stolen land. The hotel was built at the height of the Progressive Era, another crucial period of American mythology just after the Gilded Age. Aggressive expansion, capitalist beast on a leash, speaking softly and carrying a big stick. By the time I walked through the hotel's tired lobby that fall in 2007—the nation on the brink of a financial crisis—the hotel had fallen on hard times, its once grandiose marble columns covered up, encased in MDF and mirrors. Run-down, dirty, and haunted, it has since been demolished, an easy symbol for a country that has long given up on itself.

"The pay for our street fundraiser role is seven dollars an hour, and you'd come on board as a freelancer, so no benefits. And there's opportunity to move up and become a team leader, a trainer, a shift leader, and so on," said the woman interviewing me, an earnest recent Columbia graduate named Rachel. This job was her quick break while deciding whether to apply to law school or grad school. Her colleague, Ashley, had just graduated from NYU and was studying for her GMATs. I wanted to be just like them. I thought that maybe this job would get me there. We chatted for a little while longer, sharing an enthusiasm for a young senator from Illinois, the Democratic primary candidate named Barack Obama.

"Hillary's got such a huge lead, though," Rachel said, walking me to the door. "That would still be exciting if she won, but can you imagine, the first Black president?"

I couldn't imagine, because none of it was relevant to me. I was a nonvoting nonentity, useful only to be exploited for voters' compassion or hatred every election cycle, depending on the political party. All I cared about when it came to presidents and legislators was whether they saw undocumented people like me, like my family, as human. Would they give us amnesty? Or repair the broken immigration system? Give us a pathway to citizenship, which the broken system did not allow? None of these presidents ever did anything for those of us once colonized by the United States. Nothing that didn't immediately serve American interests, anyway. The Philippines fed the gods' capitalist beast, contributed to the American economy, paid duties and taxes on products imported to America. Filipinos received little in return, the United States passing on its colonial trauma to us: taxation without representation. Possession without citizenship. That was all Filipinos were. A resource, just as the American colonies once were for Britain.

Prepare a pitcher of Tang orange drink. Store in the fridge, covered, until mealtime.

I was offered the job. Like ad sales, street fundraising was only a numbers game. I didn't go back to the Spanish newspaper office after that interview. It was a beautiful autumn day, with the trees almost bare. Central Park loomed in front of me. I treated myself to a cup of coffee from a cart, which was all I would put in my stomach all day. I thought about my new job, about going back to school. Sent this wish up to the sky, where the gods of Meritocracy and Exceptionalism sat with indifference. I thought of the possibility of the first woman president, or the first Black president. Of how one of them might win next year, perhaps a marker of change in a country built on change, yet somehow so resistant to it.

The sun struggled through half-naked branches. A tiny bit of hope, for some.

Once the rice has reached room temperature, cover and store overnight in the refrigerator or a cool, dark place.

The Americans' beast of capitalist burden did not just bring their Spam and their Hershey's to the Philippines. The beast also brought the style of government favored by the god of Democracy, the frameworks for American necroeconomy. They brought their white supremacist social structures and cultural norms, an earthly disguise for the god of Exceptionalism. These structures and norms reinforced the Spaniards' leftover caste system: we were the savages, they the saviors. They brought their Boss Tweed–style political culture of graft, corruption, and nepotism, pork barrel greed that still manifests itself at all levels of Philippine government today. Corruption that still rots at the heart of American government too. We recognize this corruption and nepotism as the god of Meritocracy.

Besides Spam, Vienna sausages, and instant drink powders, the United States also brought to the Philippines their great storytelling tradition, one that still pervades today and has spread around the world. The American dream, as James Truslow Adams called it in his book, *The Epic of America*. Capitalist ideology written into mythology. Eat lots of Spamsilog to fuel that hard work, buy an American car, buy a house with a clean indoor kitchen to supplant the outdoor dirty one, buy an American refrigerator and cooking stove.

My family, like many families, believed in this mythology with the whole of our wounded Filipino hearts. We believed that if we strived to be just as industrious, just as educated, just as hardworking as the Americans, we would succeed, just like them, true meritocracy and democracy for all. It makes sense to me that after a long week of hard work, my mother cooked silog as a reward. As fuel for the week to come.

Filipinos believed in this American mythology of democracy and meritocracy so much that in 1927, Filipino politicians under the US government wrote to President Calvin Coolidge. Asked him to let us hold a vote on the possibility of a chance at independence. President Coolidge said no, using the same tactics King George III once used to say no to the American colonies' Declaration of Independence. The Philippines had not demonstrated its ability to self-rule, Coolidge wrote. The Philippine economy had not yet learned how to be self-sufficient without reliance on the American market—strange, as Philippine trade was under American control. In demanding independence this way—through a polite letter asking for a vote to merely see how Filipinos feel about independence—Coolidge wrote that we were being unruly, uncivilized, proving our unworthiness.

The next morning, remove the pot of rice from the refrigerator or from its cool, dark place. With a fork, stir it from bottom to top, letting the grains separate, removing the clumps until the rice is loose, buhaghag.

I moved up to team leader in my first three weeks, responsible for helping an assigned group of four to five street fundraisers. Their daily individual minimum goal was ten dollars, cash or credit, with a small bonus paid for signing up monthly donors. My pay moved up, a little, enough to allow for indulgences: a warmer coat from a thrift shop, slightly out of my budget, but likelier to keep me from catching a cold. Being outside in almost-winter from 9 a.m. to 4 p.m. was chilly business. After three weeks of cold and sometimes rain, I noticed a warm, pin-and-needles feeling in my toes, the tips of my fingers. The beginnings of frostnip.

I had only seven pairs of socks, washed by hand every weekend. One pair of gloves, five bucks from a street vendor, the kind where the skin showed through gaps in the thin acrylic knit. I started sitting inside cafés between visits to my street team, warming up my hands under bathroom hand dryers. Doubled up on my socks, rotating the ones I wore twice in a week.

With each day, I became more exhausted, my body colder, my brain slower. The commute from Queens to midtown Manhattan took an hour each way: one bus, then a train. To save precious subway money to manage my street team, I walked quickly between one person to the next, long city block after long city block. The walking did nothing to keep my hands and feet warm. I continued to skip meals, apart from a coffee cart cup of black coffee, no sugar. My half-pack of ramen a day was beginning to fail me. I woke up in the middle of the night to the howls in my stomach: poverty, an eating disorder, or both? Sometimes, I would remember the ulcers I suffered as a child and get up, trudging to the kitchen for half a banana.

So that I could make it through each workday, I upgraded to a full pack of ramen for dinner from Monday to Friday. My body remained cold and tired.

"I bought extra Vienna sausages and Spam and some canned tuna," my cousin told me. "Maybe have some with your ramen?" Me, skeletal, frostbitten, and shrinking before my doctor-in-training cousin's eyes.

Matty kindly shared meals with me out of his meager first-year medical intern salary. Canned tuna smeared onto crackers, the occasional luxurious box of Kraft Mac & Cheese. Even when it was free, eating felt like an extravagance, as if I was somehow rewarding myself without having earned the privilege of food. Each bite of food in my mouth, swallowed into my belly, felt to me as if I was throwing money down the toilet. My body's ability to fend off the cold continued to fail. The flesh in my pale, bluish, frostnipped toes began to harden, the skin blistering and peeling off in places, the next stage of frostbite. I couldn't afford a warmer pair of shoes, and my beat-up trail running shoes were beginning to wear down inside. I started wearing three pairs of socks. This did not help much. My toes became harder, more numb. My fingers, warmed by an extra two pairs of street vendor gloves, lessened in their redness but struggled to move for hours after each shift. I was beginning to freeze, it seemed, from the inside out. I caught the flu. With no sick pay and no health insurance, I worked through it.

Finely mince a head of garlic. Over low heat in a wok or large frying pan, fry the minced garlic in oil until lightly golden.

One afternoon in November, an older man approached. I had seen him earlier in the day, after he had pledged ten dollars on a credit card, signing my form to help the environment. I still had no idea, really, what the organization I worked for did with the funds raised. I found it hard, in my starved, penniless state, to want to know. *Do you have one minute to help us save the environment?* As long as they paid me, who cared?

The man introduced himself as a development consultant working for the Catholic church down the street.

"We're recruiting for a development associate to help with fundraising for their youth organization and media outlet. I've seen you here over the past couple of weeks. You have a great demeanor about you, so engaging and involved. Would you be interested in chatting over a coffee with me and Father Tom? He runs the program."

I agreed to meet after my shift. Coffee, their treat, at a nearby cafe. I was, by then, a deeply lapsed Catholic, bitter and let down by all the ways God didn't show up for me, no matter how good and prayerful I was. I hid this from them, emphasized my volunteer work with the Catholic youth group, my volunteer cantoring at my family's church, back when I was still playing obedient prisoner in my parents' house. I did not share that the only reason I volunteered at church was so that my father would let me out of the house.

The job sounded good, and it was full time, indoors, at a desk, keeping track of donors and donations to the institution. It had full health and dental insurance after the first month of employment, plus paid sick days and one week paid time off for the first year. I sent my résumé in that night, forcing myself to eat half a can of fried Spam with leftover rice to fuel my brain. A few days and an interview later, I was offered the job, $30,000 a year, an enormous sum to me. I was to start on the Monday after Thanksgiving. Finally, something to be thankful for.

I called Mom to tell her, wanting Dad to know that, unlike him, I was not a failure.

"What if you get caught and deported? We could all get deported."

This had not been a worry for her when I worked to give them my paychecks.

Turn the heat up to medium. Add the rice to the pan. Stir well and often to distribute the oil and minced garlic. Fry the rice until it warms and turns ever so slightly golden, but not browned or crispy.

I spent Thanksgiving and Christmas of 2007 alone. My cousin was in Chicago for the holidays, where his mother and his girlfriend were based. I bought a small turkey for Thanksgiving from CTown, thinking I could make it for myself, maybe eat a little and save the rest for lunches and dinners. The frozen bird sat on a pan on a radiator, instead, rock hard. I roasted it the Saturday after Thanksgiving, ate a couple of slices. I was so afraid of wasting it, of eating it for no reason, of not having earned the right to eat, that it stayed in the fridge, untouched, until it went rancid.

On Christmas Day, I took the long train ride from Queens to Manhattan, treated myself to a cup of coffee from a cart at Central Park South. Walked around the park, in the fresh snow, marveling at my new pair of winter socks and warmer shoes, bought with my first paycheck at the new job. I watched families play, throw snowballs, build snowmen, sled down the park's hills. I thought of their evenings, warm inside their houses and apartments, eating turkey and mashed potatoes and gravy, drinking hot chocolate, watching *It's a Wonderful Life*, a movie about a person so blessed that he could take his life for granted. The day went by without word from my mother. My sister and I traded Christmas messages on Facebook, the only mode of communication we had that was not monitored by our father. Without me there, Dad was taking his anger out on her. His new punching bag. I begged her to stay strong. She was getting ready to go to college, qualifying for a full scholarship at Brooklyn College to study as a Macaulay Honors Scholar, majoring in biology and public health. CUNY, true to its progressive tradition of serving working-class students, had changed its rules to allow for undocumented students. I remember feeling both proud and relieved. She was going to make it. She was going to be safe. Once my sister was out of the house, she could slowly build a life away from our parents. Dad might treat her better, even—his only remaining future golden goose, if he played his cards right.

I got home from Manhattan, had a Christmas meal of a few slices of fried Spam, warm leftover rice, and some five-dollar wine from Duane Reade. Alone, but free and unbruised for the first time in years.

As the sinangag rice cooks, begin cutting the Spam into ¼- or ½-inch-thick slices.

On the eve of my twenty-fifth birthday, in February 2008, I had saved up enough money for my own place. First month, last month, and a security deposit. A one-bedroom railroad apartment in the South Bronx, just off the subway stop at 149th Street and Third Avenue. Living alone was the only possible solution: I did not really have any friends in New York, and I couldn't risk the background and ID checks required by apartment rental agencies. My new landlord was an angry, short white man with a close-shaved head and a tendency to wear fatigue pants. He talked a lot about guns, liberty, the scourge of Big Government, and "cleaning up this hood." All that mattered to me was that he didn't ask any questions. He didn't care that my ID was a Philippine passport with no visa in it. He was just happy to take the rent: $1,100 a month, or over half of my monthly pay.

Matty and his dad—my uncle, Dad's oldest brother—helped me move my few belongings. I slowly filled the space with free furniture from Craigslist: a bed frame. A nearly-new mattress, checked for bedbugs and disinfected with cans of Lysol. A dresser. A fat silver cathode-ray TV that took me an hour to haul up to my fourth-floor walk-up using a handcart.

The months of relief and security went by quickly. By May 2008, I was fired from my job.

"It's just not working," said Father Tom, hostile, crossing his arms. "I'm still doing all the work."

"All of the donors message you and leave me out of the emails," I protested, and held back tears.

I took my month's severance pay, which turned into two months, perhaps a guilty parting gift from Father Tom. As an undocumented immigrant, I did not qualify for welfare or for unemployment. Or if I did, I was too afraid to try to find out. This extra month's pay was a blessing from a god that showed up, for once, for me. Within a few weeks, I found a job at a doctor's office on Park Avenue. Medical billing and front desk reception, just like my old job in New Jersey. The hourly pay was decent, but it was not the same as my previous salary. I began to cut back on food again, reducing my dinner portions. I still did not eat breakfast or lunch. It had begun to feel natural, this restriction, this control over at least one thing in my life. Less food, more savings, one dollar closer to going back to college.

I soon found another job through Craigslist. An operations associate role with a firm that called itself a hedge fund. It paid more than the medical receptionist job, and that was enough. There was no health insurance or any other benefits—I was hired as a freelancer, no papers or college degree required—but that did not matter. Anything to survive. I thought of all the millions of undocumented immigrants like me who were probably suffering worse jobs, worse living situations. Greater danger, hunger, pain. I did not allow myself to feel self-pity or despair. I was lucky. I just needed to remain disciplined.

Heat up a smaller frying pan for the Spam and eggs.

Through most of 2008, America lurched from one small financial meltdown to the next, the news warbling as background TV noise in my apartment while I fried up slices of Spam to bring to work: sandwiches made with nearly expired on-sale white bread, glued together with mayo. I was too preoccupied with each day's expenditure of dollars and cents to worry about the financial stability of the housing market or the survival of enormous banks. As I skipped meals and pinched pennies, the entire country's fate rested in the hands of a few people, the Treasury and senators and congresspeople in meetings behind tightly closed doors. Gods propping up the mythos of the American Dream.

On the day Lehman Brothers declared bankruptcy, my main preoccupa tion was to try to figure out why I only had thirty-two dollars for groceries until the end of the month, rather than my usual forty. While my coworkers crowded around the television to watch rich finance workers file out of Lehman's building, I scanned my expenses notebook. Added and re-added each day's expenditures. Where did those eight dollars go?

"I think we'll be all right," was the smug assessment of the firm's owner, squinting at the TV. He was a young guy who had inherited the business and his contacts from his father. He understood that even with a financial crisis, the firm would thrive. Its main business was to issue private loans to retail businesses, recouping their investment through credit card processing machines. The sales team targeted bodegas, furniture stores, car repair shops, and other small business owners who needed an influx of quick cash to cover other debt, repairs, or emergency expenses. Many of these business owners had employees to pay, children to feed and send to college. Mortgages to keep up with. My boss's boss understood that small businesses would need nonbank loans now more than ever, and his firm, with its 40 to 50 percent interest fees, one-year repayment term, and onerous clauses for nonrepayment, was ready and waiting for their desperation. It would be years later before I would learn that this was no hedge fund. It was just what they told assistants like us.

Take the sinigang garlic fried rice off the heat, covering the pan.

One afternoon in late October, not long after the first anniversary of my independence, my tired and hungry body gave way. I felt hot and chilly all over, my head light and dizzy. I began to black out at my desk, the Excel sheet blinking white and dark. Eliza, a fellow operations assistant who had become a good friend, put me in a cab home, pressed money into the driver's hand. The next day, I woke up to my bed soaked through with sweat, my body weak with burning fever. And the day after that, and the day after that. I do not remember anything else. I could eat only the Jell-O I had in the fridge, my throat was so sore. My body ached and shivered. By the fourth day of my illness, a Friday, my boss called.

"Look, you'd better come in by Monday, because it's not looking good for you. You know you don't get paid for sick days, right?"

He hung up on me. I mustered the strength to call my mother. An appointment at the walk-in clinic was twenty-five dollars. I asked Mom for this amount, and a bit extra for a Z-Pak, if she could.

"I can't. Dad would see the money coming out of the account. Don't you have insurance?"

I did not. I asked if she could use her client allowance so that Dad wouldn't see. She said she could not. Told me to drink water and get some sleep, she had to go, clients to see, businesses to sign up for loans and accounts. My mother, perhaps neglected herself by her mother, never really learned the simple basics of care. I sweated through the rest of the weekend, stomach empty. Straggled into the office the next Monday.

"Oh shit, you came in! We were about to replace you," the owner said. He looked me up and down. "Wow. You must have actually been sick."

I had lost about ten pounds in one week: my already thin frame, at five feet four inches, was down to less than one hundred pounds. My clothes sagged from my bones; my cheeks sank into my teeth. Eliza offered to do most of my work for me that day. I sat next to her, dizzy and weak, sipping the miso soup she had bought for me.

Increase the pan's heat to medium-high. Fry the slices of Spam, letting them lie flat and become browned on one side.

Just before my twenty-sixth birthday, around the time of President Obama's first inauguration, I moved out of my apartment. I had found my landlord's bootprints in my apartment one evening after work, along with a raised toilet seat and a small hole drilled into my bedroom wall. I was afraid of him and did not want to provoke him. He had moved into the basement of the building, had taken to wearing combat fatigues, and seemed to know my comings and goings. I made up a family emergency to break the lease as soon as I found a new place, a tiny studio in Manhattan's Yorkville, in an old tenement building on East Eighty-Fifth Street and First Avenue. It cost $200 more a month, but at least I felt safer. The new landlord, a kind older woman who had retired to Long Island, ran a criminal background check, but I was willing to take this risk. One of the perks of being an undocumented immigrant is that your crime is that of invisibility.

"Manhattan, huh? Our girl's moving up! How are you going to make rent on the new place, girl?" Leandro, an office friend, asked. "You don't exactly make one-and-a-half times rent."

How do you become good at Photoshop? By using it. My father only had a Xerox machine, scissors, and glue to doctor our Social Security card photocopies a decade and a half before. A bootlegged copy of Photoshop and a few clicks with a mouse on scans of my bank statements was much easier. But after signing the lease for the new place, forging my mother's signature as my guarantor, and paying the first and last month's rent plus deposit, I had no money left to actually move my belongings.

I had no choice but to make another dreaded phone call.

"So now that you've got our help," Dad said, standing in the middle of my small apartment, "how are you going to pay us back?"

My parents had paid $200 for two movers and a van. The way Dad saw it, this generosity negated the $100,000 or so Dad had pocketed for my "college fund." I didn't call them again after that.

Flip the slices of Spam over. Let the other side become browned and crisp at the edges too.

The loan shark firm fired me a few months later. The next two years were a flurry of job changes, one precarious position after the next. In the year of "Empire State of Mind" blaring out of bars, cars, clubs, and headphones— a dislocating kind of optimism as the recession raged, an enforcement of the capitalist myth under which we all labor—I scraped jobs and money together. I worked as: an administrative assistant for a construction firm (fired for general incompetence); a sales assistant for a company that leased advertising space on buses, phone booths, and the subway (fired for sharing salaries in hopes of collective bargaining); a real estate rental agency receptionist, then junior agent (fired for failing to sign up a single rental in three months, because I couldn't lie to prospective tenants); an operations assistant at yet another credit card processing loan shark firm (fired for refusing to sleep with the boss).

In 2010, I turned twenty-seven. The engkanto of my depression returned, took over my mind and heart. Perhaps it knew that I was weak, tired, and hungry. Saw an opportunity to feast on my spirit.

"You can't just cancel your birthday dinner," my sister said, sitting down at the edge of my bed. She was twenty-one, about to finish her bachelor's degree at Brooklyn College.

We spent that evening in my studio apartment, her big eyes brimming with concern while I laughed and cried. Twenty-seven, with nothing to show for myself. With each new job, the promise of the mythology of the American Dream drifted further away from me.

After getting fired from that second credit card processing firm, bank account emptied, unable to pay rent, I moved out of my studio apartment in the heat of July 2010. I crashed with Eliza in Kensington, Brooklyn, where she lived in an attic-level apartment in her grandmother's house. I gave her all of my furniture and electronics for free as a thank-you and as payment. We spent that summer moneyless and carefree, days spent on Brighton Beach, boiled eggs for lunch. I pretended to feel as calm and relaxed as she seemed to be. Eliza was Brooklyn Italian American, and she was working-class, like me; unlike me, she had family, love, and citizenship. I secretly envied her.

I soon found another job off Craigslist: a decent one, with a higher salary than anything I'd ever been offered, along with five paid sick days, two weeks of paid time off, and full health and dental insurance. I had no idea what a prime brokerage for hedge funds was, but it appeared to involve actual hedge funds. Whatever those were. As long as some of the funds from these hedge funds went to me, my bills, my groceries, and my college savings, it didn't really matter to me what they did. My job was to answer phones, book appointments, manage calendars, order office supplies, pay vendors' bills, and generate operational reports at the end of each week.

"Do you know whose money backs all of this?" said one of my colleagues on my first day. I peered down the high-rise to State Street and the Statue of Liberty, just beyond.

"No," I said, making a mental note to visit the statue someday. The Statue of Limitations, as Eliza fondly called it.

"Steve Cohen," my colleague said reverently. He was a recruit from Goldman Sachs, like the rest of them.

I made sounds as if I knew who this man was, tried to not think about how I, too, was now serving the same gods, feeding the same beast. It would be years later, after leaving America and watching the news of Cohen's settlement with the SEC, after seeing *Billions*, a TV show loosely based upon him, that I would come to understand his importance. None of this mattered to me at the time: not the prime brokerage's exceptional clients, not my colleagues' educational and employment pedigrees, not the billionaire whose wealth trickled down to me. I cared only about my own survival. It was all going well: after my first year, I received a pay increase and a bonus, more than I had ever been paid in my entire life.

I had enough to pay for a semester as a part-time undergraduate student at Fordham, where I was accepted to begin in September 2011, ten years after my freshman attempt in Kentucky. I began to eat better. I could afford fruits and vegetables, had the time and energy to cook and clean up afterward. I joined Asphalt Green, on East 92nd Street, and swam for two hours every day. Went to the doctor for physicals using my insurance. I had a wisdom tooth removed.

I began to plan for the future: graduation with a bachelor's degree in five years, maybe a move up the ladder at this job. Caught up in the American mythological delusion of merit and hard work, of freedom through work.

One morning, while working on spreadsheets of reports, a man holding a bike helmet and a large canvas bag appeared by my desk.

"Jill Damatac?"

"Yes?"

He thrust an envelope at my face. "You've been served."

Remove the browned slices of Spam from the pan; lay flat on a paper-toweled plate. Let the grease absorb.

The debt amounted to $6,500 for one credit card and $8,700 for another.

"We've been trying to find you for some time, Miss Damatac," said the sheriff's officer on the phone. He was tasked with either setting up my wage garnishments, or sending me to court, or to prison, or all three.

"This isn't my debt, sir."

"They're all under your name and social: 18 Berry Lane. Cards opened in 2008 and 2009, respectively."

"I haven't lived there since 2007. September 2007. My parents' house."

"Someone at the address gave us your new address, and it was easy to find you from there."

Dad had begun opening credit cards using my name, date of birth, and social security number sometime around 2003. *To help you establish a credit history, so you can have a mortgage someday,* he had said. And now here he was, overspending and destroying my credit score. I cooperated with the sheriff's officer, and gave them permission to contact my employer to set up monthly garnishments from my salary.

I made up a reason for the garnishments, told my firm's compliance officer that it was an abusive ex-boyfriend. I protected my parents even as they continued to abuse me. I nearly cried with relief when the compliance officer spoke words of compassion, rather than judgment. I felt relief that I would get to keep my job, even if it meant having to pay off the debts my father had incurred in my name.

Fry the eggs to the style preferred. Lay on the paper-toweled plate with the Spam.

Around the time I began at Fordham—a twenty-eight-year-old freshman—so did the arrival of protesters around the streets where I worked. They gathered in larger and larger groups, sat on the ground, milling around with signs and drums, shouting, singing, taunting mounted police on horses. Zuccotti Park began to fill. So did parts of Battery Park. Occupy Wall Street.

For the first time in years, I began to pay attention to the news. Saw, for the first time, that there were white people like me: fed up with believing in the American Dream, fed up with still being in debt with no way out, fed up with the lack of future. I looked down from my office desk, seventeen floors down to State Street, where they gathered. Heard the bass drums beating in unison. Felt the ground rumble as I walked past on the street, an undocumented immigrant in disguise as a Wall Street employee. Clutched my lunch, which I could finally afford.

The gods' beast, with nothing left to eat in the colonies and the territories, had turned its appetite towards the white American working and middle classes. Mortgages, CDOs, debt packaged as products, as commodities to trade. And now that the suffering had reached their comfortable suburban doorsteps, these Americans had had enough. They, too, had been forced to swallow Spam, to eat junk and believe that it was a luxury. Believe that it was good for them.

During happy hours, white friends expressed solidarity, and a couple of them—an artist, a writer, both of whom lived in Williamsburg, their rent covered by their parents—joined the protests, their signs wielding quotes from Enlightenment philosophers and Karl Marx. I could never join them, could never risk arrest and deportation. Could never afford to risk losing my job, not when I was so close to paying off the debts my father had incurred in my name. My brown and Black friends felt the same.

"Where was all this energy when we were the only ones catching it?" one of them said to me. I stayed silent. Because that is what one must do as an undocumented immigrant. Crowds of white people never thronged the streets and risked their bodies to save me. To save my family.

When Mayor Bloomberg raided the encampments at Zuccotti Park, I knew two things: first, that I had made the right decision to stay hidden, undeported, up on the seventeenth floor, crunching spreadsheets, paying my bills; and second, that I had to leave finance. Had to stop helping to feed the beast, even if all I did was answer the phones and update reports.

By month's end, I had found a new job and gave my notice, effective immediately. It was still at the peripheries of finance—a financial industry media and events company—but it was further away from the belly of the beast. I was terrified to leave, terrified of my $30,000 annual salary reduction, plus another loss of $10,000 in bonuses.

"A lifestyle writer, huh?" said a friend. "What do you know about luxury lifestyle?"

"Me?" I laughed. "Tons! I can write about how to stretch forty dollars into a two-week grocery budget. I can write about thirty ways to cook Spam. I can write about how to handwash your own laundry in a tiny studio apartment bathroom. 'The Top 5 Gallery Openings to Check Out for Free Food (Dinner).' Stuff like that."

I dropped out of Fordham later that year, no longer able to afford tuition after paying off some of Dad's credit card debts opened under my name. An assistant dean emailed to ask why. Tired of lying, I wrote:

"As an undocumented immigrant, I do not qualify for any aid, scholarships, grants, or loans. I have been paying out of my own pocket, but due to a recent job change, can no longer afford to do so."

I never heard back from that assistant dean.

Serve the plateful of Spam and eggs at the dining table. Lay the sinan-gag rice alongside in a big bowl. Put out the atchara, banana ketchup, Pinakurat, and patis. Pour coffee, Tang, and water into their cups and glasses. Eat family style.

I sit down at my dining table, a hot plate of Spamsilog warming my face. I slash some Sriracha sauce on top of the eggs, dash some Pinakurat vinegar over the Spam. I retch a little at the salty, cloying, animal-greasy richness of the Spam. My body, it seems, now knows what it is and isn't being fed. Can recognize the slickness of mythology and waste when it touches the tongue, wants to refuse to swallow its lies. Still, I scrape another spoonful together. A part of me still loves it, wants to love it. Slowly, spoonful by spoonful, I finish my plateful of Spamsilog. Wishing to be a part of the United States, a place that never wanted me, is a bit like eating Spam. I am revolted by it, unnerved by it, have no idea what is truly in it, in its past or future. But I love it, nevertheless. Even if someday, it might kill me.

7

Adobong Manok
(Chicken Adobo)

2009–2012

SERVES 2

2 heads garlic

2- to 3-inch-long thick piece ginger

6 bone-in, skin-on chicken thighs

3 cups Filipino soy sauce

2 cups Filipino cane, coconut, or rice vinegar

1 cup Filipino spiced vinegar (or use 3 cups of the above vinegar
    if preferred)

1 tablespoon black peppercorns

2 or 3 fresh bay leaves

2 tablespoons vegetable oil

1/2 cup brown sugar

1 cup coconut milk, to finish

For the mango salad, tossed:

2 green mangoes, seeded and cut into 1/2-inch cubes

2 salad tomatoes, cut into 1/2-inch cubes

1 red onion, diced

Filipino patis and vinegar, to taste

Chopped fresh cilantro (optional)

At the table:

Steamed jasmine rice or garlic sinangag rice

The sauce of soy and vinegar is swirling, dark, and tangy, in the cast-iron pot. The timer blares; I clank the lid down. Dashing to the back garden, I grab the tongs, yank the slightly black-charred chicken drumsticks and thighs off the grill. The smoky, pungent smell of it fills my nose and throat. Sets my mouth watering. I am trying something new in this batch of adobo, an added touch that I've been thinking about for years: halfway through the cooking process, I am charcoal-grilling the chicken for the adobo. I am certain that many a tita or a tito has done this to great success. I hope I don't mess it up. *Adobo is so basic*, a Filipino friend once said to me. Easy for them to say. They've never had to hide.

Finely mince 1 head of garlic. Peel the ginger and cut it into thin slices or matchsticks.

Adobo is a Spanish word for a native Filipino dish. For an indigenous method of cooking that long predates the arrival of ships bearing men who would erase the very name of that dish. There are many versions, but the one that the world knows best is simple: meat, or fish, or vegetables cooked long, over low temperatures, in soy, vinegar, peppercorns, and garlic, a sauce boiled down to its essence. A method of cooking and preservation all at once, much like what the French call confit. The salt and vinegar inhibits rot, a useful method in a time long before refrigeration, long before the Americans came and called our cooking space the dirty kitchen. There are versions of adobo with ginger, brown sugar, chilies, coconut milk, and bay leaves, all of which I like to add. Some regional versions involve turmeric. Some use patis or sea salt instead of soy. The vinegar is always there.

Some say that adobo is the gateway drug to Filipino cuisine. Salty, sweet, tangy, and garlicky, it is spooned over hot white rice, perhaps with a helping of mango-tomato-red-onion salad on the side. It delivers salt, fat, acid, and gentle heat (if one uses a bit of Pinakurat in the vinegar) in one comforting spoonful, plus a hint of caramelized sugar, in versions like mine. There is a déjà vu element to adobo, as if you have had it before, in a past life, when you were loved and well fed. It is the easiest way for us to assimilate into an America and a world that has long seen us only for the value of our labor. For the value of our care, and our ability to care.

I do not know of more than a few of us whose nose and stomach do not respond, Pavlovian and Proustian all at once, to the scent of slow-simmering equal parts soy sauce, cane vinegar, and fresh garlic. Adobo is comfort, ease, familiarity. Adobo is love and home, or the closest thing I have to it. Adobo is what I cook when I want newcomers to my life who are not Filipino to understand a small corner of our cuisine. To want more of our food. To accept me, so that I may accept myself. Perhaps to love me, even. I have been taught for so long that love and acceptance are earned, rather than a given; that they are conditional, based upon assimilation, upon obedience. That to be myself is to be punished, both at home and out in the world. Sometimes, even in this emergent, post-undocumented life, I fear that the love and acceptance of those who are not Filipino is the only way I can love myself. I know that I am not alone in this.

In our mythology, Lakapati is the deity of fertility, crops, and agriculture. Lakapati, whose name means "giver of food," is neither a she nor a he, but a siya: they/them, in English. They are one of Bathala's children and are the foremost of our rice gods. Known to be kind, generous, and loving, Lakapati gave us the gift of agriculture. Their father may have created the world, but Lakapati, through their love, showed us how to sustain ourselves. To sustain each other. During full moons, those who wish to grow crops or to start a family make offerings to Lakapati. They put out plates of rice just after dusk, perhaps small bundles of herbs or plants alongside. At harvest, workers in fields would tie small carved figurines of Lakapati to their waists, perhaps slip one into a pocket, so that the crops may grow tall and abundant, safe from disease or disaster. Unlike me, they understood that to eat our food was to be blessed.

The first time I tried to cook adobo, it was 2009, that recession year of job change after job change, constantly fired from every entry-level position I flung myself into. It was also another year of one romantic failure after another. I had a penchant for potential partners who seemed to be too good for me. I now know that they were not good enough at all.

"Are you still single, anak?" a great-aunt asked me once.

My father's aunties, the sisters of my Lola Rosing, had taken to stopping by my apartment every few weekends. I was the lost child of the family. Maybe they saw something in me of themselves, Filipina women who had been young, single, and broke in New York City and Boston, where, in the 1950s and 1960s, they studied on American government programs as master's students at places like Columbia or Harvard. They would insist on whisking me away with them to Atlantic City, where one of them, if not all of them, had free suite perks in more than a few casinos as regulars. These great-aunties earned their wealth over the decades, giving themselves over to the needs of Americans. They worked as schoolteachers and health care workers, jobs sanctioned by our governments, their bodies traded as gross national product. In those years, Filipinos migrating to the US could apply for work visas only in limited sectors, such as health care, education, and domestic labor; meanwhile, workers from other countries, often European, were allowed to apply for work visas in almost any sector.

In the casino hotels where we stayed, my great-aunties would pinch my skin and bones, insist that I eat. Have another helping from the all-you-can-eat buffet. I would comply, pile my plate high with ribs and crab legs, thankful to have something other than air and coffee in my stomach.

"I don't know if I can do relationships, Auntie," I said, cracking a crab leg open. I meant it. I had barely survived trying to end my own life. Had barely survived Tita Christy's husband. I could barely take care of myself, let alone a relationship. How could I know how to care for someone else, having never really been cared for myself?

"Still single! When will you get married?" said another great-aunt.

"Stop that!" said another, the second-oldest after my grandmother. "The girl isn't even thirty yet. She has plenty of time."

"I hope you've gotten rid of that playboy," said another great-auntie. "Unless he's an American citizen!"

The great-aunties dissolved into laughter louder than my protests of *I don't care about that* and *I would never marry for papers*. The great-aunties had known for years that my family and I were undocumented.

"Show them the picture of that girl he was seeing behind your back," said one tita.

"Naku, she showed us na! The rich white girl with the recessed chin, big teeth, and lazy eye? She is no competition!"

"We're not competing, Auntie. He was lying to us both. And she's beautiful."

The aunties only knew about the men; besides, no real relationship ever really blossomed with the women: the closest I ever got was with a woman who refused to so much as hold my hand in public, in the middle of New York City. I was never convinced that anyone I was involved with was the problem, anyway. I—the undocumented fraud, the pretender propped up by an elaborate scaffolding of lies—was the problem in all of my romances. I was never really all the way in. I always held back, and they all knew it.

Before all of them was Dean, the one my great-aunties called "the playboy." He was the first person to break my heart, and the last. We seemed fated, from the fifth grade onward, to reject each other, then to want to try again, and again. He came from a traditionally conservative family, politicians and landowners with farms and tenants. There were roads in the Pennsylvania county we grew up in named after his relatives. Like many who have inherited their wealth, they saw themselves as working class, middle class at most, until it came to selecting a partner. With Dean, there always seemed to be someone new waiting to replace me, someone with a pedigree, an education, family wealth. Dean did not know—and I swore that he would never know—that I was undocumented, uneducated, and broke. He already found it strange that I did not drive, fly, or have a career path. In the end, we knew that we were too far apart. He was closed off and judgmental of difference, too concerned with what his social circle thought of him to ever be available enough for the truth about me. I was too afraid, insecure, and distrustful.

"We're over, Auntie," I said.

"Did he even eat Filipino food?" one of them asked. Back then, it seemed like a silly and irrelevant question. I understand it now.

"I don't have time for a love life, Tita."

Place the chicken thighs and drumsticks in a large mixing bowl. Fill with equal parts soy and vinegar, plus the minced garlic.

Lakapati did not have the time for love either. They spent most days and nights tending to humanity, bringing fields to abundant life, giving children to families. Their other days were occupied by repair and revitalization: healing lands torn by earthquakes, farms drowned by floods, orchards felled by typhoons. They had many suitors and admirers, were beloved by all. Still, Lakapati was not to be distracted. They remained devoted only to humanity, to the endless task of feeding and sustaining us.

I remained devoted to learning how to feed and sustain myself. The first time I made adobo, I had just moved from the apartment with the creepy landlord, in the Bronx, to the much smaller and more expensive studio on the Upper East Side. It cost more than two-thirds of my monthly salary, leaving me with less than $400 each month for utilities, food, and subway fare. My small circle of friends decided that my new place was the perfect spot for our next potluck. None of them knew that I was undocumented, and just like Dean, they would never find out. My closest friends were Asian American—of Filipino, Korean, Malaysian, Singaporean, Chinese, Thai, and Indian descent—but that was all we had in common. They were good girls, the kind who came to New York and made it. They were raised in aspirational model minority families, American, Canadian, British, Australian citizens. They were comfortable, college-educated, and assimilated, a far cry from my own family and our secret shames. I was terrified of losing these friends, should they find out the truth about me.

"Can you make adobo, Jilly? Ligaya Mishan wrote about it in the Times *and it sounds so good!"* Kelly said in our group chat.

"Sure thing," I had written back. *"Easy peasy."*

In truth, I had never made adobo. I did not know how. Having distanced myself from anything Filipino as a form of survival, I did not cook or eat our food. Partly out of shame, but also out of pain. Out of fear of remembering who I was and couldn't be, not if I wanted to pass as American, not if I wanted to be safe and loved. Alone in New York City, I wandered streets to go home, shadowing in and out of depression, afraid of who I was, afraid of what I was becoming. I made myself act as American as possible: watched football, attended Yankees games, pretended to care about which cheeseburger was the best in town. I celebrated the Fourth of July by throwing perfectly spiraled footballs in Central Park, a Budweiser at my feet. I took the day off like everyone else for Labor Day, pretended with my white colleagues, at every MLK Day, that America was post-race. Pretended that I had forgotten how to speak Tagalog. Pretended that I was born here. I boiled down what *American* looked, acted, and sounded like to its essence, and performed it, every day.

But I had no idea who I was, really, and after seventeen years of hiding, I had no idea what it was like to cook Filipino cuisine, to understand it without a recipe, to know it by heart. Still, if I made this adobo as my friends had requested, and they liked it, then perhaps it meant that there was a chance that they might like me, the actual me. That this actual me could be a little closer to them. Unalone, unafraid of life. American and free.

Let the chicken marinate in the soy, garlic, and vinegar, covered, for 2 to 12 hours in the refrigerator.

To make adobo for my friends, I bought the cheapest cuts of boneless chicken breast and the smallest bottles of grocery store–brand soy and Heinz vinegar. Without care, I cubed the chicken breast, fished out two dry bay leaves and the small jars of garlic powder and ginger powder from my meager pantry. I hadn't bought fresh garlic or ginger in years. Couldn't afford to. I tossed everything into a pot, dashed in a teaspoon of ground pepper, poured from the jar I'd bought two years before and hardly used. I let it simmer for about two hours, then forgot about it while I got dressed. How hard could it be? This has always been the simplest dish, right?

Later in the evening, my friends gathered in my three-hundred-square-foot studio. There were homemade pork dumplings from Sam, sesame noodles from Nora, Kelly with her mother's kimchi, Kelly's boyfriend with steamed white rice. We served each other bits of our cooking on scratched IKEA plates.

"The adobo smells amazing!" Kelly said.

We ate, didn't speak for a minute. I poked at the chicken adobo, put a cube of chicken breast and some sauce on my spoonful of rice. My tongue rolled the food around, recoiled in my throat in horror. Between my teeth, the meat was hard, dry, stringy, with no flavor other than that of rice and a salty recollection of sauce. Kelly cleared her throat.

"So, Jilly," she said, gingerly, swallowing with a wince. "Um. Is this beef?"

Oh god. "Uh. It's terrible, isn't it?" I said, baring embarrassed teeth. The five of us broke into raucous laughter.

"Wait, what is it, though?" Sam asked, poking at a cube with her fork, still chewing the same bite, trying to not choke on her giggles.

"Boneless chicken breast," I admitted, between laughing gulps of air, ducking my head.

"Boneless? Chicken breast? Cooked for two hours?" Kelly shrieked.

"Two and a half!" I shrieked back. More of our laughter.

I opened another bottle of Trader Joe's Two-Buck Chuck as an apology, in relief. I had spent the entire week worried about my friends, worried that they would find Filipino cuisine, and therefore me, inferior. It turned out that they didn't care if the cooking was good or bad. They did not expect the best cooking, or even good cooking. They understood, in a way that would take me years more, in a way that their relative privilege allowed them to understand, that we did not have to try so hard. That we were not obligated to be ambassadors of our cuisine. We were not publicists for our culture, mascots for our heritage, or spokespersons for our pain. Perhaps they did actually like me for myself. Perhaps it was enough that I had tried to cook something.

Smash the other head of garlic. Add the smashed garlic, peppercorns, and bay leaves to a large preheated pot.

So 2009 turned into 2010, my eighteenth year of hiding in America. I turned twenty-seven. A dinner was planned, just my closest friends, my sister, and me. Reservations made at a favorite Thai place just north of Hell's Kitchen.

"Hi! Ready?" my sister said, perky at my front door, already a bit buzzed in the way all twenty-one-year-olds in New York were buzzed on Friday nights. She had traveled in from Brooklyn, where she was finishing her senior year as a full-scholarship Honors student at CUNY Brooklyn College.

"No, not ready," I said. I collapsed in her arms in tears.

I canceled dinner by text. By then, perhaps tired of my unpredictable ups and downs, perhaps aware that I was not quite like them, none of my friends were too bothered. I spent the rest of that birthday in my apartment with my sister. We watched *Pride and Prejudice*, paused for bouts of crying.

"I'm twenty-seven," I sobbed. "I can't keep doing this. What's going to happen to me?"

"I don't know," she said. "I'm sorry." Her big eyes sad and sympathetic.

"I'm alone," I continued. "I'm alone and I'm a fucking loser."

"No," she said, her arms around me. "You're doing your best."

"What if this is it? For the rest of my life?"

Sauté the garlic, bay leaves, and peppercorns in 1 tablespoon of the vegetable oil.

When Mapulon, the god of the seasons, first noticed Lakapati, he was taken with their devotion to humanity, their kindness and generosity. He tried to get to know them, started by trying to befriend them. But Lakapati was not to be distracted. They kept their distance. Too busy. Too many people to help, crops to bless, disasters to right. Did Mapulon wonder why Lakapati was so aloof, so hard to get? They were a deity, after all—all-powerful, all-present. Surely, Lakapati could handle love, along with everything else. But Mapulon, among other good and decent traits, was also kind, patient, and understanding. He must have known that Lakapati gave all of themselves out of a deep, unspoken need to be loved. If not by their father, Bathala, then by others. It must have been with this realization that Mapulon decided to wait. He would wait forever, if needed, until Lakapati was ready.

The way I make adobo has evolved over the years, and continues to evolve, enfolding my changing tastes, experiences, and the places where I have lived. Some of it is learned from other Filipinos, some are happy accidents, or approximations of what I think the very first adobos might have been like, cooked over a fire or in a Filipino-Spanish horno, incorporating woodsmoke and char. To me, much of being Filipino, whether at home or on other lands, is a negotiation. An exchange, a bargain, a compromise. We give so that we can feed our loved ones while having just enough to survive ourselves. In the hopes of being accepted, of contributing enough to be seen, Filipinos are taught to surrender their bodies to work, to giving, teaching, caring. Our total surrender in exchange for mere tolerance, so that America may feel secure enough to be free. In the 1930s, in the hope that our American colonizers might embrace us as a state, as more than a territory, the Philippines sent people like my great-aunts to the US to be trained, educated as workers, their intelligence and skill used within the empire rather than back home, where there were no opportunities made for them. The Manongs were brought over to work on farms in California, on sugar plantations in Hawaii, in canneries in Alaska, prevented by law from owning land of their own, or marrying white women, or having children of their own. Some Filipinos saw this sacrifice as necessary. Felt that we, as an American colony, were lucky to not be included in the Immigration Act of 1924, which barred our Chinese siblings from entry. Felt that, rather than be liberated, the Philippines needed to prove itself as worthy of the acceptance of the United States. Perhaps we saw our bodies as gayuma, to be swallowed by the empire so that we may be accepted. Loved.

I learned about gayuma from my mother.

"Gayuma," my mother said recently, "is a love potion. It's made to make someone fall in love. They put a secret spell on it, and you give it to someone to eat or put it in their food, and that person falls in love with you."

Gayuma is an ancient manggagamod's concoction of enchantment. It is still made today, both by charlatans and by real healers. It is sold on the streets of Manila as a curiosity, as souvenir. If you find the right vendor, the kind who sells her wares down quieter alleys, you just may pick up a vial of the real thing.

I wonder if the power of a gayuma is not necessarily in the herbs or other ingredients, or the spell, or the shamanic abilities of the manggagamod who makes it. Perhaps it isn't necessarily meant to be chewed, swallowed, roiled in the stomach's acids, absorbed into blood. Perhaps the secret power, the magical spell, is in the intention behind it. Perhaps the gayuma was never what the intended subject of the love spell swallowed down their throat. It was always the effort put into it by the lovelorn spell-caster.

I think—and may my ancestors correct me if I am wrong—that gayuma is actually nothing more than an act of giving, an act driven by the desire to be loved. Whether the gayuma is in the form of secret herbs in a bottle, or OFWs on a plane bound for care homes and hospitals, or a balikbayan box, or a child who only wants her parents' love, or adobo in a pot, what defines it most is the deepest longing to belong. The secret spell echoes from each beat of the heart's loneliest caves.

For the commonwealth-era Filipinos in the United States, the search for love could not be helped by any gayuma. It could often end in death. White men, angry at the prospect of brown Filipinos running off with "their" women, bombed Filipino homes, shelters, and clubs. Set fire to their places of work and refuge. Hung them from trees—the white American man's favorite pastime. And when they were allowed to live, as was the case for Filipino women who dared to fall in love with white men, it resulted in prejudice. Exclusion. Disavowal. Abandonment. It did not matter how hard they worked, or how little they were paid for that work. It did not matter how well educated they were, or how well they assimilated, tongue, body, and all. It did not matter how much America was in their hearts. Filipinos were not loved by the United States in return.

When the garlic is golden, pour the marinade—soy, vinegar, and garlic—into another large pot. Add the marinated chicken in last, with tongs.

I did not make adobo again for two years. Any manggagamod worth her salt would have told me to make adobo sooner, rather than later. To cook adobo for a lover is to make them fall in love with you, a more surefire recipe than the Americans' Engagement Roast Chicken. Still, I resisted. This avoidance was, as always, out of fear and shame.

Exactly one month after my twenty-seventh birthday, I met Steven by accident. I was out with Kelly and Sam, forced to go out because, according to Kelly, I had "holed up in that apartment for the past four weekends." It was a Saturday night in a Lower East Side speakeasy called the Back Room, and I had just enough money for one drink and a cab to go straight back home to my reruns and ready-made pizza. I had ducked into my beer when he approached and introduced himself to our circle. A tall, brown-haired, shyly confident British man in a red-and-green collared rugby shirt, accompanied by his equally tall, brown-haired, less-shy-and-more-confident British friend. The one in the rugby shirt had a smile that transformed him, and me. As an introduction, he asked our group of friends where the back room was.

"Where is the 'back room'? Really?" I rolled my eyes.

"No, I really do want to know," he said, taken aback by me, the small, angry, scowling person slouched in a corner.

"Sure. I bet it works on everyone."

He raised his eyebrows. "Let's start over, shall we? Hi, I'm Steven. What's your name?"

He paid attention only to me after that. Talked only to me in that calm, gentle, yet assured way that I now recognize is his alone. We stayed out all night that first night, till closing time at 4 a.m., talking only to each other while our friends danced and sang, downed shots and dragged us to the next place. He called the next day, insisted on dinner the night after that, and the night after that. We saw each other almost every day, a need that we recognized in each other.

"So he wants to see you every day, you talk for hours, and most of the time you cook in your apartment, visit museums, or go for walks?" said Ashley, one of the two friends I had who knew I was queer. "And he isn't a woman?"

"Nope," I said, laughing.

It was as if he and I were both under a spell: something cast by some other engkanto or, perhaps, a druidic awen from his own islands. Perhaps an engkanto and an awen, working together. He ran across Central Park every day after work to see me, called me his girlfriend after two weeks. He cooked for me: shepherd's pie, Yorkshire puddings. His dad's rhubarb crumble.

"This," he had said with a flourish one Sunday night, "is what's known as toad-in-the-hole."

"Wow. Did you spear the sausages with rosemary?" This toad-in-the-hole was, despite the name, delicious.

"I did," he said, proud of himself. "I also caramelized the onions in the gravy. Now, what are you going to cook for me?"

We soon exchanged I love yous, but I still could not tell him the truth. No, I couldn't make adobo for this man, I thought. It wouldn't be right to cook it for him. Not without being honest about who I really was, so that he can make the choice freely to stay or to go. The real me, not the version of me that pretended to work in finance and lied about having a college degree and parents who loved me. But there was risk in this, in sharing the truth about myself as gayuma. What if he decided to leave? What if he decided to go back to England, where he was due to return in a few months, at the end of his H-1B visa? Or to Hong Kong, where a colleague had invited him to transfer? If I told him about me, emerged from hiding, my safety would be at risk. No, there would be no adobo for Steven just yet. I took my turn cooking anything else, saving up for weeks each time: linguine with clams. Slow-roasted pork tenderloin with homemade applesauce. Seared medium-rare rib eyes with olive oil mashed potatoes. He was not yet worth the effort or the risk of cooking the real food that I loved.

That first summer together in 2010 was one of both romance and instability. I still remember his phone call that August afternoon, the way it stopped time, and my heart. I was between jobs, and it was late summer in Brooklyn.

"So, Jilly," he had said, a hesitation trailing after his voice. "I have some news. For next month."

Here comes the bad news, I thought. He was about to tell me that he wouldn't be renewing his H-1B visa. Or that his work was taking him back to London. I was right not to tell him anything.

"I know, it's September soon. When is work sending you back to London?" Goodbye, brief love.

"Oh, ah, no, they're not doing that. I've actually just requested to renew my visa. You know, stay for another three years."

"Really?" I stood up.

"Jill. I'm not bloody leaving New York when I've finally found someone, am I?"

He left for London two weeks later, to renew his visa at the US consulate there. September began to blow in from the Atlantic. We spoke every day, texted, emailed. Spoke on Skype every two days. I braced myself for a visa rejection, for a phone call letting me know that he wouldn't be coming back. All of my experience with the US immigration system taught me about rejection, separation, and heartbreak. Why should this be any different?

One afternoon in October, he texted a blurry photo of his new US visa, issued at the embassy in London. Three more years, just like that. A mere three-week wait. He had just booked his flight from Heathrow to JFK. On the night before Halloween, he buzzed at my apartment door, fresh from his flight.

"Oh my god," he said, dropping his duffel bag on the ground. His hands cradled my face, his face crumpling. "Oh my god, finally."

There, in the cramped entry hall of my apartment building, his six-foot-four frame folded around me. His tears soaked into my hair, wet my cheeks.

I thought of how Papa hadn't cried like this when he saw us for the first time in almost three years. Something in me began to understand time, the way it can either destroy or strengthen love.

Let the chicken simmer, on medium-low heat, in the adobo marinade. Cover with a heavy lid.

We ate paper-thin New York pizza—the kind you bless with chili flakes, garlic powder, and Parmesan—while curled up in front of the TV.

"So now, you're stuck with me for at least three more years," he said, a proud smile on his face. I remember marveling, to myself, at how easy it was to fall in love like this. How it had never been that easy before. I also marveled at how easy it was for him to get a work visa, felt overjoyed to have him here with me for three more years, should our relationship last that long (and relationships with me never lasted that long). Something else ached in me that night, an awareness of the distance between this optimistic joy and the terrified sadness that always threatened to pull me under, deep into myself. This man was staying in America for three more years because of me, an undocumented immigrant who would never have his privileges. An undocumented immigrant who might be a waste of his time or the ruin of his life. I had to say it.

"I have something to tell you," I said.

As the adobo simmers in the pot, preheat the oven broiler to medium or low.

An hour later, he was still there, on my couch, listening, in tears again. This stoic, reserved, gentle British man, often so quick with a joke.

"Are you OK?" I asked, holding his hand. I was scared. He could change his mind now that he knew absolutely everything: my family, our undocumented status, my father's abuse, my mother's enabling of his abuse. My lack of education, being raised in struggle, the immense debts my father had put me in. That I had hidden all of this from him until now. Steven could still decide to spend the next three years in New York finding someone worthy. Someone better. Someone legal.

"I should ask you the same thing," he said, hand squeezing back.

"So." I swallowed. Sat up, a little. "Is all of that . . . OK for you to know?"

"Jill," he said, nose red, eyes shining. "You're a miracle."

He repeated this three times, forehead touching mine. *You're a miracle. A bloody miracle.*

"You're not dumping me?"

"Don't be an idiot," he said, squashing my face into his chest.

We moved in together six months later, one year into our relationship. A last-minute steal, a rent-stabilized one-bedroom apartment in a brownstone on West Eighty-First Street, between Amsterdam and Columbus. It was eight hundred square feet, with soaring twelve-foot ceilings, an alcove space for a semi-second bedroom, a galley kitchen, and a brick fireplace. Steven decided, no questions asked, that I would pay only a third of the rent and utilities and half of the groceries. Said that he made much more than I did. That I had been through enough.

"Save up for school, my love," he said. "Or for our house, someday."

A house? I looked at him like he was crazy.

When bill collectors and court summonses arrived via phone, mail, and served papers—all of the debts my father made using my name and Social Security number, credit cards addressed to their house, where I had not lived for years—Steven paid them all off without telling me, taking the letters and papers from my hiding place in the alcove. The total came to over $10,000. When I found out, I yelled at him first, mostly out of humiliation and misplaced anger, and then curled up into a ball in his arms, in tears and shame.

"Don't you get it, Jilly?" he said. "It's you and me now. You don't need to owe them anything anymore. OK?"

"OK."

"Now, let's figure out how to freeze your Social Security number so they can't do this again."

It still all felt like a hallucination. I did not know how to accept love that seemed to be so unconditional. I did not know that I was worthy of this kind of acceptance, this understanding, this care and desire to keep me, and to be kept by me. My spirit began to feel the way my body had when I had started to eat again. After years of poverty-induced food deprivation, my skin, my flesh, my way of breathing changed. In the same way, after a lifetime of being unloved no matter how I tried to be good, to be loved by someone the way Steven did—without judgment or question—made me feel less imprisoned. More human, seen, and acknowledged. Open, moving, strong. Free, despite being trapped in the US. Being undocumented and unloved by a country mattered a little less now that I had someone—just one person—who loved me.

Steven, as it turned out, had his own form of gayuma: understanding, compassion, and care.

Still, I had trouble sleeping at night, even with his soft trusting snores next to me, long legs wandering over to my side of the bed, feet asking to be warmed next to mine. I struggled to sleep all the way through the night without being chased by sweat-soaked, screaming nightmares. As if eventually, reality would come crashing through the movie set that my life had become.

"Jill! What is it? What's wrong?"

He would often find me sitting up in bed, legs curled up to my chest, shaking, crying. My body was purging itself. Perhaps it was an engkanto or a friendly manggagamod, trying to displace the fear and sadness in my blood to make room for happiness. For love.

Still, during the day, my anxieties clutched at me. What kind of future could we really have? Me, an undocumented immigrant with deep, two-decade-old roots in a country that I couldn't leave and couldn't return to. Him, a white-collar British immigrant with all the freedom in the world to live and work wherever he wished: New York, San Francisco, London, Paris, Hong Kong, Singapore, São Paulo. He could turn around tomorrow and say I've met someone, and she is an American/Australian/Canadian/British citizen, and she is a lawyer/doctor/investment banker, and she has money and no baggage, and her parents are very nice, unlike yours, and we're moving to Hong Kong next month.

I also couldn't tell him about what my uncle had done to me. I wouldn't tell Steven for a very long time. All love, I believed, had limits.

Turn the pot's heat down to medium-low.

Eventually, perhaps after centuries, maybe millennia, Lakapati finally noticed Mapulon. They saw that he made an effort to support them in his capacity as god of the seasons. When the crops needed rain, he brought the right clouds to make Lakapati's work easier. When the trees needed to grow fruits fat and juicy, Mapulon cajoled the sun so that Lakapati could rest. Lakapati saw that Mapulon was not there to compete with them or to disempower them, and they found this attractive. Mapulon, simply by being himself, supported Lakapati willingly, without conditions. This was how Lakapati began to understand love.

Add the brown sugar and coconut milk to the mix, gently stirring to evenly distribute.

That first summer of living together, my body began to feel New York as more than a battleground. As more than something to be survived. This newfound love and its material safety had begun to break down the protective outer layer of me, the one no one else before Steven could get past. I was slowly becoming myself. Reducing down to my essence. I decided that it was time to cook Filipino food for Steven, that it was time to show him who I was from tongue to stomach. To feed my old body the food it had quietly craved for so long. Adobo, done the right way. I trawled through the internet for recipes, websites, forums, a digitized substitute for calling my mother.

Do not marinate the chicken for too long. The acid toughens the meat!!!

Two hours is plenty for chicken

I would say 6 hrs is fine, I have done it this way for 30 years!

6 hours is too long yata.

There is something to be said about cooking with love. As gayuma. I took an entire Saturday afternoon to make it, starting while Steven was still prone under the covers, sleeping in till noon. Bone-in, skin-on chicken thighs, marinated for three hours. Two fat heads of fresh garlic patiently peeled and minced. A chubby, two-inch piece of fresh ginger, peeled and sliced into thin slivers. Fresh bay leaves. Whole peppercorns. Datu Puti cane vinegar and Silver Swan soy sauce from a Filipino store in Queens. The chicken, fried in

a separate pan halfway through to caramelize the brown sugar, then placed
back in the sauce, which had by then reduced and caramelized a little, too.
The rice, cooked the day before, left to dry out a little in the refrigerator,
tossed with minced garlic in a wok for the perfect sinangag rice. Green mangoes cubed with tomatoes and red onions, dashed with patis and a bit of
vinegar, bowled and chilled on the side. I'd even picked up some bottles of
Filipino San Miguel beer for the meal.

"Holy fucking shit," Steven said, stuffing another mouthful into an already full mouth. "This is incredible."

"It actually is," I said, not at all humbly. The adobo was perfect: the sauce
just the right consistency of syrupy, striking the balance between the salty
soy, acidic cane vinegar, and softly sweet brown sugar. The skin was pan-
seared just enough to have some bite, its Maillard reaction–burnt bits con-
trasting against the soft, juicy chicken within.

"I haven't had adobo this good, maybe ever," I continued, still not being
humble. Thank you, mothers and titas of the internet.

It is impossible to know if this acted as a gayuma of any kind for Steven.
After all, he already seemed to be in love with me. If anything—and perhaps
the elders and engkantos can clarify—it taught me to begin to love myself.
To accept myself.

Heat a frying pan on high.

Later that summer, I invited Kelly over for dinner. Made her my new,
perfected chicken adobo.

"To make up for last time," I said with a wink.

Steven proudly laid down the garlic rice, the first of many batches he
would master making for us.

"Jilly," Kelly said a few minutes later. "I don't even know what to say. This
is better than all the chicken adobos I've had in all the restaurants!"

"Really?"

"Steve," she said, giggling. "Let me tell you about Jilly's first adobo two
years ago."

At our front door, saying good night, Kelly requested pork adobo for our
next potluck.

When the pan is hot enough to sizzle droplets of water, add the remaining tablespoon of vegetable oil.

On June 22, 2011, I spotted an op-ed in the *New York Times*, just published that day. "My Life as an Undocumented Immigrant," written by a journalist named Jose Antonio Vargas. A Filipino. I remember cradling my laptop, disbelieving as I read. I walked around the apartment, read every word out loud.

Steven found me sitting on the floor between the dining table and the couch, laptop on my thighs.

"Hey, you OK?"

I said nothing, let my red face, tears and snot shining it, do the speaking for me. He sat down on the floor next to me, pulled the computer over to his thighs. Read Jose's op-ed.

"Whoa," he said. "He's just like you."

"Yeah," I said. "Photocopies and Disneyland and everything." The same disappointment in the system, in a country that told us to find salvation and freedom in work. The same mad desire to be excellent so that we could be accepted, loved.

For the rest of that week, Jose's words felt like a rising drumbeat in my chest. *I'm exhausted. I don't want that life anymore.*

I'm tired too, Kuya Jose, I wanted to say. I wanted to find him, make him my friend. Invite him for some of this adobo I had just learned to make. To go for a walk with him, talk to him about our undocumented lives. To ask him how he became a writer. To find solidarity, to be tired together. My parents had taught my sister and me that we were alone for all of this time, that there was no one out there like us, and no one who cared. Yet here was someone just like me, an undocumented Filipino American almost exactly two years older than me.

I began to admit, in the most gloaming hours of each night, that I did not want this life of terrified hiding anymore. As each day passed, the canyon between my life's outward joy and its internal acknowledgment of inalienable truth became wider. But what did this admittance mean, really? What would I do? I was a nobody, just an office worker who worked on spreadsheets for a living. I was not a journalist, I was not an activist. What did admitting to myself that I was unhappy in America really mean, as an action? If I were to stop running, to stop hiding from place to place, job to job, lie to lie, what would I do next? I began to think about quitting my job at the prime brokerage, where I had watched Occupy Wall Street from my seventeenth-floor window each day. To think of where I wanted to be—the embodiment of American imperial power and inequality—so that I could do more than just survive. To think of the possibilities of my lifelong dream of becoming a writer, like Jose. To maybe write about this life, someday. Still, I was too afraid to really work out the details. I let the engkantos in my nightmares work the rest out for themselves.

When the oil begins to smoke, take 2 or 3 pieces of chicken from the pot. Place them skin side down in the pan. Do not crowd the pan.

"So, Jilly," Steven said in his gentle way one night in January 2012. "I had a chat this week with Janet. From the Hong Kong office."

"Oh?" I said, not looking at him. Her again. She persisted, on a regular basis, that my boyfriend come and join her in Hong Kong. Whenever she visited the New York office, she insisted on going to lunch or drinks with Steven alone, giving him gifts of snacks and coffee. *Come to HK. It's so much better.* He would come home with packs of dried squid snacks, which I would refuse to eat, declaring Filipino ones to be better (they tasted exactly the same). She made me nervous.

"She's saying there's a position opening on her team. Wants me to apply for a transfer."

We fought long, loud, and hard that night—a Friday night, wasting our movie tickets and dinner reservations. He couldn't understand my terror, my fury. I couldn't understand his desire to move out there, his lack of understanding of my limitations. And, I can admit now, I was also jealous of Steven's privileges as a British citizen, as a white man with a white collar job, the kind that allows people like him to call themselves expats rather than migrant workers. To become green card holders or citizens of any land they wish to set foot upon.

"Good for you!" I had shouted. "You can just go anywhere you want, get any visa you want! Fall in love with anyone you want, make them feel like they can count on you! And then just leave!"

"I wouldn't be leaving you, Jill!" he had shouted back. "Don't you under-stand? I want you to come with me!"

"You know I can't come with you!"

I accused him of cheating. He accused me of being dishonest, of blaming him for whatever it was I was really afraid of. He was right, and I was too proud to admit it. After more tears and shouting, we fell asleep on our anger. We were awakened by our rescue dog, Farley, snuggling into the covers be-tween us. Our foreheads touched above his snoring face. Eyes open, looking at each other.

"If you leave for Hong Kong," I said, "I can't come with you. And Farley can't either. He's eight."

"We can figure out the dog. Why can't you come with me? Don't you want to be with me?"

"You know I can't come back if I leave. You're asking me to leave my entire life. My whole entire life, and to never come back. I'm not like you—you can go wherever you want and always come home again. I know I'm not technically American, but I am. I grew up here. My life is here. Even if we stayed together, what happens after Hong Kong?"

"None of that matters if we're together. And aren't we your life too?" He took my hands, clutched them against his bare chest.

"You're asking a lot of me, Steve." How could I say *What if we break up in Hong Kong? Then what?* How could I say *I'm not sure I can trust this, trust you to not leave me stranded. The way Papa left us stranded.*

We agreed on a break from arguing. Walked the dog, came back to our apartment. Made coffee, opened the Saturday edition of the *Times*. Tried to find some peace. Eventually, he turned to me, tired of pretending to read about the NFL, which he called "American football" and knew nothing about.

"There's absolutely no way you can fix it, right?"

"There hasn't been since I was a child. I could marry an American for papers. Unfortunately, I'm in love with a non-American."

"Your life is stuck in limbo here anyway. We can just start over elsewhere, right?"

"In Hong Kong? With a Philippine passport? What would I do out there? I don't have a degree. What if we ... what if ..." I couldn't finish my sentence.

I thought of his oddly persistent colleague in Hong Kong. Thought of having to start over, alone, jobless, and broke in another new city. Steven and Janet and her packets of dried squid snacks.

"Is that what you're afraid of? That we might break up? Jill. We've been together for almost two years. We live together. We adopted a dog together!"

"I would have nowhere to go but the Philippines if we broke up," I babbled, panic in my chest, my throat. "I haven't lived there in twenty years. What would I do there?" Twenty years away in what we had been taught to think of as the greatest country on earth, only to come back to Manila as an unqualified, unskilled worker. Broke and broken.

"Is that all?" He frowned, disturbed by the thought. "You're worried that I would leave you, like that?"

I said nothing. He sat up, a determined look on his face.

"So you're saying that if you were my wife, and I were your husband, that you would come with me to Hong Kong? Live with me wherever we decide to go?"

"No! I—I don't know! I'm not saying anything about marriage now, or ever, or—! I'm just saying I—how can you expect me to just leave or to just get married just so you can transfer to Hong Kong? This is all I have. This life. It's shitty, and it's going nowhere, but it's all I have. If I leave this, then what do I have for sure?"

"Oh. OK. For sure, huh," he echoed, frowning. He pulled out his iPad. "For sure. Fine. Let's do this."

"Do what?" I sat up too. The newspaper slid off my lap.

He was typing *city hall wedding new york city* into Google.

"What the hell are you doing?"

"I'm solving the problem," he said. Ever the data man. Numbers and statistics to my splashed paint and jumbled words.

"Are you assuming that I'm going to marry you?"

"Sorry," he said. He put the iPad down and turned to face me. Took my hands in his.

"Jill Gonzales Damatac," he intoned. Paused. A smile fought his tears. "Will you marry me?"

"Is this just so you can transfer to Hong Kong?"

"Say yes, and then I'll tell you."

I paused. "Yes." Palms cold. Being with Steven for the rest of my life was what I wanted, but did I want it to be like this?

"Good. OK, here's what we're doing. We won't move to Hong Kong, now or ever, unless you want to live there. I'll tell work I'm not moving. I would never take you away from here unless you want to leave. I just want to be with you."

"Oh."

"Do you hear me? Our life is here, but it's also anywhere we decide—together—where to go."

"OK."

"Do you believe me?"

I began to shake a little. This was scary. Why was I so scared?

"You're safe with me. OK?"

I nodded, started to cry. Steven did too.

"We're getting married. You and me. I keep telling you this." Our bodies crumpled into each other, relief. The dog sighed, kicked at us for squishing him under the comforter.

"We can't move to Hong Kong anyway," he said. "Our New York City Filipino food spreadsheet is incomplete."

As the skin on each piece of chicken browns to a good—not burnt—crisp, remove from the pan. Let rest on a paper-toweled plate.

That evening, after a celebratory dinner, we walked back to our apartment, holding hands in the January cold, block by block. A kiss on each street corner, a cliché we have since turned into a tradition in every city we would live in.

I called home, excited. My father refused to come to the phone.

"I don't know what to say, Jill," my mother said, upset, anxious. "He didn't even ask your Dad for permission."

Of course that was her reaction. For all of her life, from the age of nineteen, my mother's sense of self, her consciousness, has been molded by my father to prioritize him, and him alone. The condition for their marriage was: Dad first. Dad only.

I would have been happy to elope at City Hall. Maybe a red dress from

Salvation Army, blue shoes borrowed from Kelly's extensive shoe closet, dinner with friends and my sister at Maharlika, my favorite Filipino restaurant in the city. Steven, however, wanted to have a celebration: music, a first dance, an open bar, cake, music, friends and family. He also insisted on an engagement ring, despite my protests: I chose a ring of amethyst, my birth stone. We decided that the wedding—just a small one—would be in March, two years after we first met.

We went to City Hall to register: presented our passports, signed documents to make our union official. Visible. Documented. Signed into something legal. It felt strange, somehow out of order. I was not allowed to drive, work, or study legally in America, but I could still get married to the person I loved. I thought of Jose Antonio Vargas. Of how same-sex marriage, at the time of our wedding, was still illegal. This inequality, compared to heterosexual couples, grated at me. I may have been unlucky in many ways, but I was still a bisexual woman lucky enough to not be too gay in the eyes of the law. To remember my own sexuality, I shaved off my hair. It would be extremely short, almost showing my scalp, on the day of our wedding.

I tamped down my sadness, my anxieties that spread beyond my own life. Focused on the minutiae: cake, dress, shoes, menu, music, beverages, photographer, venue. Life's bigger problems—papers, career, education, housing, a future for this legal union I was about to enter—could wait until April.

While the chicken rests on the plate, check the adobo sauce in the uncovered pot. It should be reduced, thicker, clinging to the spoon.

The wedding rehearsal was staged in our newly rented apartment in Brooklyn Heights, on Orange Street (we had a knack for finding rent-stabilized gems). Our living room was crowded with Steven's parents, his sister, his brother-in-law, and my sister, her boyfriend, my aunt and uncle, and friends taking part in the ceremony. Kelly, ever the organized leader of every pack, corralled us all.

"One more run-through of the entire wedding march, and then we can have dinner!" she hollered. She picked up her violin. Another good friend, Fiona, began to strum on her guitar. We practice-marched to their rendition of Pachelbel's Canon. Farley hopped around, tail wagging madly with happiness at all of the human attention.

After three practice runs, I declared dinnertime. I had spent the entire day making an enormous batch of chicken adobo, mango-tomato-red onion salad, and steamed jasmine rice. Enough to feed fourteen people. I still don't quite remember how I cooked everything, alone, in that one-bedroom apartment's modest kitchen. A massive wok, bought last-minute from Chinatown, was involved. And instead of frying the chicken, I used the oven broiler. Five rounds to cook everything. Bottles of empty Datu Puti and Silver Swan in a corner by the garbage can, where bottles of wine and beer would soon join. All I knew was that I wanted our guests to love it. To love me.

"Well, I am relieved that my soon-to-be daughter-in-law can cook," Steven's mother said, leaning against the kitchen door as I served up rice. We had just met for the first time, in person, the day before.

"What did you think?" I said. *Please love me.*

"I think we're going to have to have you back in the UK so that you can make this for us every weekend!" She smiled. "It was delicious. And what was in the mango salad?"

I pulled the bottle of Rufina patis from the cupboard to show her. We might be OK, after all.

When the chicken pieces have adequately rested, oils absorbed by the paper towel, place them back in the pot to finish cooking.

My in-laws made it from Wales and England, but my father, an hour away in New Jersey, was absent. Until 4 p.m. the next day—the time the wedding ceremony was scheduled to begin—Steven and I held on to the hope that Dad would show up. Mom had arrived late, unsure if he would come. She spent most of our time getting ready griping at my lack of hair, at my lack of makeup or a makeup artist, at the inadequacy of my wedding outfit, the disappointment of having to get ready in our apartment and not a fancy hotel room. She had turned down my request to shop for a dress with her, ignored my invitations to look at the venue, to select food. They had contributed nothing to the wedding, and I had not expected them to. For my wedding dress, I had bought a tea-length tulle skirt made by a seamstress from Etsy. She had color-matched the tulle to a cream corset top I bought from a clearance rack. Total cost: $472.

"This isn't even a real dress, my God," my mother had muttered, while I held back tears.

"Mom," my sister glared. "Stop it."

Levi, our photographer and my friend, whispered a request to my sister and to Kelly. They both ushered my mother out of the room.

That afternoon was mostly a happy blur. Pre-ceremony photographs at Brooklyn Bridge Park, shivering in the early springtime air. A walk through DUMBO, my sister telling jokes to cheer me up, keeping our mother away from me. Our chosen venue was a warehouse gastropub and movie theater on Front Street, an all-inclusive package for $3,500, paid for mostly by us and by Steven's parents. Tito David—my father's oldest brother, my cousin Matty's dad—waited for me, tall and handsome, in his best suit. Fifty of our family, friends, and loved ones were inside, in the gastropub's movie theater, where the ceremony would be. This life as a film. The ultimate narrative arc. The fictional, made real, except for one crucial, life-giving detail.

"Looks like it's going to be me walking you down the aisle, anak," my uncle said, a shy smile tinged with sadness on his face. Though he and Dad often fought, I always found my Tito Dick to be gentle, kind, and fun.

"I think so, Tito. Salamat po." Steven had called my parents' house the night before, after the rehearsal dinner. *Please come, Andy. I love your daughter, and we are getting married tomorrow. It would mean everything to her if you came.* No response. Dad had blocked my emails and let my phone calls go to voicemail for weeks.

Taking my uncle's arm, I shook thoughts of my father and his latest abandonment out of my head. Kelly's and Fiona's violin and guitar began to sing over the gentle chatter in the movie theater. I took a deep breath. This was all I had to be, right now. A someone made real by the love of someone else, waiting for me at the end of this aisle. No conditions, no doubts. The start of a life together witnessed by others who, for the most part, loved us simply for being ourselves. This was all there was for today. No fear, no loneliness. Beyond documents, greater than any citizenship, unprovable by any bureaucracy, pledging allegiance to no institution. There was only this, the kind of belonging we search for from the moment we are born. A search that can take us across decades. Across oceans.

I teetered on high-heeled red satin shoes towards Steven, beautiful and tall in his suit. His brown eyes shone with tears. Here, there was nothing and no one we had to measure up to. Only each other. Only love.

Using a thermometer, check that the chicken, at the thickest part, is cooked to temperature. If so, remove from the heat.

Lakapati and Mapulon married each other too. They joined their lives together, the deities of life and abundance, of goodness across all weathers and seasons, for better or for worse. Devoted to each other, to their life's work, to their life together. For our people, their union symbolized the equality that we should strive to achieve in a marriage, the bond of mutual support and protection. Soon, Lakapati and Mapulon gave birth to a child. They named her Anagolay. She would grow up to become the goddess of all lost things. It is this goddess, I think, who has looked after me. Made sure that I was found.

Serve the chicken adobo family style, with rice and mango salad on the side.

A little more than one year later, over plates of fish stewed in ginger and soy—something close to, but not quite, adobo—I asked my father why he did not come to our wedding. We had agreed to meet at a restaurant a few blocks from where Steven and I lived.

He struggled to find the words.

"Your Mom did say I would regret it. It's just . . . I try to be a good Catholic, true to my faith. And it wasn't in a church, and Steve never asked my permission, and you were living in sin. And . . . you know what, it's not important. Sorry na lang, anak." A pat on my hand.

At the end of the meal, I waved goodbye to my mother and my father. Goodbye to my father's hypocrisy, the good Catholic who was repeatedly unfaithful to his wife. To my parents' conditional love, which demanded my suffering for their comfort. As I began the walk home—my true home, where love involved no tricks, no demands, no gayuma—I thought only of my husband. Of our life together, no matter where we chose to live next.

> Build the perfect bite on a spoon: rice, chicken, chicken skin, sauce, a
> bit of mango, onion, tomato.

The wood charcoal–grilled chicken adobo is magnificent. Crisp, smoky charred skin contrasts with the fatty, salty, acidic elements. My version of adobo, like everyone else's, is built upon so many others' versions. Some may not recognize this way of eating—perhaps their family's adobo is oven-baked, others' stewed, confit-like, others simply tossed and simmered, thin-sauced, in a pan. Some may associate mango salad with other dishes only, their adobo eaten on its own, without accompaniment; some may associate adobo with a side dish of garlic-sauteed kangkong. Adobo, I suppose, is a lot like love: everyone has their own way of giving, of receiving. But we always know what it is when we taste it.

8

Halo-Halo
(Mixed Shaved Sweet Ice Dessert)

2012–2023

SERVES MANY

Shaved ice, store bought or made with a shaver
Preserved sweet jackfruit
Nata de coco
Sweet red munggo
Ripe plantain
Young shredded macapuno
Canned corn
Fresh-made sago
Leche flan
Ube ice cream
Cheese ice cream
Vanilla ice cream
Condensed milk
Evaporated milk
Kellogg's Rice Krispies or Corn Flakes

"OK, Jilly," Steven says, rubbing his hands together. "Where do we begin?"

My husband towers over the array of jars, bowls, and bottles. I have set out all of the ingredients for our halo-halo. The shaved ice, freshly made, is in the freezer, waiting.

"Anywhere you want. Just layer ice and milk between ingredients."

I lay five slices of leche flan on top of my glass of shaved ice. Pour a generous amount of evaporated milk over it. Ponder adding a spoonful of jackfruit, which I used to hate as a child. What is time for, if not change?

There were floods reported not far from here, just like the ones everywhere else on this planet. Floods and fire, droughts and storms, an awful glimpse into our planet's melting future. It seems that no matter where I run, there is always something else to run from, to not run to. Is any place or time truly safe? I push away the anxiety. Stir the fatty milk into the ice and thick slices of leche flan, the slippery yellow slivers of jackfruit. Focus on this glass of comfort, just for now.

Prepare the store-bought ingredients by laying them out in their containers, jars, and bowls. Keep a small serving spoon in each for all to use.

Halo-halo is a dessert, a street snack, a cool oasis in the belly, a relief. It is both new and old at the same time, just like the Philippines. True to its name—*halo* is Tagalog for "mix"—it is anything and everything all at once, its base of shaved ice able to carry whatever sweet thing you might wish to mix-mix together. It adapts to place and person, to palate and preference. It is anything you want and need it to be. In the end, regardless of ingredients, halo-halo is always recognizable as itself.

The Japanese call their version of this dessert kakigori, which they brought to the Philippines. It is the much simpler origin of our now-riotous version. Ice was new to us in the 1940s and 1950s, made possible in the tropical heat by appliances imported by GE, Westinghouse, and Frigidaire, which is what we still call this appliance to this day: *prigider*. We love halo-halo for reasons far beyond its war-torn beginnings. We sell it on our streets, serve it in our restaurants, make it at home. Halo-halo is a glass of unabashed joy, a savior, if only for less than an hour, from sticky heat and postcolonial malaise. It is the gleeful, anarchic mixing, long spoon between fingers, of disparate parts that should not make sense together, but do. Jackfruit. Coconut. Tapioca. Preserved saba banana. Leche flan. Ube ice cream. Cheese ice cream. Canned corn. Buko pandan. Nata de coco. Condensed milk. Corn flakes. Pinipig. Evaporated milk. This list is incomplete. There is always some other variation, some other suitable ingredient to add to the mix. No hesitation, only joy. For no matter what has happened to us as a people—whether it be in the indigenous north, where my father is from, or in the Muslim south, where I wish to visit—we have always been able to find joy. We have had to. We stir in the bad with the good, swallow it whole and cold. Let the sweetness of lessons and hope linger on the tongue. Let the ice numb whatever it is we wish to not feel, teeth to throat, chest to stomach.

Kakigori was not all that the Japanese brought to us. On December 8, 1941, they also brought their bombs. I grew up to know this day as the attacks on Manila and Pearl Harbor, a distinction that is not taught or remembered anywhere but by my people. It was taught to me by my grandfather. His war stories were my bedtime stories. As he spoke, his arthritic fingers would graze over the three-inch scar on his forehead, the mark of a Japanese bayonet. Aside from bombs and dessert, the Japanese also brought their troops, their guns. They placed Filipinos in labor camps. Across the ocean, the American government placed Japanese Americans in concentration camps. Terror and torture spreading out to terror and torture, prison camps from Pacific shore to Pacific shore. People stirring the evil and the good inside themselves, mix-mix, halo-halo.

In 2012, I was only beginning to consider leaving America. The summer after Steven and I married, President Barack Obama announced an executive order called the Deferred Action for Childhood Arrivals, which we know as DACA.

"These are young people who study in our schools, they play in our neighborhoods, they're friends with our kids, they pledge allegiance to our flag. They are Americans in their heart, in their minds, in every single way but one: on paper," the President said. "They were brought to this country by their parents—sometimes even as infants—and often have no idea that they're undocumented until they apply for a job or a driver's license or a college scholarship."

I cried as I read the news article again and again. Knees on the kitchen floor, tears on tile. I did not know it then, but even as he gave that speech,

President Obama's administration was in the midst of deporting undocumented people who simply needed work, an income, something to help feed their children back home. This would amount to three million people by the end of his two terms. His administration was not alone in this, of course. Deporting immigrants from a nation of immigrants is one of the United States' favorite settler colonialist traditions.

With an ice shaver, grind ice cubes into medium-sized shavings. Not too fine, so as to keep the melting rate slow. Keep these shavings in the freezer.

I was just eligible for the program, making the age cutoff by one year. My sister and I could have work permits for two years at a time, though it provided no pathway to further legality or citizenship. My heart was a mix of feelings. Happy to be acknowledged. Relief for millions like me who were forced to come here, stay here, and hide here. Still, as I learned more about DACA, I began to distrust it. Was it worth it, raising my head above the parapet like this, giving my name to the system? Undocumented immigrants already had the ability to obtain taxpayer ID numbers, which was often all that was needed for many jobs. Who did this program serve? This current administration may support DACA, but what about the next president? What if the next one hated immigrants, or needed us as a scapegoat for another financial crisis, or used us to hide their corruption, their malfeasance? The government would have my name in a database; in a worst-case scenario, a xenophobe with an entire highly militarized state at his disposal could access that database to hunt down people like me. I decided to not apply. Changed my mind the next day. And again, the day after that.

The measure, which was the best that could be achieved in a bitterly bipartisan Congress, was inadequate, a political play. What we really needed was a path to legalization and citizenship. The last efforts at legalizing undocumented immigrants were in 2001, with the original, bipartisan-led Dream Act. It was killed at inception by a Republican majority, and again in 2007, when President George W. Bush had tried to pass a comprehensive immigration reform act that conferred temporary worker status on undocumented immigrants. How was DACA any different from the conditions the

Filipino Manongs worked under almost a century ago in the fields of California? Like them, we would be migrant workers with fewer rights and no recourse to permanency or equality. Legal to work, and nothing more. That was all we were. DACA was an underscoring of how we were not quite one thing, never another, always an other. To make matters worse, the process was complicated, needing dozens of documents, many lost, and a complex submission process. Some applicants worked with lawyers. How many of us undocumented people could afford a lawyer?

"A lot of them are crooks, anyway," said one lawyer friend when I broached the subject, hoping I could ask him to help "a family friend." This lawyer friend defended white-collar criminals for a living. "Illegals are prosecuted for crimes all the time."

"That's not really my specialty, and I don't know any immigration lawyers," said another lawyer friend. She said that her practice focused on B Corps, ethical corporations doing good for the world, using their profits for poverty alleviation, or the environment, or gender inequality.

"Tell your friend to go home and come back legally," said another, someone I knew from high school. She had just passed the bar and was of South Asian heritage, the first-generation child of immigrants. "All these people do is overstay and waste everyone's time."

I gave up on finding a lawyer. And then: my sister texted me in the spring of 2013. She had begun applying for DACA with the help of a nonprofit legal organization. Did I want to check it out?

The office of the Asian American Legal Defense and Education Fund, known as AALDEF, was on Hudson Street in Manhattan. Pro bono, they were helping people like me apply for DACA. In a windowless basement room, their volunteer lawyers instructed us to gather evidence of our arrival date and as much proof as possible that we have stayed and lived in America for a continuous amount of time since arrival.

I felt inspired by my sister. I pushed down my fears and worked on my application. I had tax documents to gather, elementary, middle, and high school transcripts to request. An official copy of my birth certificate procured by Dad's youngest brother, in Manila. Photographs from as many years as I could find. Copies of the newspaper in Pennsylvania that showed me competing in the 1997 National Spelling Bee as a child. Rental agreements under my name to dig out from under my bed. Utility bills, library records, college enrollment forms, bank statements. Proof of the debt judgment and liens from my father's debts under my name, debts that Steven and I paid off. Everything to prove that I have lived every year of the past twenty-one years in America. Two decades' worth of paper trails. Proof of place. Proof of personhood. Undocumented, but not really. Here, but not really. Educated and raised here, but don't tell anyone. An illegitimate personhood, illegible, ineligible.

I was still missing a crucial document: my I-94, also known as the Arrival/ Departure Record. Required and definitive proof of my arrival within the eligibility timeframe for DACA. To obtain this original I-94 from August 13, 1992, I needed the passport I had when we first arrived. I called my mother.

"I don't know what you're talking about," my mother said. "What proof?"

"Of arrival. My passport, Mom," I said. "The one with the stamp that says I arrived here on August 13, 1992. I need my passport with the I-94 stamp in it."

"No, I don't know what you're talking about," she said. "We don't have that. I don't have your passport."

"Mom, yes you do," I insisted. "You have my passports, my Social Security card, everything."

She pretended to have a work call coming through and hung up.

The AALDEF lawyer tried to hide her disbelief. She had probably never encountered such a mother.

My sister could not get our parents' cooperation either.

"They're probably scared that they'll get caught if we do this," I said. The same fear kept me awake, after all. I hated myself for empathizing with parents who never cared about their children's future. My sister and I were not surprised by this latest failure.

With those meager hopes for DACA dashed, Steven and I considered another long-term plan: legalization through his green card, which he could obtain through his job. It took less than a year for him to receive the card, processed for free by his employer, delivered to his desk by HR. I ignored the mixed feelings of excitement and envy in my belly. My husband would be eligible to apply for citizenship after five years, though the process could take up to ten years. Steven could then petition me for legal status as his wife. I would be eligible for a green card in five to ten years, then citizenship in another five to ten years after that.

I would be in my fifties, maybe my sixties, before I became a citizen of the only country I had ever really known.

"That's shit, isn't it?" Steven said one evening, at dinner. "Do you want to wait till we're fifty?"

I looked down at my hands. Dad's hands, minus the arthritis and the skin hardened by manual labor. My father was fifty-eight, my mother fifty-four. They were still waiting. I was thirty. Did I want to keep waiting, as they have? I felt grateful to have any kind of choice at all. Felt ashamed of my need to feel grateful. Ambivalent about my choices, or lack thereof. Guilt at having a way out.

Add the first layer of sweetness to a large, wide glass or deep bowl. Start, perhaps, with preserved saba banana, something solid that can be eaten last, while upholding the rest of the ingredients well.

In 2014, we decided that it was time to leave. It had been twenty-two years since I first arrived. Twelve years since I first tried to end my life, since I was raped and had swallowed pills to end an unwanted pregnancy. Seven years since leaving my parents' house, blood in my hair and eyes, used up for money and credit cards. Four years since finding one person, just one, who could love me. Two years since marrying that person, his trust in my hands, our promises of eternity in an uncertain future. I felt ambivalence about this exhaustion, ashamed that I should complain. I often thought that as a Filipino raised in America, the center of our lifetime's empire, my life as an undocumented immigrant was still better than millions of others' lives, others still living in the postcolonial remnants of imperial extraction. I felt that perhaps I should remember the good, the privileges I had. Still, I stopped short of feeling grateful. Everything my family and I eked out of our time in America was not without self-destructive effort, consequence, or price. For my mother and father, and so many Filipinos who have migrated to the United States, America was a place in which to seek—and often not quite find—refuge. For me, the United States was a place from which I wished to find refuge. It was not a place to be. It was a place to flee.

We executed our plans each month. Steven requested a transfer to his company's office in London, booked the journey to England for himself and our dogs. I booked a separate trip to Manila, alone, to submit my printed documents at the UK embassy there. Since I was undocumented, I couldn't finalize my online application for a British spouse visa from the UK embassy in New York. Even the act of leaving was made cruel, difficult.

These moves required money, which neither of us really had. My husband had spent the past few years covering credit card debts my father had incurred under my name. He had also covered my income shortfall from year after year of menial jobs with menial pay. I needed a job that would pay more without a college degree, and quickly. I took a course in photography at the Pratt Institute, each class paid for by an almost full-time job. By day, I worked thirty-five hours a week as an office manager for a start-up in DUMBO, Brooklyn. While the men in the office sat at their desks coding and testing prototypes, I did basic data entry, washed dishes, made coffee, caught mice, and took out the garbage. By night, I was at Pratt: shooting and processing medium-format film, 35 mm film, entire weekends in red-lit darkrooms. I took classes on advanced lighting, studio digital photography, and practical classes on Photoshop and Lightroom.

My body was tired of numbing itself. I wanted to express something in my life other than want and survival. To allow myself to see and feel the world's beauty and horror, no longer closing my eyes in denial; to see the light of the golden hour, rather than the shadows of hiding. On nights and weekends, I worked as an assistant for some local wedding and editorial photographers in Manhattan and Brooklyn, carrying bags, setting up lights, backing up memory cards, mass-processing photos for the photographer to finalize. Six months later, I also began booking small weddings of my own to shoot. I found that in New York, the more you charged for your services, the likelier you were to be booked by clients willing to pay you. I set up an LLC called the Little Photography Company and charged $3,000 per wedding. I booked two weddings per weekend, for most of the spring, summer, and into autumn. I continued to do assistant and editing work on the side at $400 per gig. I continued to pay taxes, as always (my tax forms also provided useful evidence of being a good immigrant for my UK visa). It was the most I had made in years. I wished I had started sooner. Steven and I saved as much as we could for the move, plus the cost of the spouse visa, which was around $2,000.

In that final year in America, I became an anxious mix of fear, anticipation, excitement, and sadness. This mix was topped with bravado and defiance. If my parents, like so many other immigrant parents, could forge new lives while knowing and having less than I do, so could I. If I could survive a lifetime of being undocumented, I could survive anything.

For a third layer, add a spoonful or two of evaporated milk. Something to help soften the added layers of sweetness to come.

Did Filipinos embrace kakigori because they liked it, or because they needed to swallow survival during occupation?

"We lived for a little while in the house where Yamashita surrendered to the American Allies, in Kiangan," Dad recalled, a few years ago. "It was one of the houses we lived in while your grandfather was the superintendent of schools up there."

I began to understand my parents. Despite everything, I still felt a measure of awe at how they uprooted their lives for a new country. Unlike me, they did not have the internet to scroll through in 1991, had no online forums or websites to guide them. They only had some conversational guidance, a mix of ill-informed and well-intentioned suggestions. Hearsay and assumptions. Did they have the same sunken, mixed feeling of fear and excitement, blood running hot and cold, like a pasma?

"Naku," a grandmother, or an aunt, or a yaya might say. "Don't take a cold shower immediately after coming in from the heat. You may get pasma. It might make you sick or kill you."

Pasma is a term that describes the unholy clashing of hot and cold within one's body. Pasma may result in chills or hot flashes. In fevers, numbness, immobility, or death. It is sometimes believed that the duwende are to blame. That they seek to punish the afflicted. Duwende are creatures who live in fabulous wealth. They hoard gold, steal things. If a person offends a duwende, they may afflict that person's body with pasma as revenge.

In my anxiety-ridden hot and cold flashes during that last year in America, I sometimes thought, *Who did I offend now?*

It must have been even scarier, the hot-cold pasma swing from terror to anticipation greater, for our elder Filipino immigrants. They left the Philippines with nothing more than hope and a vague promise of work, of better wages than the ones back home. In conditions much more inhospitable and inhumane than mine, our elders persisted through violence at the hands of racist American men. Photographs from the 1930s show a California where signs, hand-scrawled in xenophobic rage, proliferated:

Work no Filipinos or we'll destroy your crop and you too.

Get rid of all Filipinos or we'll burn this town down.

Positively No Filipinos Allowed.

These Filipino workers found solidarity with Black liberation groups, with Chicano activists, with fellow Asian Americans. They came together to form labor unions and political movements. America is not a melting pot. It is a halo-halo of oppressions, a glass of melting inequality laced with icy death, sweetened by the fight for freedom.

So why was I leaving? Was my life that hard? Maybe if I waited a little longer, as my parents were, a change could happen. Maybe DACA was the first step. Maybe movements could form together with my fellow Dreamers, with other people working for liberation. I wobbled for weeks. Thought about withdrawing my UK visa application. Reconsidered waiting until I was fifty, or fifty-five, to become a legal resident in America, if all went well. It could all work out. I did not like my odds.

"It's like leaving our parents' house," my sister said, when I told her about my plan to self-deport. We were having brunch somewhere in the West Village. "Or an abusive partner. You start to doubt yourself, start to think maybe it wasn't so bad. Maybe you're the problem."

"Am I the problem?" Maybe I haven't tried hard enough. Maybe I was a failure at life because I wasn't good enough at it.

"Hell no," she said. "I might follow you outta here."

January 1, 2015, the morning of my flight to Manila, of my self-deportation, I was numb. New York was in a deep freeze, ready to unleash a blizzard of snow and ice. A cold farewell. In my carry-on, I had only seven items: my Philippine passport, an accordion folder, six inches thick, with all of my papers for my UK visa application, James Baldwin's *Another Country*, headphones, lip balm, a notebook, and a pen. I thought that I might write something, a poem, a draft for an essay, on the flight. Something, anything to document what it was I was about to do. To name it, so that I could recognize it as real. There is no name for those of us who choose to deport ourselves. The Huddled Masses, yearning to breathe free from the nightmare of the American Dream. American Escapees. Refugees from America.

JFK's Terminal 4 was quiet. In my left hand, I held my phone, flashing with texts of farewell: beloved friends, my sister. I pushed away the thought that I might not see her again. *Call me when you're at the gate*, Steven had texted from JFK's check-in area, where I had left him. He was to continue clearing our rented Brooklyn apartment, then board the *Queen Mary 2* for Southampton, England, with our two rescue dogs, both too old to fly. His belief that we would reunite in London was stronger than mine. Our goodbyes were a fading, sweet pressure on my lips, my fears a rising, cold panic in my throat. In my right hand, I held my one-way ticket to Manila. In my left hand, a cell phone, my only remaining line to the life I was about to leave behind.

Will you still love me if they don't let me join you? I typed.

Don't be silly, he replied. *I'd move to Manila. The food is better.*

The TSA agent, bored of her power, waved me forward with her long acrylic nails, spangled for New Year's. She flicked through my passport's blank pages, raised an eyebrow. She swiped my passport across the scanner, the careless flick of her wrist severing me from the place I had grown up to call home. She chinned her head towards the turnstile with a nod. Not a word. Behind me, a baby cried. I could see the edge of someone's long, fat ski bags to my right. I heard the laughter of a group of teenagers. My eyes swung from side to side. Scanned the periphery. I was shivering. Heart racing.

I hesitated at that turnstile, frozen in fear for maybe a few seconds or years. My hands, my feet could not move. My breath shallowed. The guards would be coming out to arrest me at any second. TSA agents, or ICE. I tried to turn my head, looked for Steven. Would my husband be able to see me from here? How would he know if I was detained?

A scuffle of shoes behind me. I jumped. Just the teenagers.

"Ma'am," the TSA agent sighed, meeting my eyes for the first time, both eyebrows raised, now. Her acrylic-pointed nail jabbed towards the turnstile. "You may proceed. Next!"

Sometimes, the most powerful gods are also the most idle.

I stepped through the barrier, that thin place where past and future meet, but never mix. I looked back through the crowd, found Steven. He stood, waving, tall and handsome as ever, a hopeful smile on his lips, my winter coat draped on his arm. There is no need for wool in the Philippines.

So this won't be the last time I see you? I wrote back, swiping away with a shaking hand.

The US government website glared from my phone's browser.

If you are an alien and are not a lawful permanent resident of the United States, you may be inadmissible for 10 years if:

- You accrued one year or more of unlawful presence during a single stay in the United States on or after April 1, 1997; and
- You voluntarily departed the United States or were removed from the United States under any provision of law.

The 10-year unlawful presence bar applies whether you leave before, during, or after removal proceedings.

I closed my eyes against tears and tried to see Manila, but saw nothing. Only the parts of myself that would never, could never mix, separated from each other by laws and borders made and enforced by those who do not have to adhere to their bounds. By those who have never had to leave and be banned from the only home they've ever known.

I was early to my gate and regretted it. Thought of Steven, headed for the subway, and could not stay still. My feet, restless, wandered around the terminal in no particular direction. In stores in the JFK departures lounge, I sniffed perfumes, touched scarves, looked at whiskies and shoes. Breathing in the scented air, I wished that I, too, could be imported, duty-free.

In the midst of applying for my UK visa two months before, I had gathered a stack of documents. Letters, tax forms, marriage certificate, wedding and couple photos with dates, bank statements from our joint account, pay stubs, birthday cards, lease papers bearing both our names going back years.

"This is insane," Steven had said, hands on his hips. "It's easier to get the dogs into the UK."

"I'm just relieved I can apply."

Add a second layer of sweetness, perhaps sweet red beans or munggo.
Something that can also bear weight.

I thought of how these would be my last few moments in the United States, and remembered eighth-grade English, of all things. Our teacher had us read many short stories, but three stayed with me: "The Lottery," "The Most Dangerous Game," and "The Man Without a Country." Stories I immediately understood, as a loser in America's biopower lottery, as undocumented game lured in and hunted down, as a person without a country.

There, by a tall, wide window, looked out at airplanes, vessels of freedom and travel for so many, I stood, gasping a little. Thought about leaving my gate. *Let me out let me out let me out.* I wanted to run out of the terminal, out of the airport, to catch up to Steven as he swiped his MetroCard through. I wanted to feel our bodies in wool coats sitting next to each other, rocking together to the sway of the tracks in the dark. Back to Brooklyn. J to Broad Street, transferring at Delancey Street for the F to Coney Island. Exit at the Seventh Avenue Station. I wanted to sit in our rented 350-square-foot studio apartment on Eighth Street and Eighth Avenue in Park Slope, where it was warm and quiet except for the dogs' snores. With my husband and our two dogs, I could sit by the bay window, Prospect Park at one end of our street and the Eighth Street Mini Market at the other end. I could step into that beloved bodega, stamp the snow off my boots, buy bread and milk, butter and eggs. Return home. Make coffee. Make french toast. Make plans with our friends for a blizzardy dinner party in, affogatos for dessert, a kind of halo-halo. We could live there forever, my husband, our dogs, and me. Nothing needed to change.

Before I boarded, Steven called, one last time. A wordless call. Air, tears, a shared sadness. Fear. *It will be OK, my love. Just breathe,* he whispered against my quiet sobs.

In my airplane seat, I watched the routines of other people. I sent my husband one last goodbye text, which was Delivered but not yet Read. I checked the time. Time slowed, turned upside down. We lingered on the tarmac for an extra 45 minutes. I entertained thoughts of asking to get off the plane. I thought of that itchy wool hand-me-down dress I wore when we flew from Manila to Newark, twenty-two years before.

As I cried into the blanket we were each given, the plane began to move, fast and high, higher still, black asphalt merging with gray sky. Buckled into my seat, my body rose into the air. My bones, flesh, and blood vibrated, my jaw clenched against the rising. The skyline blurred, shrank, tilted. I placed a palm on the window as New York slid away from me, down into the lower corner of the rectangular window. Obscured by tears and the winter mist. I breathed goodbye to the homeland that never wanted me. Twenty-two birthdays, twenty-two Americaversaries. The roar of engines filled my head, drowned out my sobs. For my father, my mother, my sister, for what we could have been and what we became, instead. For my husband, and the life in America he could have had, if it weren't for me. For myself, for having no choices except the wrong ones. For the millions like me I had left behind, who had no choice at all.

I fell asleep for the rest of the flight, waking up only to change planes in Tokyo, at dawn. Part of me wanted to exit that airport too. Have a walk around, take an extended layover. See all of the wealth and beauty that Japan had gained at the expense of countries like mine.

I landed at Ninoy Aquino International Airport late at night. The air, warm, familiar, and heavy, was a hug from a long-lost relative. At customs, the officer waved me through, glanced at my passport.

"Where is your US visa in this passport, ma'am?"

"I don't have one," I said, looking directly at him. "Why?"

"Oh. Were you working over there, ma'am?"

"No, I grew up there, and I was a TNT." A term he would recognize.

He startled at my frankness, shifted uncomfortably at my direct gaze. *Go ahead*, I thought. *Judge me.*

"We left here in 1992, and this is my first time back. My mother lost my old passport, which is why this is blank."

His face registered condescension, maybe pity. He glanced over to the other line, for Overseas Foreign Workers. Glanced back at me.

"OK, so not an OFW. Welcome to the Philippines, ma'am."

After twenty-two and a half years away, Manila was changed. It was also not changed at all. In 1992, when we left, Corazon Aquino had just stepped down from the presidency, in accordance with the one-term limit she set for all presidents after the Marcos dictatorship. In 2015, when I returned,

Corazon's son, Benigno Aquino III, was in the final year of his term. In the years I'd been gone, I'd watched my post-dictator country fight itself, a halo-halo of self-determination and corruption learned from our occupiers, our colonizers.

I called my parents' house the morning after I landed. We had not spoken in years.

"I know," Dad said. "Your uncles told me. I don't know if I should be scared or proud."

"Doesn't Steve have a green card?" Mom wailed, and I already knew where this was headed. "He could have petitioned you, then you could have petitioned us!"

"Sure, Mom. I can help you when I'm fifty-five, and you're seventy-nine, and Dad is eighty-two."

They asked no questions about our plans, our future, though I did not expect them to—my future had always been an afterthought for my parents. I wonder if they thought about leaving America too. My sister would begin to plan her way out, not long after me.

The city of my birth had become tall, shiny, and modern in places. It also remained old and run-down in others. The squatters were gathered in camps along the sides of roads and highways, more dense and numerous than what I remembered. Those roads and highways led to large, air-conditioned, multi-level malls, where there were now Krispy Kremes, Starbucks, and Apple Stores. Gucci, Louis Vuitton, and Hermès. Huge American pickup trucks and SUVs now dominated the roads, all the better to tower over small children begging for change. The televisions had the same variety shows and classic teleseryas, sounds that mingled with K-dramas and American comedies streaming on Netflix. Their cacophony mixed in with new musicians and artists, new songs in Tagalog on streaming platforms alongside American hip-hop and the latest EDM. The Manila I spent my first nine years in was a halo-halo of post-dictatorial want and aspiration. The Manila I returned to, at thirty-one, was a halo-halo of simultaneously neocolonial mimicry and decolonial pride.

I submitted my UK visa application at the center in Makati, the Manila district where white American, British, and European migrant workers who called themselves expats tended to live and work. Tito Ed, one of Dad's older brothers, had let me stay at the big marble house, which was now his house.

He had woken up at dawn with me for the drive, had waited hours with me for the submission process. Afterward, he took me out for lunch.

"Do you want to visit your Lolo and Lola?" he asked, trying to appear casual. We had just finished a dessert of sago at gulaman after lunch.

At the cemetery, we drove on a road that was exactly like the one my grandfather and I walked on ten years before, during the dream walk we had on the night he died. The trees, as in the dream vision, were the same, one, two, three. And where Lolo Pedring said "This is me, for now" in that dream walk, stopping on the side of the road, his hands on my shoulders, was where he now lay buried, next to his wife, my Lola Rosing. This was where he said goodbye in my dreams. It was real.

I fell to my knees and sobbed. *I'm so sorry I couldn't be here for you, Lolo and Lola. What is in me, Lolo? What did you mean? Who am I supposed to be?*

In those weeks of waiting for my UK spouse visa, I woke up dreamless. Alone in a rented studio apartment, anxious about moving to a new country I had never even seen before. I took long walks to reacquaint myself with Manila, to calm my stomach. I ate food and sipped drinks from street vendors, paid in peso coins and bills depicting men with noses and lips like mine. I swallowed taho. Cheese ice cream. Fish balls. Halo-halo. My cousins teased me for my Taglish, which I deserved. My uncles said I looked pale, like I needed the sun. They were right, and I bathed in it, letting my shoulders burn, my hands brown. The light in Manila was different, an all-encompassing, equatorial kind of light. It shone down at a direct angle, its rays warmer, more golden. My body and mind responded, a calamansi tree in the right kind of light. Slowly, I felt happier, my New York seasonal winter depression faded by the sun. Every day, I ate food from a different karinderya, a new turo-turo, a street cart I hadn't seen before. My daily ashtanga yoga practice melted away, replaced by meditations at dawn.

To heal the person afflicted with the duwende's pasma, which may be feverish and itchy or chilled and numb, there are remedies that a healer can attempt. Massages in ginger, coconut oil, and garlic to encourage the circulation of blood and energy. Hot soaks in rice water and bayabas leaves. Steam therapy. Drinks made of holy basil leaves. Often, this course of natural ingredients from the land is effective, and the pasma withdraws from the body in the course of a few days. The afflicted is advised, going forward, to avoid overly cold things, especially in the cool of night.

"You're glowing, Jilly," Steve said during one of our twice-daily Skype calls. Our London apartment, rental contract signed for two years, echoed with his voice and my absence. Next to him, one of our dogs, Ron, tried to eat Steve's sandwich.

"I do feel pretty good, yeah. I look like myself."

I squinted at my laptop. I could see only the tall walls and high ceiling of the London apartment, a converted warehouse rental. I tried to imagine London as a real place, with air and sidewalks and a river. Could only imagine what I had read from Charles Dickens. Gas lamps and horses, inequality and gruel, monarchy and subjugation. On our Skype calls, I fought to stay upbeat, stirred up whatever optimism I could find. Steven was not nervous about the UK visa application at all. Despite knowing how deeply I was scarred by my years of living undocumented, he still could not comprehend the fear and anxiety I felt, and I did not expect him to. In his experience, visas were mere paperwork, an administrative chore, nothing to worry about. *Why wouldn't they approve your application?* he often asked, as I cried, body shaking with anxiety.

Add another layer of ice, not too thick, to make room for more.

"My god," I said to my Tita Renee. "This is incredible!"

My aunt and I were at a branch of Razon's in Manila's Mall of Asia, celebrating having just picked up my British spouse visa from the UK's visa center. She had taken me under her wing on this first trip back, ever the warm, generous Tita I remembered from childhood. This glass of halo-halo was her way of celebrating for me. I stuffed another spoonful of leche flan, shaved ice, and condensed milk into my mouth. It had been a very fast five weeks. Part of me could have stayed another month, turning brown and Filipino; part of me wanted to be in London weeks ago, with my husband and our dogs.

"It's so good, no?" She smiled. "They're from the same part of Pampanga your Lolo Baldo is from."

This version of halo-halo was an exercise in elegant minimalism. Milk, ice, leche flan, jackfruit. It focused on the essential sensations of halo-halo:

its milkiness, its softness, its contrast of sharp ice and melting leche flan, the texture of jackfruit. It dispensed with the coyness of mixing up to a dozen ingredients in an effort to find a harmonic whole. It said: life is simple, be happy. Could life ever be simple? Could I be happy?

"I wish you weren't leaving yet, Jill," she said, her hand on my arm. I placed my hand on her hand. I wished there was no such thing as leaving.

I told Steven the good news: I received a full UK Partner Visa, good for two and a half years, renewable once, then a five-year track to permanent residency and citizenship one year after that, in 2021 or 2022. The US and the UK vastly differ from each other in their visa policies. For all of its flaws, the UK's immigration system is more efficient and process-driven than the US's, with its racist quotas, red tape, biased interviews, and bureaucratic sluggishness. As we talked on the phone, he walked home from his office in the City of London to our apartment, just by the Barbican.

"I'm buying your flight right now, my love," he had said, his voice wobbling. "Is the twelfth OK, next week? We can spend Valentine's Day together?"

"I'd go today, if I could." I laughed. "But my old school friends want to take me out for my birthday tomorrow night."

All I remember about turning thirty-two was shots of whiskey and tequila at a bar called Finders Keepers and being found by my friends behind a curtain, passed out while my phone glowed calling Steven. My friends were still as raucous and fun as when we were nine, when we were at the School of the Holy Spirit, a group of foul-mouthed little girls obsessed with Sanrio. If I'd stayed in 1992, my life might have been just as beautiful as theirs.

As a farewell, my mother's family took me out on my last day. We visited Mount Taal and had lunch at one of the beautiful mountainside restaurants overlooking the volcano-lake-within-a-lake. We feasted on lechon, kare-kare, pinakbet, bulalo, barbecue skewers, and, for dessert, halo-halo. This version contained a galaxy of ingredients, stripes of color and sweetness, of ice and milk. This halo-halo said: life *is* complex. Be happy.

It was strange, paying a departure tax at the airport before my flight to England. All Philippine citizens have to do it, a fee paid for exiting the country. I did not have the cash for this departure tax; I had used up the last of my pesos in my Philippine bank account. I called Tito Nathaniel, Mom's second-oldest brother, in tears and panic. What if I missed my flight because of this tax?

"Don't worry, anak. We're just outside. I'll come give you the money, ha? Don't cry."

They were all still outside, waiting until I was safely at the gate. I still remember Tito Nathaniel's face as he handed the cash to me: torn, wistful. Like Tito Raynold, he only saw my mother when he looked at my face, so much like hers.

The warm, magenta dusk of Manila at takeoff and the hot, tangerine dawn at the layover in Dubai gave way to the pale, gray clouds and fat raindrops of England at touchdown. At Heathrow's passport control, I nearly hugged the border control officer when he said, "A very warm welcome to the United Kingdom, madam."

Steven met me at Heathrow. Still as tall and handsome as ever, my winter coat draped on the same arm, folded the same way, as if he had carried it with him for all of the weeks we were apart, taking it with him to bed, to work meetings, to grocery runs. A talisman, a lucky charm, a fervent, wooly prayer to the petty, hostile gods of the Home Office. I ran to the open gate, a willing and happy cliché from *Love Actually*.

For my first meal, Steven took me to what would become our local pub: the Jugged Hare, just off Old Street, across from the Barbican. We ordered steak and ale pies with chips, two pints of Guinness on the side. I dashed brown sauce on my plate and dabbed in forked bites of gravied beef and crispy, hot potato. We let the head settle on the Guinness, then clinked our glasses together, ankles entwined beneath the scratched wooden table. Thankful fingers laced in shared relief. We walked home to our flat on Dufferin Street, winter coats wrapped around our stuffed bellies.

For dessert, we dug into my suitcases until we found two Filipino ensaymada buns—softer, fatter, and sweeter than their Mallorcan cousins. There, sitting on the floor of our bare, clean kitchen, we chatted through happy, chewing mouths, licked sugar, cheese, and cream from our fingers. Our two old dogs, still tired from transitioning to a new land and a new time, snored on me, one drooling face on each thigh.

"You're safe now, Jilly," my husband said to me, licking the cream off the ensaymada packaging.

"I am," I said. I thought about my father, my mother, and my sister. When will they be safe?

There was a discomfort in the air in 2015, that final Obama year, though it at first felt certain that America's first Black president would be followed by its first woman president. I watched from afar in London. Began to see the country I hid inside for two decades, understood the feeling of seeing the self only after leaving America, as James Baldwin once wrote about. And as America descended into rhetorical flames the color of those red MAGA hats, Britain soon followed, leaving the European Union in a fit of nativism. My adopted nation cut off its arms, feet, and nose to spite an imaginary enemy conjured up by its politicians to paper over their other failures. The same old story, which I could not seem to escape. The UK was retreating into its scared, isolationist corners, too afraid to look beyond their fears, let alone at themselves. At their real problems. Brexit and Trump. Blame the immigrants. Blame the poor.

Drizzle some condensed milk onto this ice. Work quickly, against the melting.

In those first few years in London, I felt myself melting. After twenty-two years of hiding, violence, pain, and want, the world had opened itself to me. I could begin to see what life was like for people made legible and legitimate by papers.

In October 2015, eight months after arriving in London, I matriculated into the Master's in Documentary Film program at the University of the Arts London, at the London College of Communication. I was accepted based on my professional experience as a writer and a photographer, with letters from my former magazine editor, my mentor in photography, and lecturers from Pratt helping to assure my acceptance. An impossibility in America, where education was more of a rigid hierarchy, a points program, an explicit class system. A multilevel marketing scheme that left millions in debt. For such a class-strangled structure, Britain still had its surprises. I qualified for university loans and rejoiced. After so many years of qualifying for absolutely nothing, this was a miracle greater than being accepted into university.

I already knew what my dissertation documentary film would be. I was going back to the Philippines. To my father's family's mountains. I did not know where my future was headed. It made sense to look back and finally see where I came from, not just in this lifetime, but in my ancestors'. I wanted to understand this feeling in my stomach of being from nowhere in particular. Of longing to belong.

"All your Dad is asking," said my mother, "is that you don't mention that he is from up there."

"Mom," I sighed. "Is that really all you have to say?"

I had spent the past hour telling her about my week in the Cordilleras, about the journey to see the legendary Indigenous tattooist Apo Whang-Od, the center of my documentary film. It was to become a meditation, a poetic film, something like Kidlat Tahimik or Werner Herzog or Agnès Varda would make. An experiment, an autoethnography. The discovery of myself through blood and ink. The title of the film.

Apo Whang-Od had touched my chin, tilted my face upward when she first met me.

"Ah," she had said through a translator. "A beauty. You look like a Tadian girl."

I beamed with pride. One of the translators said that his brother knew of some Damatacs from Tadian. I felt my feet connecting to the soil. My lungs inhaling the air. As if the ancestors were reaching up and out through my body.

"You know, I think we're partly white," my father once said, in a fit of delusion common to many Filipinos who claim whiteness or European ancestry. "We have a French ancestor."

"Really?" I had said. "Or was that just another name one of our ancestors was forced to take?" This is the likeliest explanation for almost all Filipinos with European surnames. A forced surname from a missionary or a conquistador for the sake of colonial recordkeeping. Like my father, many Filipinos pretend that they have Caucasian blood mixed into their veins. They recycle their relatives' dubious tales of whiteness.

Denial like my father's, like many Filipinos', like Spain's, like America's, is a way of reconciling mixed feelings. Spain wishes to erase its colonization of the Philippines, as if one less country might make up for their subjugation of other continents. America denies its colonial history so that it may feel like an exceptional, benevolent power and not what it truly is: the latest in a long line of greedy, bloody empires. The Philippines' leaders deny their complicity in their citizens' suffering so that they may continue to place their own survival above all others.

When I feel particularly guilty about how much better my life has become since leaving America, I notice that I want to deny my privileges. But I cannot deny: my sexuality (not too gay), my skin (not too dark), my material comfort through marriage to a man with his own privileges (white, which has the power to eclipse his working-class origins), my education (awarded with distinction from just off-center of empire), and where I live (just off-center of empire).

Continue layering the lighter ingredients on top: tapioca, sago, nata de coco.

Filipinos speak hundreds of tongues every day, an intersection of all the people who have come by, who have come before, who have come and stayed. A genetic test says that I am 96 percent Austronesian, primarily from our northern mountains. I am also partly Chinese, specifically from Guangdong. In smaller percentages, this test claims that I am also a bit South Indian. I have trace ancestry as an Indigenous American, from the Yucatan, perhaps through our shared colonial past. My first language is English, followed by Tagalog, with a bit of Ilocano. Somewhere between our languages, suspended in the murk of translation, we exist as Filipinos. If you ask some Filipinos today if I am Filipino, they may say that I am not. If you ask some Americans today if I am American, they may also say the same. Say that I will never be. As for Britain, time will tell.

In 1946, the United States finally granted the Philippines independence, forty-eight years after they first ignored our declaration at the end of the Spanish-American War. They chose the date of July 4 with no self-awareness. Before granting this independence, the Americans committed a final act of betrayal that would reverberate through to my life. In February 1946, President Harry S. Truman, the Democrat from Missouri, signed into law the Rescission Act, which had just passed Congress. This act stripped Filipino soldiers who fought for the United States of veterans' benefits and American citizenship, which was promised to them by FDR's administration. Congress decided that the cost of $3 billion for veterans in the Philippines was too much. Instead, they gave the Philippine government—not the veterans—$200 million as a lump sum. My grandfather never saw a dollar.

Of the sixty-six countries that fought for the Americans during World War II, only Filipino veterans like Lolo Pedring, my grandfather, were stripped of their monetary benefits and right to citizenship. Many Filipino soldiers are still owed restitution. Decades later, my grandfather appealed to American senators like John Kerry and Ted Kennedy. He sought to claim the citizenship promised to him, so that he could petition my father, my mother, my sister, and me. We were languishing in America at the time, and he worried for our future. John Kerry's office wrote back. The letter said something like: *We understand, and we are so sorry, but there is nothing we can do.* The Clinton scandal was unfolding at that time.

A small handful of living veterans in the US eventually received a small restitution in 2009. A single payment of $15,000 each, for Filipino veterans living in the US; $9,000 and still no citizenship for those outside the US. Lolo Pedring died in 2004 still in hope that this might someday change.

To heal the pasma for good, it may also be necessary to ask the healer to address the offended duwende so that they might stop harming the body. The ritual, called tawas, involves the soaking of a crystalline alum stone, which leaves a pattern in the water. The healer reads this pattern to determine the cause of illness. Often it is a duwende. To help the afflicted, the healer anoints the ailing, pasma-ridden part of the body with this tawas water. And then, speaking a few words to the duwende, the healer throws the water westward, into the setting sun. If it is effective, the sick person's pasma—the immobile numbing of the self—is soon released by the duwende.

I turned thirty-six on my fourth year as a legal British resident. Even after a few years of freedom, I still felt afraid, angry, and hungry. I was writing almost every day. Essays, short stories, attempts at novels. Terrible poetry. I needed to write, needed that writing to be seen beyond the pages kept secret in my laptop. I needed to write about my life in America, now that I felt safe enough to do so. Needed to talk about being undocumented, which I did, privately, dinner by dinner, drinks by drinks, with people I could trust. I needed to write about everything that had happened. To make myself legible and legitimate. For my story to no longer be written in invisible ink.

I applied for two creative writing master's degree programs. I must have thought it would help me to be more brave, help me to write towards being seen. I submitted bits of a novel, a magical realist one that had a protagonist who could move between dimensions, and would later find out that she belonged to none. Wrote a statement to explain my lack of undergraduate degree.

On March 13, 2019, after a call with a commercial film client one afternoon, I checked my emails. I was working from home, sitting on the living room floor of our small apartment in Hampstead, London. Bored and disillusioned with my job as a video producer for a corporate film production company. My dream of working in documentary film had slipped away years before. Despite my short film's early success—an official selection at DOC NYC, the winner at a film festival in Ireland—a career in documentary seemed to be the refuge of people who could afford financial tenuousness, people who still had the nerve for it. People who had the right connections. Men who were taken seriously by other men, simply because they were men.

Two new emails arrived, one titled "MSt in Creative Writing." My hand shook as I clicked on it. Our new puppy, Gus, snored on my lap.

I am delighted to inform you that it has been decided that you will be offered a place on the course . . .

My hands slid off my keyboard. I had interviewed at Cambridge University just the week before. I had applied there and at Oxford as a joke to myself. An hour before going inside Cambridge's Madingley Hall, I sat in the parking lot, in our rented car, while Steven walked our puppy around the Capability Brown gardens. As I practiced certain lines, thoughts, ideas for my interview, an enormous black crow landed—thud—on the car's hood. Stared at me as if it knew me. Watched me mouth words while gazing into my eyes. One minute, maybe another thirty seconds, passed. When I tried to take a picture, it flew away.

As I read the acceptance email over and over, my body began to shiver. I could not control my hands, could not hold the glass of water in front of me. Sobs issued from deep inside my belly. I cried for maybe fifteen minutes, maybe longer, to exhaustion. I fell asleep while still shivering from tears. As if my body were leaving itself.

When I opened my eyes, Lolo Pedring was there, on the couch, next to

Gus. I sat up, felt the rug marks on my face. He was younger, his hair more black than white, the version of him that I knew best.

"You see? I told you," he said, in Tagalog. "What did I tell you?"

I stared at him. "It is in you."

"Now you know." He smiled.

When Steve came home from work, I was still there, sitting on the living room rug, my hands in my lap.

"Hey babe," he said, hanging up his scarf. "You OK?"

Outside, on our windowsill, an enormous black crow flew off.

"Ooh," my husband said, coming over to kiss my forehead. "Look. Your bird!"

Add another layer of ice.

I wrote the beginnings of this book as part of my master's degree at Cambridge. My dissertation supervisor, Dr. Midge Gillies, had gently encouraged me to move towards memoir. I had been second-guessing the novel I had begun writing.

"I think it might be a really useful exercise to just get this part of your life on the page," she had said during one of our calls. It was April 2020, deep into the first COVID lockdown. She was right. Until I could imagine myself on the page, make my life real and legible on the page, I would be unable to imagine anything else.

It was strange, to suddenly become legible. To "articulate the situation of the victim," as Baldwin once said, to have "ceased to be a victim." At the end of the master's program, I was accepted onto the PhD in English Literature, also at Cambridge. My broad aim was to study contemporary Filipino American novels as a critique of American empire. It was one hell of an achievement, with no undergraduate degree, no less. Still: I could not ignore the mixed feeling of disappointment, mostly in myself. I felt a deep ambivalence and confusion about who I was becoming. Was this what all of my suffering was for? So that I could become a part of the same imperial machinery that, for two decades of my life—arguably all of my life—had chewed up my family, spat us out? I was slowly becoming swallowed by the very empires I sought to criticize. In becoming a part of these exalted circles—book publishing, academia—my own argument for liberation had been, I felt, diminished.

"I get what you're saying, Jilly," a friend said at dinner one night, "but you're hardly a sellout. You suffered in empire. You left empire. No one can call you a hypocrite for that."

"For that, anyway," I said. "And I moved to England. Hardly liberatory."

"You are allowed," said another friend, "your own measure of relief."

In this new life, where I am an author, a grad student, and the co-owner of a small house with my husband, I am still frozen in place by depression. I am still shredded by anxiety over my place, traumas, desires, and privileges. I do not know what to do with these bitter and sour ingredients in the increasingly sweet halo-halo that is my life now. I am still riven with the desire to prove myself, with the belief that excellence is required in order to be seen as equal. I am proud of myself; I am ashamed of myself. I am convinced of my true potential; I am convinced I shall fail, as I always do. I deserve to be here; I am here only through the goodness of others.

If desired, add a layer of leche flan.

After five years and thousands of pounds paid to the UK for visa applications, I became a permanent resident, one step closer to British citizenship. To earn permanent residency, applicants were required to pass the Life in the UK exam. It was short, just twenty-four questions over forty-five minutes. I could get up to six questions wrong and still pass.

It was a strange exam, a mix of bland nationalism, sweetened monarchism, and frozen solipsism—questions about dead kings, bank holidays, roast beef, the Beatles, Mo Farah. Nothing about civic knowledge that really matters in everyday life in the UK, such as: How to register to vote. What the political parties stand for. How to obtain a driver's license. How to get an appointment with the NHS. How to register children for school. How to fund the NHS. How to raise the poverty cap to feed more children in need. How to live with neighbors who do not know how to interact with a woman of color. How to properly care for Filipino health care workers in the NHS who were dying in record-setting numbers during a pandemic.

Still, I stirred my criticisms in with a small scoop of gratitude. In all of my decades in America, I had never come close to even thinking about a citizenship exam.

"I understand your gratitude," my sister said, her big eyes full of understanding. "And your guilt." She was also preparing for her citizenship application in the Netherlands, where she had been since 2017, having escaped America through a neuroscience PhD program just outside Amsterdam. She, too, was seeking refuge in another former empire.

I passed the exam with only one question wrong. I mixed up King Charles I and II. The first one was executed, not the second.

"I wouldn't get half of these bloody questions right," Steven said, tapping through the app I had used to practice. "By this standard, most Brits would lose their citizenship."

Add another thin layer of ice.

For most of 2021 and 2022, I did not speak to my parents. I worried that they were only rebuilding a relationship with me in the hopes that I would sponsor their visas. Some days, I believed that it was the right thing to do, that I could at least help get them out of America. But on other days, they felt grasping, artificial, more concerned with speaking to my husband, their white, British son-in-law with a good income. My sister had long stopped speaking to them, feeling the same distrust.

When I graduated from Cambridge one May afternoon, words in Latin pronounced in an old hall, my shoulders cloaked in a graduate's silken hood, I held my master's degree in front of me, posed for pictures outside Senate House with Steven. I looked at all of the parents and thought about my own. Even at thirty-nine, I needed them. Would my parents' pride be real, or would it be the kind that is wielded publicly, like a weapon, in salu-salo parties, in WhatsApp chats with friends, in Facebook groups? As a father took photos of his daughter on the Senate House steps, proud and present, I thought of what Dad had said when he had found out about my acceptance to Cambridge, two years before.

"Can you get a university sticker? Two of them, for the Lexus and the Land Cruiser." The vehicles he had bought in lieu of my undergraduate education.

After my graduation, late on a July evening, my first summer as a PhD student, I was working on an exciting rewrite of this book's first chapter, changing the recipe from tinola to pinikpikan. I wanted to incorporate an indigenous ritual of divination, complete with chanting women and embodied spirits, old grievances from dead ancestors, screaming prayers and blood-soaked animal sacrifice, sourced from an old academic text by a Filipino researcher. The words flowed, as if someone else were speaking through me, like in the ritual.

It was, by then, impossible to not constantly think about my father and his illnesses of mind and body. I had failed to call for his recent sixty-seventh birthday, hadn't talked to him since his birthday the year before. Our parents' wedding anniversary was in a couple of weeks. Maybe, I thought, I'll call then.

A ding! softly rang through the dining room, as if from a bell. Loud enough to not be an accident. I shot up from my chair. What was that sound? I tapped the wineglasses in the kitchen, empty wine bottles by the back door, a mug on the counter, but the sounds were wrong. I spotted an old brass Las Vegas! hotel call bell on a shelf in the dining room, across from where I was sitting. Tapped the brass with my fingernail. Yes, that was the sound. Weird. How? I looked at the clock. Just after 12:05 a.m.

My phone vibrated against the dining table, shuddered through the cold, quiet chill in the room. My sister.

"Dude, I've been calling you. Did you not get Mom's texts? It's Dad."

I took the phone off my ear, scrolled through my messages. A dozen missed calls.

He's gone. Paramedics declared time of death 7:05 p.m.

US eastern time, 12:05 a.m. here. When the bell rang.

Drizzle a generous amount of condensed or evaporated milk on the top layer of ice.

"He was trying," our mother wailed on the phone. "We were packing up the house, getting ready to sell it. We were going to go back to the Philippines."

Dad had mowed the house's wide, deep lawns that morning. There was a heat wave going through New Jersey, and my parents did not have an air conditioner. The house was becoming too much for Dad to maintain, with its tall trees, large lawns, and extensive roof gutters.

"He said he was tired, that he was dizzy. He napped for a bit, and when he woke up, he was so pale. So pale!" she sobbed. "He had spent all week packing up the house, throwing things away. He was so overwhelmed. I told him to not work so hard!"

My father died just after he woke up from his afternoon nap, while sitting on the edge of their bed. While trying to put his clothes on. He had finally agreed to go to the hospital. Had fretted about the cost without insurance. He was putting on his socks when he fell back onto the bed. There, on his side, he took his last breaths, gasped for air as his heart struggled, each breath deeper and deeper, until no more breaths followed. He was dying as the paramedics raced into their driveway, as they tried to revive him in their bedroom. As they carried him out of the house. As their machine pumped his naked chest, his body jerking up and down, no clothing except for his boxer shorts, on the front walk of the house. As my mother sobbed over his jaundiced skin. As she tried to call their daughters. As the neighbors watched. As I sat in my clean, comfortable house in England, ready to apply for citizenship. As I wrote my book and praised myself for thinking of calling my father, of calling my mother, in two weeks. As I congratulated myself for being a forgiving, magnanimous daughter.

This was no pasma, no duwende, no folkloric diagnosis that an albularyo could cure. My father died of diabetes-induced cardiac arrest, brought on from years of eating poorly, drinking, and being too afraid to go to the doctor. My father died from years of being undocumented and without health insurance. Frozen in place by fear and by the cost of health care.

Despite my permanent resident status in the UK at the time, I was unable to return to the US for the funeral.

"The only way you might be able to return to the US is ten years after you left, so 2025, or through a British passport, once you have it," an immigration lawyer said, not unkindly. "I am so sorry."

My sister, similarly stuck in between visas and citizenships, could not go home to America either. She and I drifted apart at this time, as we tended to our own grief. To our own separate relationships with our father. To our own broken hearts.

We watched Dad's funeral on YouTube, livestreamed by Saint Veronica's Church in Howell, New Jersey, a funeral workaround that began during COVID lockdown and remains in place today. His last picture, from a recent birthday, was blown up, poster-sized, and placed on an easel next to his bronze urn, which I had ordered online with next-day shipping. A cousin read our eulogies. Our mother wore a black dress I helped her pick out over a video call. She cried alone.

When the funeral ended, I went upstairs to the bathroom and locked the door. Howled in rage.

Finish off the halo-halo with a scoop of ice cream, perhaps two, if there is room.

The Philippines may have become independent in 1946, but we remained a dependent, a regional ally, and a military outpost for the Americans for decades to come. Air force and naval bases abounded until 1991, when the Americans were told to leave by the post-dictatorship government. Now, with the dictator's son's government in place, the Americans have returned, with four new military bases aside from the ones they have agreed to reopen. Chinese aggression—the theft of our islands, the theft of our waters—is the new fear. American military protection is the old, ever-present answer. To this day, there is still no true reckoning, let alone recognition, of the United States' exploitation of the Philippines. In this world, there is no such thing as free independence. This applies to me, of course.

On an overcast November day in 2023, nine months after my fortieth birthday, sixteen months after Dad's death and thirty-one years since my family first arrived in America, I had my British citizenship ceremony. I slipped on a black Filipino barong, a traditional men's dress shirt often made of piña or silk. This one, made by women artisans for Vinta Gallery, was tailored for women, embroidered with Filipino flora and fauna. Visayan hornbill and Anahaw palm fronds embroidered in black thread on sheer black silk. I wore the barong with a long black skirt of raw-edged leather. I left my hair undone, a mess, like me. A bisexual third-culture kid's dress of mourning and celebration. Steven changed into a suit and drove us to Alconbury Weald, a small town on the outskirts of Cambridge.

"Ready?"

"No." I smiled, a little. "Let's do it."

In a modern, high-ceilinged room, forty-eight citizens-to-be gathered to pledge allegiance. If, like me, they had paid around 2,500 pounds for each visa renewal round, this room represented nearly half a million pounds' worth of revenue for the UK's Home Office. We would each pay 93 pounds after this to apply for a passport. I thought of a Filipina friend, a journalist who had married a British man in the 1980s. *It was free, back then. One day, I just got my passport in the mail.*

A local councilman stood up to speak. He said something about the natural beauty of Cambridgeshire, the ancient cathedrals and the university. Something about contributing to the fastest-growing economy in the country, about contributing our cultures to Britain. And what, I wondered, was Britain contributing to our lives, besides passport privileges?

The councilman was followed by a man wearing a medal of sorts. The king's representative. He said that five hundred years ago, he would have had the power to conscript citizens to fight for the king. In a regretful tone, he said that he no longer has that right. And that while we no longer fought for the king, we were to represent the king.

And how, I wondered, did the king represent us, besides on banknotes?

A third speaker, the woman running the ceremony, told us about the ancient Greeks, where democracy began. That the word *citizen* was Greek ("Wrong—it's Latin. Greek is *polis*," I hissed to my husband). She said that in Greece, citizens were people considered to be upstanding members of society, that it was an earned privilege to be a part of a democratic society. And how, I wondered, did natural-born British people earn their citizenship in this particular democracy?

Before we were allowed to receive our naturalization certificates, we were required to make promises. We were divided into two self-selected groups. Half of the attendees had chosen to speak an oath to God. They said, "I swear by Almighty God." The other half of us had chosen a substitute for God, an affirmation. We said "I do solemnly, sincerely, and truly declare and affirm." I believed in myself. Still, this sense of autonomy was short-lived. The first line of the mandatory oath and affirmation was followed by these words:

> ... *on becoming a British Citizen, I will be faithful and bear true allegiance to His Majesty King Charles III, his Heirs and Successors, according to law.*

The pledge, the second part of all the words we had to say to earn our piece of paper, was more civic-minded:

I will give my loyalty to the United Kingdom and respect its rights and freedoms. I will uphold its democratic values. I will observe its laws faithfully and fulfill my duties and obligations as a British citizen.

In the video Steven took of me, I choked up, teary, at the words "uphold its democratic values." I was thinking of the Windrush immigrants brought in by the British government on a ship of the same name, Black citizens of the Commonwealth used for labor and then deported without legal rights, decades later, by the UK Home Office. I was thinking of the refugees who washed up on British shores, dead, or were turned away and detained, against international and human rights law. I was thinking of the frozen class mobility in this nation, of generations of working-class people struggling to pay bills, to feed their children, while the government paid for wars and weaponry to be wielded on people overseas. I was thinking of the people in the room, forced to pledge allegiance to an unelected figurehead as a contingency for naturalization. A mandatory pledge that turned us into subjects of the crown. A pledge that classed us, separated us as artificial, state-made. Natural-born citizens never had to make a pledge, could feel and say whatever they wanted about monarchy, and were never threatened with the loss of their citizenship should they refuse to "bear true allegiance" to any monarch. The British government's official guidelines regarding citizenship states:

A person aged over 18 cannot be registered or naturalised as a British citizen unless he or she has made the relevant citizenship oath and pledge at a citizenship ceremony.

"Have you ever had to pledge allegiance to the royals to keep your citizenship?" I whispered to my husband.

"No."

"Not even when you were a baby?"

"No. So bloody weird."

We were finally given our citizenship certificates. The near-equivalent of my husband's birth certificate. A tiered membership. In the envelope was a letter with a picture of the home secretary, the one who was in the news for turning away refugees and contravening international law. Her smile did not reach her eyes in the photo. Tucked underneath my citizenship certificate, her letter, with its vague platitudes about earning naturalization, felt like a threat.

Before we could leave, we were asked to sing the British national anthem. A familiar melody, though I did not want to save anyone's king. I wanted only to return to the land where my father died, back in time. I wanted only to save my father. This British citizenship could have been one way to do it. Too little sweetness, too late. Could I have saved my father? He was a terrible person, but I did not want him dead. Britain was a confused country regressing into its past, but I still wanted to be a part of it. Who was I to complain? This was better than my life in America had ever been. Better than many people's lives.

A better life, Mom used to say to me, when I was wailing about leaving Manila for America.

At home, I cried and could not explain why. The ceremony felt empty, contradictory, unsure if it wanted democracy or monarchy. What did I go through all of this for—years of paperwork and exams, ten thousand British pounds—if it meant that at the very end, my rights as a citizen, to freedom, to my own political beliefs, were still to be held hostage, given only with contingencies, as long as I swore to uphold an antiquated system of inequality? What had I agreed to? What had I become? A subject?

"Don't take it too seriously, my love," Steven said, in an attempt at comfort. "They had the British flag draped over a massive television, for god's sake. It's just ceremony. Very weird, inappropriate ceremony."

"The flag over the television was a little too symbolic," I sobbed.

"Let me put this away for you," he said, taking my citizenship certificate. "Before you get tears and snot all over it."

The citizenship certificate is an A4-sized sheet of paper. We keep it in a safe, along with my other papers. All of them unassuming, but life-altering. These papers say that: I am married to Steven, and he is married to me. We own a house together. I was born in the Republic of the Philippines. I am a citizen of the United Kingdom of Great Britain and Northern Ireland. These papers confer rights and expectations. Despite everything, it is a relief to have these papers speak for me, for once.

For a crunchy topping, use Rice Krispies or Corn Flakes, or pinipig, if you're lucky.

"So," Steven says. "How do you feel now?"

It is weeks later, and we are staying in for the weekend. My brand new UK passport has just arrived. As someone who grew up rootless, trapped in my father's house of hoarded things, I treasure being safe and warm in our house in Cambridge, with its joyous mix of Filipino textiles, art, and carvings, of Welsh bells, ceramics, and chairs. It is my second year as a homeowner, which is still a strange thought. This patch of land may be small, but it belongs to us, just another pair of Brits.

We clink our glasses of halo-halo to celebrate. Shaved ice and sweets as brief relief from the inferno of the world. The chewing of preserved fruits and coconut meat between fat blobs of ube ice cream, leche flan, nata de coco, and condensed milk, shocking the gums between teeth. Halo-halo is deliberate, a purposeful mixing of what may or may not go together, ingredients thrown in according to your own personal liking and need. With the stir of a long spoon, the sense of purpose gives way into a melting, a surrender into whatever the blend may turn out to be.

"Tired," I say. I scoop a piece of leche flan and ice into my mouth. And I am. A three decades kind of tired. I tell my husband that I feel only relief at being able to travel more freely, often visa-free. I want to see my sister in the Netherlands. EU travel is easier as a British citizen, even after Brexit. I now have access to British freedoms, which are rooted in its once-global empire, in its hundreds of colonized countries. I feel like a hypocrite. Complicit. The most guilty of survivors.

At the age of forty-one, after everything, I no longer have the energy to be angry. With exhaustion, there is a surrender to the ambivalence that comes from a lifetime, from twenty years undocumented in the United States. It does not matter to which country I pledge allegiance. I no longer believe in the goodness of any country. Countries mean boundaries. Boundaries mean exclusion. Exclusion often means death.

"What do you want from a country?" asked Alexander Chee, a writer whose time, space, and wisdom on this plane is broader, deeper than mine. He sighed as he said it, looked up and off into the distance, perhaps answering his own question for himself. Two queer Asian Americans, sharing lunch and ambivalences in a Cambridge University cafeteria.

I have no answer. I know we seek to be freed of, or at least less bound by, the poor, starved imagination of countries, laws, and borders. I know we seek to be cured of the numbed pasma of nationalism and the grasping duwende of the state. I know we seek to have the right to swallow something sweeter than the false, brief relief of patriotism and identity. What this means materially and in practice, none of us know.

No one knows, I can hear my Lolo Pedring saying to me, a crow on my study's window ledge. *This is why we have halo-halo.*

EPILOGUE

Bayah ng I-pugao
(I-pugao Rice Wine)

The Present

YIELDS ABOUT 1½ QUARTS

Banana leaves
2¼ pounds glutinous black Ballatinao rice
4 ounces bubod (rice yeast)

"Should we try them?" Steven says.

These three wines have been resting for one year, six months, and three months. I made them after Dad died. My grief and rage, boiled, rotted, fermented, clarified, aged. Sealed inside glass. I am faced by three bottles in the kitchen of this Cambridge house, which my husband and I are selling in exchange for a new journey. Each bottle asks me to look back in different shades: berry red, melon pink, ripe peach. Made by my two searching hands, grasping for a goodbye, they now soften, fade with time.

"Let's go for the one year," I say. Steven pours.

This glass of bayah is sweet, bready, gentle, lingering in the back of the throat. My spirit waits for the wine to take hold. When it does, we will mourn and celebrate all at once. Dance with the future and walk with memory, that still-developing ferment of beauty and terror, omissions and lies. With a sip of this wine, my throat will awaken and speak a humble offering up to Sky World, so that the god Liddum may look after us.

Our rice wine is known in my father's mountains as tapuy. The I-pugao, with whom I share blood and whose process I mimicked through YouTube, call theirs bayah. Aged in banana leaves, the rot fermented with rice yeast, it is simple in its creation, complex in its purposes. The I-pugao drink this wine for weddings and funerals. Conjurings, divinations, and healing rituals, also.

My husband and I clink glasses. I pause by my father's urn, moved from its secret nook inside one of the fireplaces. It sits atop Dad's piano, my prized and only inheritance.

"Mom will meet you in Manila," I say to the cylinder of engraved copper. As in the last year of his life, Dad says nothing to me in return.

With a fresh cloth soaked in warm water, wipe the banana leaves clean until no dirt remains.

The squat, heavy box arrived at our doorstep almost one year before, on December 22, 2022.

"Ooh!" I had said to the courier, holiday tipsy, a glass of Laphroaig 18, my favorite, in hand. "What's this?"

"Ma'am," he said, looking sadly at the box by my feet. "Do you need help to bring it in?"

I smiled, said no thank you, happy holidays. He backed away, his eyebrows knitted in worry. I hauled the box inside, slashed the top open. Bubble wrap, paper, a hard, cold lump. I pulled the cold lump out of the box, unfurled the final layer of bubble wrap. Freezing cold, metal cold. Heavy.

Not a present.

"What is it, Jilly?" Steven said, coming down the stairs. I was sobbing.

It was Dad's urn. Dad's ashes. So heavy, even without his blood, his soul. I did not know that it was coming. The only indication of what was inside was a line of small print under our address. HUMAN REMAINS—CREMATED. Mom, in her usual neglect excused as forgetfulness, had not told me that it was coming.

"I thought you'd know," she said. "You sent me the USPS packaging."

"Months ago, Mom."

Clean a pot with soap and hot water. Dry over the stove, on gentle heat.

If we had honored my father the way our elders' elders honored their dead, we would have slaughtered three pigs and danced around his body, cups of sweet bayah in hand. One of us would have offered a short, singing prayer to the gods. One of us would have spilled the bayah onto the ground, consecrating the soil. One of us would have swallowed the wine into our blood until the present disappears and all that we are is what we remember. These would have been his true last rites, more ancient and sacred than the priest's lines of printed text, words mumbled up to their short-tempered, solitary god.

For over a year, Dad rested in this house, as if to make up for the last year we could have had. Awkward phone calls and video calls, misinterpreted text messages. He rested in the living room fireplace breast, behind a museum exhibit print titled ALL THAT I HAVE, waiting for Mom to follow him to England, which was my original plan. In the time that his ashes—and two months later, his piano—have been here, he changed the energy of this house. Perhaps he haunted it, consecrated it. Steven and I changed, also.

"Would it be worth sending it to your Mom before we move, or should we just get the movers to ship it to Manila?"

Mom was no longer joining us here. The profit she made from the house sale was diminished after paying off Dad's debts. I still did not make enough each year to support her. And after thirty years of paying her taxes, the US government still denied Mom her Social Security pension. A government all too happy to benefit from undocumented immigrants while giving back nothing in return.

"You've done enough to support us," Mom said when I told her, ashamed, of my financial precarity. "It's time for me to go home to Manila. My money will last there."

I had cried in relief. She did too. It seemed that we were both letting go of who we were and who we thought we should be. None of us were the same. I felt like thanking my father for this. Out of the rot of my family's unhappiness and out of the ferment of time, a new start for Mom. For my sister. For me.

Roast the rice on the stovetop, in the pot, until the scent is deep and nutty. Pour water to cover the rice. Cook halfway.

The year-and-a-half point of grief is the beginning of the spirit's great turning. We begin to reorient our bodies and our hearts, begin to stop feeling guilty for doing so. Our senses return to the self, to our own needs. Our dreams are no longer visited as often by the dead. Our dreams change.

My sister became a Doctor of Philosophy in neuroscience. She bought a large flat with her partner, an Art Deco two-bedroom in a quaint town square just outside Amsterdam. She has just become a Dutch citizen, a process speedier and more humane than the UK's. She has learned a new language, a new culture. I am so proud of all that she has done. Our mother says she is, too, and shares the news with her friends, people we do not know. My sister is someone that our father—now on the spirit plane and wiser than when he was in his body—is proud of. I know this because in a dream, he tried to help me cross a road.

"Let's see your sister. She is already there," he had said, offering his hand. "Where the sun is high."

I waved at my sister, who waved back. And then, letting go of my father's hand, I walked towards the ocean, calm and waiting, where the sun goes to rest.

Remove the half-cooked rice. Let cool by spreading onto banana leaves laid flat on large pans.

The decision to go towards the ocean rather than the land came suddenly, after I left my PhD at Cambridge. I had taken up the PhD for the same reasons many would: curiosity, prestige. I was the first Filipino or Filipino American PhD student in the university's Faculty of English; its first to arrive without an undergraduate degree. The feeling of unbelonging in academia entered and remained in me after reading "The Race for Theory" by Barbara Christian. I was never comfortable: I preferred to theorize, as Christian wrote, in writing this memoir, in drafting a novel.

It was not until after my father's death, when Mom found his secret love letters from a mistress, that I realized I had been doing it only for the approval of a dishonorable man. I had wanted him to see me for who I had become, to stop calling me stupid, weak, and useless. Dad's death clarified that it did not matter what he said, what I did with my life. The judgment, hatred, and violence he meted out was not for us, but for himself.

Dad knows that he can never say anything to me again, now that we know who he truly was. I know this, because Mom told me about a dream she had recently.

"We were in our old bedroom, you know, in the old house. I was sitting at the foot of the bed, next to where he died. He walked in, and he had all of these photo albums. And when he opened them, the entire room filled with hundreds of pictures floating in the air. Pictures of you, just you, anak, you and him together, when you were a baby, when you were a toddler, when you were a kid and a teenager. The two of you laughing, happy. Scenes of you two that I had never seen before. Each of the pictures were moving, like little movies. And he stood there, watching them all float around the room, and he looked so sad. He kept saying, 'I have to fix things with Jill. She is so angry. I have to fix it.'"

It was after this call that I began to let go. Of who I was, and the story of who I was. Of what I thought I was becoming, of what I thought I wanted.

I began my spirit's great turning, towards a future for me and Steven, the future that Dad's spirit, now freed of his body, knows will give me a draught of peace.

Evenly and thinly sprinkle the bubod onto the rice. Turn the rice over with a spatula. Repeat.

Whenever friends asked, I always said that I had no interest in ever returning to the United States.

"They had me for twenty-two years and fumbled the bag," I would joke. "I'm the one that got away."

I still have no answer for what made me change my mind, made me turn towards the ocean, rather than the land. My PhD withdrawal at Cambridge was approved on the same day that I submitted my application for British citizenship. My world felt as if it had become a little wider. Possibilities, rather than fears.

Steven and I had a celebratory drink in the back garden. It was its second full summer under my care. Where there had once been three unkempt bushes, dirty paving, and an overgrown tree in this garden, there were now roses of a dozen varieties climbing everywhere, clematis—fourteen of them—scrambling over fences and trees. Rosemary, lavender, and star jasmine perfumed the air. The young magnolia tree I had planted the year before would be ready to blossom the following spring.

"Now that we're done here, when should we sell," Steven asked, "and move back to London?"

"What do you think of San Francisco?"

"What?" He frowned. "Where'd that come from?"

I looked at him. "Your work is mostly there, right?"

"But you said you never wanted to go back to the US," he said. "What happened?"

"You know, I have no idea."

Wrap the banana leaves to cover the rice, and keep in a warm, dark place. Let ferment for three days.

The City by the Bay had called to me long before I met Steven. It was the first place I had landed in America, the place I had told all my school friends I was moving to. It had called to Steven, also. Before we met, we had each attempted to leave New York for San Francisco and failed.

Newly married in 2012, we had talked about our shared wish to try moving to San Francisco again.

"It would have to be a road trip," I had said. "I can't fly without papers, remember. And you would have to drive."

He had stared at me, hands on his hips. Back then, he was still beginning to understand the debilitating limitations of being undocumented.

"What about a train cross-country?"

"I hear they search those now too. Like old-timey 1930s Germany."

"Oh," he said. "Then no. We're not doing this. There's no point moving there or anywhere here if you're still undocumented."

"You're telling me."

"Let's go to England and sort you out first, shall we?"

Ten years later, I had become the kind of person I used to hate, out of envy and helplessness. Degrees, a career path, citizenship in a country that had decent freedoms. Poured out of America, separated from the rot of my undocumented life, I had clarified in dark English winters. Aged gently into something sweeter.

My mother says that my father had always wanted to move to San Francisco, but was too afraid.

"Now that you can do it, you should," she said. "You are ready. We were never ready."

Open the leaves. With a large spoon, scoop the fermented rice into a large, lidded jar.

Within two months, Steven's work transfer from London to San Francisco was approved and in process. There was nothing for us to do except to sell the house. Our first house, under both our names, purchased at the expense of our emptied retirement savings, at the expense of our credit scores. Our first house, sanded, plastered, painted, sawn, hammered, and scraped by our own hands.

"I'm happy, excited even," I had said to my sister. "But young, bitter, angry me? I can't help but think: it's so easy for them, and so hard for us."

"What do you mean?" she had said.

"Mom tried to get a work visa in 1992 as a banking industry worker. Same industry as Steve. But she was rejected on the grounds that Filipinos are eligible only as health care and domestic workers. She tried three times, until we became undocumented. Meanwhile, Steve and I are just waltzing in, like it's nothing."

"Wait. Really?"

My sister had no idea. Perhaps this has helped her to soften towards our mother too. To clarify that though she was not the mothering kind, Mom did make an effort towards legality. That she was stymied by a classed and racist immigration system.

Cover and let rest, undisturbed and sealed, in a dark, cool place: a cellar, a cabinet, underground, for at least seven days and up to one year.

My relationship with our mother is still dark, sharp-edged, a shattered glass bottle. We fight often. My sister tells me to expect less, to want nothing, to not speak to her for a while, which, after Dad's death, I cannot do. She married her first boyfriend too soon, a man who manipulated her for forty-five years to think only of his own happiness. Mom remains unable to recognize her own needs, her children's needs. My sister and I do what we can to respond, but having been abandoned by her for most of our lives, we are unable to do much.

Strain through cheesecloth into bottles. Store the bottles in a dark, cool place.

From just outside New York City, on an aunt's couch where she has slept every night for the past year, Mom smiles on our video call. She says she is ready to go back home to Manila. To see her brothers and her friends. I want to ask how she feels about going back to the same life she had in 1991, when she first decided we would follow Dad to New York. I want to ask: If she had known, then, that thirty-one years later, she would be returning to her parents' house, still with nothing, still without her husband, would she have chosen differently? Would she have taken that aunt's advice and chased after a man who had left her behind with their children? Who was making plans to start over in America with a mistress? These are questions that young, bitter, angry me would have asked. Instead, I tell her all about how much Manila has changed too. How much more like other major Asian cities it has become—that is, identified as a middle, upscale, and luxury retail market. How she won't miss America at all.

Drink to celebrate, to mourn, and to dine, just like any other wine.

There is no moving on from grief; there is only learning to move through the rest of one's life with grief. Yet I can devote only so much of my spirit to my past. To my father, my mother, and all of the ways we have failed each other. Now, I choose to accept the final, lasting gift that Dad has given all of us. This freedom—from his expectations, his judgment, his violence—is one that can be understood only by those of us who have survived such rot. With clarity, I choose to see the ocean and the land on the other side. Places where my husband and I can go, together, having learned from the ferment of our parents' lives.

Steven pours another glass of bayah for each of us. He presses play, and the music begins. In our living room, which is beginning to fill with storage boxes, we dance to Nina Simone's "Lilac Wine," which I had just been playing on my father's piano, my voice breaking along the edges of each lyric.

"Are you ready to go back?" he asks. His head bends down towards me.

"I don't know," I answer, my cheek on his chest. "Maybe. At least this time, it'll be different."

"Different. Better."

Acknowledgments

There is a tradition that was taught to us as children, a gesture of gratitude and honoring that stretches back to precoloniality and across shared Southeast Asian waters. An elder's hand gently taken by the fingers, knuckles pressed to one's forehead. In places like Malaysia and Indonesia, this gesture is known as salim, or salam. We Filipinos share this word in how we say thank you in many of our languages: salamat, rooted in *salaam*, the word for peace. In gratitude, we wish you peace. Today, lowlander Filipinos call this gesture of thanks pagmamano, or mano, one of the few Spanish words we were allowed to use, perhaps because the gesture flattered the vanities of our then-colonizers. Before family feasts, there might be rooms full of elders for pagmamano: one relative after another; a kiss on the knuckles for a beloved great-grandmother. To obediently do pagmamano felt, to little kid me, like a silly ritual that took up precious time that could be spent playing with cousins, a half-eaten lumpia clutched in my dirty fist. What I would give now to press my forehead to the wrinkled hands of my Lola Luisa, my Lola Rosing, my Lolo Pedring, my Lolo Baldo, my Tito Dick, my Papa. Maraming salamat po sa inyo, agyamanak unay. I hope you are watching from the spirit plane.

This book began as a response to an exercise during my MSt in Creative Writing at Cambridge University. The prompt was given to us near the end of our first year by Dr. Midge Gillies, my dissertation advisor and mentor for the beginnings of this book. Without Midge's warm, empathetic, patient, yet persistent guidance, I may never have written this memoir. Midge, your friendship has made me feel seen and understood in a wider university whose sheer magnitude has sometimes made a working-class Filipino immigrant like me feel a bit lost and sometimes unwelcomed. To the University of Cambridge's

Centre for Creative Writing and to the MSt in Creative Writing: thank you for being a home for writers from all walks of life, for encouraging the act of making art and the decolonized, expressive questioning of our world.

Dirty Kitchen's beginnings as a nonfiction essay exercise would not have developed into something more had it not been for the Asian American Writers' Workshop, for their literary magazine *The Margins*, and for the writer and editor Joseph V. Lee. Thank you, Joseph and the AAWW, for taking my submitted essay and sharing it with the world. It was through *The Margins*' publication of "Dirty Kitchen" that my amazing literary agent, Charlotte Seymour, found me. Charlotte, you have been an advocate and a believer not just in this book, but in me, as a writer and a formerly undocumented person. Thank you for being my friend, for changing how I see myself: as someone with something worthy to say, rather than as someone to be silenced. Thank you for finding the most incredible editor this book could have asked for: Alessandra Bastagli at One Signal. Grazie, Alessandra, for your genuine passion and care. For seeing me in these pages and for championing not just my writing, but also the younger me in these pages, wondering if anyone might ever care enough about what is happening to her. Charlotte and Alessandra, I will have utang ng loob, forever. Thank you to the amazing team at One Signal, Atria, and Simon & Schuster for your support, hard work, and brilliance in making this book real. To Rola Harb and Abby Mohr, and to Abby Velasco, my fellow Filipino American, for being a diasporic early reader. Without all of you, this would just be another file saved to the cloud, just another set of memories.

To the incredible writers I am so lucky to call friends, my fellow women of color from the MSt who encouraged the beginnings of this book: Maxine Sibihwana, Gloria Huwiler, and Jessica Chan, your writing and your companionship have made me a bolder, more expressive, and more honest writer. Here's to our circle of joy, pain, and beauty. To Anne Elicaño-Shields and Rogelio Braga, my siblings in Filipino diasporic writing: maraming salamat for being here, with your beliefs and philosophies on how to be ourselves in a world that doesn't quite know what to do with us. To Qian Julie Wang, my ex-undocumented Asian American sister, I am so glad to have met you while writing this book; your memoir spurred me on to write mine, for as we always say, we are not a monolith. To Saeed Jones, a new friend who felt like an old friend from our first voice note, onward: thank you for helping me feel less alone as a debut author, for showing me how to expand as a writer. I am also so thankful to the friends I have been lucky to make and keep in New York, London, and Cambridge, especially those of you who have stood by me as I disappeared into this book and, for a time, into my grief. To Melissa Victor-Burkhardt and Phoebe Salvador, thank you for your belief in this book, your hard work, your time, and most of all, your friendship.

It feels strange to thank my sister, a best friend, a karmic companion for past lives, for this life, and for lives to follow. Christienne, you have been through everything with me, have been through your own worst times, your own pains. You are my truest family, both given and chosen. Thank you for letting me tell this story. I love you. To my parents, who did all they could with what they were given, with what they could give: I will always have love for and utang ng loob to you both.

Steven, Steve, my Bear. There are no words and also not enough pages for everything I feel about you. You have seen my worst, most broken parts, and have helped me carry on in this lifelong project of putting myself back together. I still cannot believe that in a life of so much rotten luck and violently bad circumstance, you have appeared as if you were a gift, a blessing. You have stuck by me, have held me close, and have taught me to love without fear. Thank you, my love, for giving me the strength to be brave, to be myself in this book and in everyday life, knowing that you will always be there, loving me. Being loved by me.

I touch my forehead to all of your hands. Salamat.

Bibliography

AUTHOR'S NOTE

Febos, Melissa. *Body Work*. Catapult, 2022.

Fernandez, Doreen G. *Tikim: Essays on Philippine Food and Culture*. Brill, 2021.

Kirshenblatt-Gimblett, Barbara, and Doreen G. Fernandez. "Culture Ingested: On the Indigenization of Philippine Food." *Gastronomica: The Journal of Food and Culture*, vol. 3, no. 1, Feb. 2003, pp. 58–71, https://doi.org/10.1525/gfc.2003.3.1.58.

Orquiza, Alexander. *Taste of Control: Food and the Filipino Colonial Mentality under American Rule*. Rutgers University Press, 2020.

Proust, Marcel. *In Search of Lost Time, Volume 1: The Way by Swann's*. Penguin Classics, 2003.

PROLOGUE: Itak at Sangkalan *(Cleaver and Chopping Block)*

Beyer, H. Otley. *Origins Myths among the Mountain Peoples of the Philippines*. Pantas Publishing, 2021.

Demetrio, Francisco R., et al. *The Soul Book*. GCF Books, 1991.

Eugenio, Damiana L. *Philippine Folk Literature*. University of the Philippines Press, 2007.

Francia, Luis H. *History of the Philippines*. Abrams, 2013.

CHAPTER 1: Pinikpikan *(Beaten Chicken in Broth)*

Barton, Roy Franklin. *The Mythology of the Ifugaos*. Literary Licensing LLC, 2011.

Beyer, H. Otley. *Origins Myths among the Mountain Peoples of the Philippines*. Pantas Publishing, 2021.

Carino-Fangloy, Judy, et al. *Indigenous Earth Wisdom: A Documentation of the Cosmologies of the Indigenous Peoples of the Cordillera*. Maryknoll Ecological Sanctuary, 2015.

Dulawan, Lourdes. "Ifugao Baki: Rituals for Man and Rice Culture." *Journal of Northern Luzon*, vol. 15, no. 1-2, 1985. eHRAF World Cultures.

Food and Agriculture Organization of the United Nations. "Republic Ac No. 8485: The Animal Welfare Act of 1998." 1998, www.fao.org/faolex/results/details/en/c/LEX-FAOC019221/.

Kohnen, Norbert, and Perta Kohnen. *Igorot: Traditional Ways of Life and Healing among Philippine Mountain Tribes*. SDK Systemdruck Köln GmbH, 1986.

Lico, Gerard. *Edifice Complex: Power, Myth, and Marcos State Architecture*. Ateneo De Manila University Press, 2003.

Rizal, José. *Noli Me Tángere*. Penguin Classics, 2006.

Santiago, Arline, and UN Human Rights Office of the High Commissioner. *The Cordillera Indigenous Peoples' Right to Land*. 2018, www.ohchr.org/sites/default/files/Documents/Issues/IPeoples/EMRIP/RightToLand/SantiagoPhilippinesCordillera.pdf.

CHAPTER 2: Sisig na Baboy *(Pork Cooked Three Ways)*

Clem, Andrew. "The Filipino Genocide," *Historical Perspectives: Santa Clara University Undergraduate Journal of History*, Series II: Vol. 21, Article 6, 2016.

Demetrio, Francisco R. *Myths and Symbols*. Independently Published, 1981.

Fineman, Mark. "Close Subic Base by End of '92, Manila Tells U.S." *Los Angeles Times*, 27 Dec. 1991, www.latimes.com/archives/la-xpm-1991-12-27-mn-909-story.html.

Francia, Luis H. *History of the Philippines*. Abrams, 2013.

Immerwahr, Daniel. *How to Hide an Empire*. Farrar, Straus and Giroux, 2019.

Javate, Aurora, et al. *Dictatorship and Revolution: Roots of People's Power*. Conspectus, 1988.

Karnow, Stanley. *In Our Image: America's Empire in the Philippines*. Random House, 1989.

Limos, Mario Alvaro. "Quiapo Gayuma: How an Occult Practice Still Captivates Filipinos." *Esquiremag.ph*, 2020, www.esquiremag.ph/long-reads/features/searching-for-gayuma-in-quiapo-a00293-20200207-lfrm.

Mijares, Primitivo. *The Conjugal Dictatorship of Ferdinand and Imelda Marcos*. CreateSpace Independent Publishing Platform, 2016.

Nicdao, Alfredo. *Pampangan Folklore*. Unknown, 1917.

Pineda-Ofreneo, Rosalinda. *The Philippines: Debt and Poverty*. Oxfam, 1991.

Sanger, David E. "Philippines Orders U.S. To Leave Strategic Navy Base at Subic Bay." *New York Times*, 28 Dec. 1991, www.nytimes.com/1991/12/28/world/philippines-orders-us-to-leave-strategic-navy-base-at-subic-bay.html.

US Geological Survey, et al. "The Cataclysmic 1991 Eruption of Mount Pinatubo, Philippines," 2005, pubs.usgs.gov/fs/1997/fs113-97/.

CHAPTER 3: Lengua Kare-Kare *(Oxtail, Beef Tongue, and Tripe in Peanut Stew)*

Bulosan, Carlos. *America Is in the Heart*. Penguin Classics, 2019.

Constantino, Renato, and Letizia R. Constantino. *A History of the Philippines: From the Spanish Colonization to the Second World War*. Monthly Review Press, 2008.

Cole, Mabel Cook. *Philippine Folk Tales*. BiblioBazaar, 1916.

Espiritu, Yen Le. *Home Bound: Filipino American Lives across Cultures, Communities, and Countries*. University of California Press, 2009.

Fish, Shirley. *When Britain Ruled the Philippines, 1762–1764*. AuthorHouse, 2003.

Francia, Luis H. *History of the Philippines*. Abrams, 2013.

Karnow, Stanley. *In Our Image: America's Empire in the Philippines*. Random House, 1989.

Natividad, Ivan. "Why the Story of the United States Needs to Be Challenged." *Berkeley*, 2022, news.berkeley.edu/2022/04/12/why-the-story-of-the-united-states-needs-to-be-challenged.

Pimentel, Benjamin. "White Man's Forgotten War." *SFGATE*, 31 Jan. 1999, www.sfgate.com/news/article/White-Man-s-Forgotten-War-One-hundred-years-2949359.php.

Roque, Mela Maria. *Tales from Our Malay Past*. Filipinas Foundation, 1979.

Tracy, Nicholas. *Manila Ransomed*. University of Exeter Press, 1995.

CHAPTER 4: Sinigang na Hipon at Isda sa Sampalok *(Prawns and Fish in Soured Tamarind Broth)*

Demetrio, Francisco R. *Myths and Symbols*. Independently Published, 1981.

Eugenio, Damiana L. *Philippine Folk Literature*. University of the Philippines Press, 2007.

Ramos, Maximo D. *Legends of Lower Gods: Stories about Creatures from Philippine Mythology and Folklore*. CreateSpace Independent Publishing Platform, 1990.

Ramos, Maximo D. *Philippine Myths, Legends, and Folktales*. Phoenix Publishing House, 1990.

CHAPTER 5: Dinuguan na Baboy *(Pork in Blood Stew)*

Clodfelter, Micheal. *A Statistical Encyclopedia of Casualty and Other Figures, 1492–2015, 4th ed.* McFarland, 2017.

Constantino, Renato, and Letizia R. Constantino. *A History of the Philippines: From the Spanish Colonization to the Second World War.* Monthly Review Press, 2008.

De Bevoise, Ken. *Agents of Apocalypse.* Princeton University Press, 1995.

Demetrio, Francisco R. *Encyclopedia of Philippine Folk Beliefs and Customs, Volume 1.* Independently Published, 1991.

Demetrio, Francisco R. *Myths and Symbols.* Independently Published, 1981.

Foner, Philip S. *The Spanish-Cuban-American War and the Birth of American Imperialism Vol. 2.* New York University Press, 1972.

Francia, Luis H. *History of the Philippines.* Abrams, 2013.

Karnow, Stanley. *In Our Image: America's Empire in the Philippines.* Random House, 1989.

Ramos, Maximo D. *The Aswang Complex in Philippine Folklore.* CreateSpace Independent Publishing Platform, 1971.

Ramos, Maximo D. *The Creatures of Midnight.* CreateSpace Independent Publishing Platform, 1990.

Ramos, Maximo D. *Creatures of Philippine Lower Mythology.* CreateSpace Independent Publishing Platform, 1971.

CHAPTER 6: Spamsilog *(Fried Garlic Rice, Egg, and Spam)*

Alvaro Limos, Mario. "History of Tapsilog." *Esquire.com*, 2019, www.esquiremag.ph/culture /food-and-drink/history-of-tapsilog-a00293-20190729-lfrm2.

Coolidge, Calvin. "Message to the Governor of the Philippine Islands Returning without Approval an Act to Hold a Plebiscite in Philippine Islands on Independence." The American Presidency Project, 1927, www.presidency.ucsb.edu/documents/message -the-governor-the-philippine-islands-returning-without-approval-act-hold-plebiscite. Accessed 12 July 2024.

Francia, Luis H. *History of the Philippines.* Abrams, 2013.

Lewis, Michael. *The Big Short: Inside the Doomsday Machine.* Penguin Books, 2011.

Lopez, Mary Stachyra. "One Community's Complicated Relationship with SPAM." *The Atlantic*, 29 Mar. 2022, www.theatlantic.com/podcasts/archive/2022/03/spam-wwii -history-hormel-canned-meat/629416/.

Mydans, Seth. "Marcos Flees and Is Taken to Guam; US Recognizes Aquino as President." *New York Times*, 26 Feb. 1986, www.nytimes.com/1986/02/26/world/marcos-flees-and -is-taken-to-guam-us-recognizes-aquino-as-president.html.

Orquiza, Alexander. *Taste of Control: Food and the Filipino Colonial Mentality under American Rule.* Rutgers University Press, 2020.

Truslow Adams, James. *The Epic of America.* Routledge, 2017.

CHAPTER 7: Adobong Manok *(Chicken Adobo)*

Bautista, Kimberly John. "How Anti-Filipino Racism Triggered California Riots in 1930." *Esquire Philippines*, 2023, www.esquiremag.ph/long-reads/features/manilatown -watsonville-riots-filipinos-america-racism-1930-a2836-20230727-lfrm.

Bulosan, Carlos. *America Is in the Heart.* Penguin Classics, 2019.

Choy, Catherine Ceniza. *Asian American Histories of the United States.* Beacon, 2022.

Demetrio, Francisco R. *Myths and Symbols.* Independently Published, 1981.

Equal Justice Initiative. "On Jan. 19, 1930: White Mobs Attack Filipino Farmworkers in Watsonville, California." *A History of Racial Injustice*, calendar.eji.org/racial-injustice /jan/19. Accessed 2022.

Espiritu, Yen Le. *Home Bound: Filipino American Lives across Cultures, Communities, and Countries.* University of California Press, 2009.

Gancayco, Stephanie. "Lakapati, Transgender Tagalog Goddess of Fertility and Agriculture." *Hella Pinay*, 20 Nov. 2016, www.hellapinay.com/article/2016/11/20/lakanpati -tagalog-transgender-goddess-of-fertility-agriculture.

Jocano, F. Landa. *Outline of Philippine Mythology.* Centro Escolar University Research and Development Center, 1969.

Limos, Mario Alvaro. "Quiapo Gayuma: How an Occult Practice Still Captivates Filipinos." *Esquire Philippines*, 2020, www.esquiremag.ph/long-reads/features/searching -for-gayuma-in-quiapo-a00293-20200207-lfrm.

Mishan, Ligaya. "Reveling in Pork, Filipino-Style." *New York Times*, 7 Oct. 2009, www .nytimes.com/2009/10/07/dining/reviews/07unde.html?searchResultPosition=30.

Oakland Museum of California. "Depression Era: 1930s: Watsonville Riots." picturethis .museumca.org/timeline/depression-era-1930s/watsonville-riots/info. Accessed 2022.

Ramos, Maximo D. *Creatures of Philippine Lower Mythology*. CreateSpace Independent Publishing Platform, 1971.

Ramos, Maximo D. *Legends of Lower Gods: Stories about Creatures from Philippine Mythology and Folklore*. CreateSpace Independent Publishing Platform, 1990.

Ramos, Maximo D. *Philippine Myths, Legends, and Folktales*. Phoenix Publishing House, 1990.

Torres-Gomez, Lucy. "Gayuma." PhilStar, 2002, www.philstar.com/lifestyle/sunday -life/2002/11/10/183386/gayuma.

Vargas, Jose Antonio. "My Life as an Undocumented Immigrant." *New York Times*, 22 June 2011, www.nytimes.com/2011/06/26/magazine/my-life-as-an-undocumented -immigrant.html.

CHAPTER 8: Halo-Halo *(Mixed Shaved Ice Dessert)*

American Immigration Council. "The Dream Act: An Overview." *American Immigration Council*, 16 Mar. 2021, www.americanimmigrationcouncil.org/research/dream -act-overview#.

Baldwin, James. *Nobody Knows My Name: More Notes of a Native Son (Penguin Modern Classics)*. Penguin Classics, 1991.

Bush, George W. "President Bush's Plan for Comprehensive Immigration Reform." *Archives.gov*, White House Archives, 23 Jan. 2007, georgewbush-whitehouse.archives .gov/stateoftheunion/2007/initiatives/immigration.html.

Caronan, Faye. *Legitimizing Empire: Filipino American and U.S. Puerto Rican Cultural Critique*. University of Illinois Press, 2015.

Cerio, Calyd T. "Albularyo Folk Healing: Cultural Beliefs on Healthcare Management in Partido District, Camarines Sur, Philippines." *Journal of Southeast Asian Studies*, vol. 25, no. 1, 2020, www.researchgate.net/publication/342674455_Albularyo_Folk_Healing_Cultural_Beliefs_on_Health_Management_in_Partido_District_Camarines_Sur_Philippines.

Francia, Luis H. *History of the Philippines*. Abrams, 2013.

Gov.uk. *Oath of Allegiance and Pledge of Loyalty*. assets.publishing.service.gov.uk/media /5a7c9f4ded915d6969f462e6/oathofallegiance.pdf. Accessed 2023.

Guillermo, Emil. "Forgotten: The Battle Thousands of WWII Veterans Are Still Fighting." *NBC News*, 2016, www.nbcnews.com/news/asian-america/forgotten-battle-thousands-wwii-veterans-are-still-fighting-n520456.

Obama, Barack. "Recognizing the Extraordinary Contribution of Filipino Veterans." *Whitehouse.gov*, 9 July 2013, obamawhitehouse.archives.gov/blog/2013/07/09/recognizing-extraordinary-contribution-filipino-veterans.

Obama, Barack. "Remarks by the President on Immigration." *Whitehouse.gov*, 15 June 2012, obamawhitehouse.archives.gov/the-press-office/2012/06/15/remarks-president -immigration.

Ocampo, Ambeth R. "Japanese Origins of the Philippine 'Halo-Halo.'" *Inquirer*, 30 Aug. 2012, opinion.inquirer.net/35790/japanese-origins-of-the-philippine-halo-halo.

US Citizenship and Immigration Services. "Unlawful Presence and Inadmissibility." USCIS, 24 June 2022, www.uscis.gov/laws-and-policy/other-resources/unlawful-presence -and-inadmissibility.

EPILOGUE: Bayah ng I-pugao *(I-pugao Rice Wine)*

Norbert, Kohnen, and Perta Kohnen. *Igorot: Traditional Ways of Life and Healing among Philippine Mountain Tribes*. SDK Systemdruck Köln GmbH, 1986.

About the Author

Jill Damatac is a writer and filmmaker born in the Philippines, raised in the US, and now a UK citizen living in San Francisco. Her film and photography work has been featured on the BBC, in *Time*, and at film festivals world-wide; her short documentary film *Blood and Ink (Dugo at Tinta)*, about the indigenous Filipino tattooist Apo Whang-Od, was an official selection at the Academy Award-qualifying DOC NYC, and won Best Documentary at Ireland's Kerry Film Festival. Jill holds an MSt in Creative Writing from the University of Cambridge and an MA in Documentary Film from the University of the Arts London.